NAFTA and Trade Liberalization

in the Americas

NAFTA and Trade Liberalization

in the Americas

Elsie L. Echeverri-Carroll
Editor

Bureau of Business Research
Graduate School of Business
IC² Institute
The University of Texas at Austin
Austin, Texas

The editor gratefully acknowledges the contributions of the following authors:

Leonard Waverman, Director, Center for International Studies, University of Toronto.

Joseph F. Francois, General Agreement on Trade and Tariffs, Geneva.

José Romero, El Colegio de México, Mexico, D.F., and *Leslie Young,* Economics Department, University of Texas at Austin.

William C. Gruben, Senior Economist and Policy Advisor, Federal Reserve Bank of Dallas, *John H. Welch,* Economist, Lehman Brothers, and *Jeffrey W. Gunther,* Economist, Federal Reserve Bank of Dallas.

Antonio Yúnez-Naude, Professor, El Colegio de México, Mexico, A.C.

Elsie L. Echeverri-Carroll, Head, Economic Development Program, Bureau of Business Research, University of Texas at Austin.

María Beatriz Nofal, President, Nofal & Associates, Buenos Aires, Argentina.

Raimundo Soto, Professor, Graduate Program in Economics, ILADES-Georgetown University, Santiago, Chile.

Francisco E. Thoumi, Professor, Universidad de los Andes, Bogota, Colombia.

William Glade, Professor, Department of Economics, University of Texas at Austin.

Contents

Acknowledgments

A published volume is as remarkable for what is left out as for what is in it. Of the list of things not obvious in the final publication—the papers that never arrived, those that the authors decided to drop after they had already been edited, and the untimely death of Mr. Peter Field from the North-South Center at the University of Miami, whose paper on the impact of NAFTA on Chile I reluctantly removed because there was no one to answer editorial questions and update his paper—it is the efforts of colleagues and friends who agreed to our editorial suggestions that most deserve recognition. Although communication with authors in Europe, Latin America, Mexico, Canada, and the United States was difficult, I was fortunate in having such agreeable colleagues as contributors, and I would like to thank them for their cooperation.

The idea of this book emerged from a conference organized jointly by the Bureau of Business Research at the University of Texas at Austin and the Instituto de Estudios Superiores de Monterrey (Monterrey Tech, Mexico City campus), held at the University of Texas at Austin on June 11, 18, and 25, 1992. The purpose of the book is to cover the impact of NAFTA on Mexico's financial and agricultural sectors and the maquiladora industry. The book also discusses trade liberalization efforts in the most active countries in Latin America, Chile, Argentina, and Colombia. Finally, it concludes with a discussion of the need for capital in Eastern Europe and Mexico.

I would like to express my gratitude to Lois Shrout, Associate Director of the Bureau of Business Research, as well as Vijay Mahajan, Associate Dean for Research at the time of the conference, for their support, not only for the conference but also for the publication of this book. Michael Ambrose, CBA Media Services, patiently reformatted the papers, and Robert Jenkins, Bureau of Business Research, helped with final page makeup. Finally, I wish to thank Isabel Morales, a graduate student, for administering the operation of the conference.

I alone bear responsibility for what is in the book.

I would like also to thank Aida and David. They tolerated my frustration in many instances during this process and shared many of the good moments of it.

E.E.C.

Austin, Texas
February 1995

Special Acknowledgment

This book would never have been completed without the contribution of Sally Furgeson of the Bureau of Business Research at the University of Texas at Austin. Her main contribution was to make the prose of this collection of papers more precise and more readable. Sally did this wonderful job with an enthusiasm that I appreciated, especially in the most difficult moments of the publication of this book.

E.E.C.

NAFTA and Trade Liberalization

in the Americas

Introduction

Elsie L. Echeverri-Carroll

The Arduous Road to Free Trade

Free trade and regional integration are not new to Latin America. Until the 1930s, the external sector in the great majority of the Latin American countries was open: exchange controls were almost nonexistent and import tariffs were very low (Edwards and Savastano 1988). The situation changed significantly during the 1950s and 1960s. Under the intellectual leadership of the United Nations Economic Commission for Latin America (ECLA/CEPAL), most Latin American countries embarked on industrialization programs based on import substitution. The result, in most of these countries, was a largely inefficient industrial sector, which was developed under the barriers of protection and used highly capital-intensive techniques (Krueger 1980, 1983).

Import substitution policies paralleled government efforts toward regional and subregional integration. The first modern attempts at commercial integration in Latin America date to the 1960s with the creation of four subregional integration areas: the Latin American Free Trade Area (1961), the Central American Common Market (CACM) (1960), the Caribbean Free Trade Association (1965), and the Andean Group (1969). Edwards and Savastano (1988) attribute the lack of success of these subregional and regional integration arrangements to the fact that they overlooked the basic *inconsistency* between the ambitious goal of establishing a common market of a regional (Latin American Free Trade Area) or subregional (Andean Group) dimension and the need of each government to satisfy the demands of highly protected and influential competing import sectors.

In the mid-1980s, the extreme protectionist tendencies of developing countries gave way to free trade fever. Simplification of import procedures, reduction or elimination of quotas, and the rationalization of tariff structure were the most common reforms (Rodrik 1992). Trade liberalization efforts in Latin America came to be seen both as a way to address the need for foreign exchange during the economic crisis of the 1980s and as a recognition that the resumption of sustained growth requires a major effort to enhance the role of the external sector. The objective is not to protect the domestic industry, but rather to make it more competitive by reducing trade barriers, thereby increasing both its chances to sell in the international market and the country's foreign exchange. According to Dornbusch (1992), the new enthusiasm for more openness of the economy stems from four overlapping sources: antistatism, in which protection is seen as one of the manifestations of an overly intrusive state; poor economic performance, characterized by debt crisis and hyperinflation; more readily available information on prices and new products in other countries; and World Bank pressure and evidence of the success of trade liberalization efforts.

With the opening of economies came a renewal effort toward regional and subregional trade integration. The new subregional agreements in Latin America have been more successful than earlier ones, in part because there is greater consistency among policies. Moreover, in contrast to the inefficient product-by-product strategy adopted in the 1960s and 1970s, most of these agreement negotiations are based on automatic reduction of average tariff levels (Edwards and Savastano 1988). Latin American countries also changed their strategy in free trade negotiations with developed countries. Dornbusch (1992), for instance, points out that the issue of market access and preferential access to the markets of developed countries previously had been a chief item on the agenda of the United Nations Conference on Trade and Development (UNCTAD).[1] What is new is the willingness to practice free trade as a two-way street. In other words, Latin American countries allow companies from developed countries free access to their markets.

The free trade movement encompasses several countries in Latin America, the most notable examples being Mexico and Chile. Mexico began to dismantle its tariff and nontariff trade barriers unilaterally in 1985 and joined the General Agreement on Tariffs and Trade (GATT) in August 1986. The reward for Mexico was a free trade agreement with the United States and Canada, the North American Free Trade Agreement (NAFTA), which significantly enhanced Mexico's possibilities for selling in one of the largest markets in the world.

The process of negotiation for NAFTA started on June 10, 1990, when President George Bush and Mexican President Carlos Salinas de Gortari endorsed a comprehensive bilateral free trade agreement as the best means to enhance economic relations and meet the challenges of international competition. Talks began in 1991, with representatives from Canada also taking seats at the negotiation table. NAFTA went into effect January 1, 1994, after a difficult ratification by the U.S. Congress and approval from the Canadian and Mexican legislatures. Approval in the United States was hard won. To placate critics, who expressed dissatisfaction with the labor and environmental side accords set forth by the U.S., Canadian, and Mexico trade representatives, the three countries agreed to establish two North American commissions (or secretariats): one in Canada to handle environmental complaints and the other in Washington to deal with labor issues. These side issue agreements do not require the member countries to enact new laws, only to enforce those already on the books.

NAFTA is the most comprehensive free trade pact ever negotiated among regional trading partners, and the first reciprocal free trade pact between a developing country and industrial countries (Hufbauer and Schott 1994). Furthermore, as Wonnacott (1991) notes, a free trade agreement among Canada, the United States, and Mexico marks a major step toward free trade throughout the Western Hemisphere. In fact, efforts to elaborate a broader vision of the Western Hemisphere awaited the results of NAFTA negotiations. After NAFTA, Chile signed a free trade agreement with Mexico in September 1991, with Venezuela in April 1993, and with Colombia in December 1993; and Cuba signed an agreement in mid-1993, establishing the Joint Commission for Technical Cooperation agreement with Caricom (the Caribbean Community).[2] In addition, several bilateral and trilateral agreements have been signed: Colombia, Venezuela, and the Central American Common Market (CACM) (February 1993); Mexico and Costa Rica (March 1994); El Salvador, Guatemala, and Honduras (May 1992); Mexico, Colombia, and Venezuela (G-3) (May 1994). According to Hufbauer and Schott (1994), progress in Latin America to date has been most pronounced in liberalizing trade in goods and services and in building supraregional institutions. By contrast, coordination of monetary and fiscal policies has not advanced, which is not surprising given the limited European and North American achievements in these areas.

A more ambitious integration process is the Enterprise for the Americas Initiative (EAI), announced by President Bush on June 27, 1990, shortly after the announcement of U.S.-Mexico trade talks. It lists several objectives: the creation of a Western Hemisphere Free

Trade Area (WHFTA), the promotion of investment in the region, and the development of mechanisms for debt relief of Latin American countries to spur both new private foreign capital and the return of Latin America "flight" capital to the region (U.S. International Trade Commission 1991).

The Summit of the Americas, held in Miami in December 1994, was the first one since 1967, when the last inter-American summit was held in Uruguay, and it represented a significant step in the creation of a WHFTA. At the time of the previous summit, Latin Americans were all expanding state enterprises, raising barriers against imports, nationalizing American companies, and blocking American investments (Brooke 1994). With all the countries of the hemisphere, except Cuba, governed by democratically elected leaders, traditional themes like human rights and democratic rule took a back seat to business at the Miami summit. However, some human rights and labor groups in the United States criticized the summit for failing to acknowledge the need to protect worker rights and the environment. As Hufbauer and Schott (1994) note, the post-NAFTA paradigm ensures that human rights, labor, and environmental issues have become an integral part of trade negotiations, and this decidedly raises the readiness threshold confronting Latin America in WHFTA talks.

During the three-day summit, the leaders of the three NAFTA countries agreed to admit Chile to the North American Free Trade Agreement, a significant acknowledgment of a country that started its most important trade reforms in the 1970s, much earlier than other Latin American countries. The inclusion of Chile will pave the way for larger economic powers, including Brazil and Argentina. Indeed, the admission of Chile to NAFTA is seen as the first step in an agreement between President Clinton and 33 other leaders from the Western Hemisphere—only Cuba was excluded—to conclude a treaty within a decade to create a free trade zone in the Americas.

The summit made clear both the interest of Latin American countries in opening their markets and the need for the United States to open its market. The percentage of a country's total exports that goes to the United States will, in part, determine the short-term benefits derived from transacting or selling in a more open U.S. economy. For instance, Mexico and Canada, each of which export 75 percent of their products to the United States, will benefit significantly by an elimination of U.S. trade barriers.

In light of this, one can understand European Union efforts

toward creating its first significant free trade links with Latin America. Europe has been the largest trading partner of Common Market of the South (MERCOSUR)[3] countries, accounting for 27 percent of their imports and exports between 1985 and 1992, compared with about 20 percent for the United States. In 1994, officials from the European Union started negotiations with the MERCOSUR countries for the creation of a free trade zone, first, for industrial goods and services and later, for agricultural products. The negotiations continue, with formal links probably not to be established until 2001. The economic links with Latin America could certainly benefit Western Europe, considering that economic growth in many Latin American countries since 1990 has created lucrative markets at a time when purchasing power in Europe is nearly stagnant and expansion in European markets is expected to be modest (Nash 1994).

Meanwhile, U.S. merchandise exports to Latin American have picked up since 1990, reflecting radical decreases in tariffs in the region. U.S. exports in 1989 were $24.1 billion; in 1993, $37 billion. Latin America now accounts for 8 percent of total U.S. merchandise exports, up from 6.6 percent in 1989. Latin America is the fastest growing region for American exports and the only region where the United States consistently enjoys a trade surplus. In 1994, the Clinton administration announced that U.S. trade emphasis was being shifted away from Japan and toward markets in Asia and Latin America. Japan is perceived as an already mature market in which it is expensive to operate, with strong domestic competitors and numerous regulations and other barriers (Pollack 1994). By comparison, emerging economies in Latin America and East Asia, with a strong record of exports from the United States to these economies in the first half of the 1990s, are expected to create an increasing demand for U.S. products.

The Mexican Crisis

Contrasting the U.S. euphoria about increasing trade surpluses with Latin America was the Mexican concern about its ballooning trade deficit. Since 1988, global investors (mainly U.S. investors) had been drawn into the Mexican market with promises of economic growth and a stable exchange rate. President Ernesto Zedillo's administration assured a continuation of key economic policies implemented by President Salinas, predicting for 1995 high annual growth (about 4 percent), low inflation (about 5 percent), and a stable currency (an exchange rate of 3.2 peso to the dollar). It came as a shock when on December 20, 1994, the Mexican government approved a 12.7 percent devaluation in the peso. The devaluation was part of a dramatic change in economic focus aimed at correcting the nagging trade deficit (about $17 billion in 1994). The country then embarked on a bold new economic agenda, putting stronger economic growth aside to attack its most nettlesome problem: a ballooning trade deficit.

After the December 20 devaluation, market participants perceived—correctly— that there was no plan to support the currency, and they started to sell their Mexican papers. Confidence weakened in Mexico's ability to back its short-term debt, particularly the dollar-index government bonds, *tesobonos*. The sell-off of the peso and capital outflows continued. On January 3, 1995, President Zedillo finally announced a much awaited *economic emergency plan* that contained a strong dose of fiscal and monetary restraint and ratified an accord among representatives of labor, business, and government to limit wage increases to 7 percent. However, the plan did not explain how the government intended to stabilize the exchange rate, an omission that left open the possibility that the currency could continue to sway unpredictably. This concern was directly addressed by the announcement, on the same day, of an international financial rescue package structured by the U.S. Treasury and the Federal Reserve. The package would provide Mexico with $18 billion in credit lines to be used to create a stabilization fund to support the peso. However, this fund did not increase the confidence in Mexico's ability to back its short-term debt, particularly the *tesobonos*.

Concerned about the implications of the Mexican crisis for other emerging markets in Latin America and the impact on U.S. jobs tied to exports to Mexico (about 700,000), the Clinton administration offered Mexico, in addition to the $18 billion credit line, a financial package that included up to $40 billion in loan guarantees. However, many members of Congress objected, complaining that the biggest beneficiaries of the loans guarantee plan would be some of the richest American and Mexican investors. In the face of widespread opposition and opinion polls showing little public support, Clinton abruptly abandoned a two-week effort to get congressional approval for $40 billion in U.S. loan guarantees for Mexico and acted unilaterally to tap into a Treasury fund. Created by Congress in 1934, the Exchange Stabilization Fund provides resources for the Treasury Department to buy and sell dollars during periods of currency turmoil. Experts believe that the law creating the fund—intended to defend the U.S. currency—could be extended to provide $20 billion in support to Mexico.

In a parallel move, Mexican officials announced that the International Monetary Fund (IMF) had tentatively agreed to lend Mexico $17.8 billion, the largest loan made by the organization in its 50-year history. To make this loan, the IMF had to make a rare exception to its rules. Mexico still owed the fund more than $3.6 billion of a $4.8 billion loan authorized in 1989. Each of the 179 member nations may borrow against a established quota, but outstanding loans from the fund must be deducted from the amount. Usually, approval of IMF assistance—along with agreement by the receiving country to institute fiscal and monetary reforms—is given to cover a small portion of the monetary needs of a country in financial straits. Then the country can seek financial help from commercial banks or other countries. European officials complained that the $17.8 billion was several times what Mexico would qualify for under normal circumstances (Nash 1994). This amount was part of the package of assistance for Mexico announced by President Clinton after he failed to muster support in Congress for U.S. loan guarantees. European banks will put up $10 billion in loans from the Bank for International Settlements, based in Basel, Switzerland, in addition to the $20 billion from the Exchange Stabilization Fund and the $17.8 billion from the IMF.

In return for the new loans, Mexico put up revenues from its oil exports as collateral and promised austere economic policies to achieve 1.5 percent economic growth and 19 percent inflation in 1995. If these goals are not met, IMF officials are expected to demand further cuts in government spending and stricter limits on the money supply (Golden 1995). CIEMEX-WEFA (1995), a private consulting firm, predicts, however, much lower rates for GDP growth (-3.0–0 percent), higher rates of inflation (23–25 percent), and a current account deficit totaling $16 to $20 billion for 1995.

The Mexican crises—financial and, in the case of Chiapas, political—as well as Venezuela's decision to roll back many of its trade reforms as the threat of political revolts heightened, show that the road to free trade is a difficult one. It is especially hard for developing countries, for which the choice of free trade not only means increasing the welfare gains occurring from a more efficient economy, but also the need to built democratic institutions and social programs that counterbalance the short-term adjustment for the poor (a large majority in developing countries). Why, then, are countries willing to walk the uphill road to free trade? The answer is the *expected*, although difficult to quantify, benefits from free trade.

Expected Benefits from Free Trade

Hufbauer and Schott (1994) suggest five elements in the integration process: the liberalization of barriers to trade in goods and services; the elimination of restraints on investment (free movement of capital); the provision of freer labor movement, at least for specialized workers; the harmonization of monetary and tax policies; and the establishment of supraregional institutions to administer the arrangements and to resolve disputes among the partner countries. However, not every element is addressed at each stage of integration. In Latin America the emphasis has been on trade liberalization in merchandise and on border measures, rather than behind-the-border policies.

What are the benefits of free trade? Traditional analysis of the effects of economic integration weighs positive "trade creation" against negative "trade diversion." Trade is created between the members of a customs union when barriers to trade are eliminated, allowing for increased specialization according to static *comparative advantages* and, consequently, greater gains from trade. Simultaneously, some trade is diverted from low price suppliers outside the free trade area, who still face trade barriers, to high cost suppliers inside the free trade area, who do not. Consumers gain because they pay less when the country specializes in the production of goods in which it has a comparative advantage.

Since the late 1970s there has been a fundamental rethinking of the theory of international trade. As Krugman (1993) points out, international specialization and trade cannot be explained simply by an appeal to comparative advantages, that is, speaking loosely, by countries trading in order to take advantage of their differences. While comparative advantage due to differences in resources and exogenous differences in technology is clearly important, so is specialization driven by noncomparative advantages, such as:

• Economies of scale. Trade liberalization expands the market for efficient firms as they can sell now in a wider area. Thus, it opens for them the possibility to take advantage of economies of scale (arising from distributing fixed costs in a large volume of production).

• Efficiency gains. Trade liberalization may induce inefficient firms to exit and push remaining firms down their average cost curves as prohibited market access barriers—visible and invisible—are eliminated (Flam 1992).

• Agglomeration economies. Krugman and Venables (1990) contend that integration offers incentives for concentration because the reduction of trade costs (i.e., products no longer have to adjust to different national product regulations) favors concentrated production to take advantage of economies of scale. However, they also argue that geographical location of new production is uncertain. The combination of economies of scale, transportation costs, and input cost differences may, in some cases, dictate a central—in others, a peripheral—location.

The importance of noncomparative advantage sources of specialization, however, is not news. What has happened since the late 1970s is that the role of increasing returns has been codified in models (Krugman 1993). Empirical studies suggest small gains from free trade, basically because it is difficult to quantify many of the large benefits associated with free trade policies and also because in many cases a domestic policy designed to correct for the market distortion would be more effective than a free trade policy. Although the noncomparative advantages of free trade, often termed the dynamic benefits of trade, are notoriously hard to formalize and measure, many economists believe they are of far greater importance than the more theoretical tractable static benefits from the comparative advantage theory (McCulloch 1993). As Dornbusch (1992) points out, measuring the benefits of trade reforms has been a frustrating endeavor. Summarized evidence on the proposition that outward orientation is beneficial, whatever the channels, has been hard to document in a clear-cut way. The most plausible evidence comes from case studies and from the more novel work of modeling imperfectly competitive economies in computable general equilibrium models. These models highlight that, in specific market structures or with specific scale economies, the gains from liberalized trade can be substantial. In fact, in some examples, the gains are far larger than the static resources allocation effect and come to more than 10 percent of GNP.

The presumption is that trade reforms work, but in the long term, and so will eventually yield perceptible economic gains. But, as Papageorgiou et al. (1990) note, the short-term benefits are less clear. Most theoretical arguments, old and new, overstate the benefits of change by comparing alternative equilibriums without considering the costs of moving between them. Yet real-world discussions of trade policy often center precisely on problems of adjustment (McCulloch 1993). As Papageorgiou et al. (1990) point out, trade reform will succeed only if it shifts resources from inefficient uses to new tasks. However, this short-term reallocation of resources carries economic costs and political risks. In fact, when barriers to imports are first lowered, there exists the danger that the balance of payments might deteriorate. Another is that unemployment might rise if workers displaced from inefficient jobs are not quickly re-employed. Thus, even if the long-term gains are substantial, the short-term pains may make liberalization politically unfeasible (Papageorgiou et al. 1990). Displaced resources that remain idle for an extended period are both costly in terms of foregone output and politically troublesome (McCulloch 1993).

The practical case for free trade recognizes the formidable obstacles to translating theoretically optimal intervention into real-world welfare gains. Real-world policies are chosen not by omniscient social welfare-maximizing technocrats, but by incompletely informed government officials vulnerable to influence from interested parties (McCulloch 1993). Moreover, implementation of optimizing intervention requires detailed information on industry cost and demand—future as well as current. The most reliable, though far from neutral, sources are the industries themselves.

The Structure of the Book

Our purpose is to provide concise analyses of trade liberalization efforts not only in Mexico, but also in those Latin American countries that have been active in implementing trade liberalization policies: Chile, Argentina, and Colombia. The literature available on NAFTA is overwhelming, but *relatively* fewer studies are available on trade liberalization in other Latin American countries. Also, the focus of analysis is different: many NAFTA studies rely on models, while studies on other Latin American countries are more policy-oriented. Moreover, the book analyzes some of the most controversial sectors—agriculture and financial—in the NAFTA negotiations, as well as the effect of the agreement on maquiladoras, an important industry for the United States and Mexico.

I. Modeling NAFTA's Economic Effects
Leonard Waverman finds that, among the three member countries (United States, Canada, and Mexico), trade patterns are broadly consistent with the comparative advantage story. Then he compares the hypothetical effects upon Canada of a Mexico–U.S. free trade

agreement (MUFTA) with the effects of a North American free trade agreement (NAFTA). His estimates indicate that the total static effects of NAFTA would be smaller than the one estimated from MUFTA. Thus, he suggests that a Mexico-U.S. free trade agreement would result in some costs and few benefits for Canada. Only a true NAFTA can provide both Canada and the United States with the real benefits of free trade.

Joseph F. Francois reviews some of the Computerized General Equilibrium (CGE) models developed to measure the impacts of NAFTA. He points out that, given the variety of structures employed to assess NAFTA, there is a surprising degree of uniformity regarding the aggregate implications for Canada, Mexico, and the United States. However, he contends that while these results can be viewed as highly suggestive, they are in no way conclusive because of the ad hoc manner in which most of these models assess capital flows. Moreover, as he indicates, the experiments conducted generally contemplate immediate liberalization. Because many, if not most, nontariff barriers will be phased out over a ten to fifteen year period, the annual effects of the actual implementation of a NAFTA will be even less noticeable for all parties than the results reviewed here suggest.

José Romero and Leslie Young use their dynamic dual model to simulate the effect of complete tariff elimination without and with a drop in the interest rate. They point out that the assumption that the interest rate will not change is not valid, especially if one considers that NAFTA represents a commitment from the Mexican government not only to an open market economy, but also to *stable, predictable policies*. Stable policies remove a great deal of risk from investment in Mexico. Access to international capital markets will greatly improve as the international community removes the "political risk premium" from the interest rates that they charge for investment in Mexico. Adding to this trend is the reversal of capital flight from abroad, characterized by a repatriation of Mexico's capital. In a second simulation exercise, they assume not only that tariffs are eliminated but also that interest rates fall from 15 to 12 percent, resulting in a higher real GNP, 11.9 percent, than the constant interest rate scenario of 3.1 percent. These results highlight the importance of capital flows in the welfare effects of trade liberalization in Mexico.

II. Industry Effects of NAFTA
William C. Gruben, John H. Welch, and Jeffrey W. Gunther begin

their chapter with a brief history of the Mexican financial system from 1940 to 1974. At this time, the system was highly regulated by the Bank of Mexico. These high levels of regulation left commercial banks at a disadvantage relative to nonbank intermediaries. To correct this situation, reforms were instituted to give banks the market opportunities formerly restricted to nonbank intermediaries. The liberalization of the financial sector in Mexico that began in 1988 was advanced further by NAFTA. But, they state, even after the phase-in period ends, NAFTA's characterization of national treatment is limited. Mexico still will be able to treat U.S. and Canadian-owned subsidiaries differently than it treats domestic firms. Moreover, although banking is extremely profitable in Mexico, most U.S. banks are not familiar enough with the Mexican market to compete effectively in this part of the market. On the other hand, the more liberal treatment given to nonbank institutions suggests that equity and bond markets may prove somewhat more attractive than de novo banking.

Antonio Yúnez-Naude uses a CGE model to simulate the impact on the Mexican agricultural sector of reforming the Agrarian Law concerning the *ejidos*.[4] The first scenario captures what would happen if liberalization of North American trade was accomplished without *ejido* system land reform. It is therefore assumed that there is no market for rainfed lands dedicated to the production of corn. The second scenario quantifies the impacts of trade liberalization and internal reforms in the context of free markets for all lands. Estimations results indicate that whether or not there exists a market for rainfed lands for the production of corn (scenarios one and two), the general effect of trade and price liberalization is to depress Mexico's agricultural production. However, if we take into account that, under the assumption of a free market for *ejido* lands (scenario 2), rainfed corn production is less affected, it is possible to argue that domestic price reforms and trade liberalization, together with property rights reform, would bring about a more favorable outcome for poor rainfed corn producers.

Elsie L. Echeverri-Carroll highlights three variables that will influence the growth of the maquiladora industry. The first variable is the capacity to increase flexibility, not only within maquiladora plants but also in the relationship with assemblers. A second variable is new trade policies, specifically NAFTA's tariff and nontariff provisions. The most important changes introduced by NAFTA are related to nontariff provisions. Japanese maquiladoras, with their significant participation in the assembly of televisions and their use of a large percentage of Japanese components and machinery, could be among the most affected by changes in non-tariff provisions. A third variable that will influence the growth of the maquiladora industry is the quality of the infrastructure used to move goods between countries.

III. Trade Liberalization in the Americas

María Beatriz Nofal analyzes how the process of integration of the Southern Cone has worked, what changes and/or adjustments are needed, and what challenges await. She highlights the key role that the process of economic integration between Brazil and Argentina has played in the creation of an integrated regional market. This process has been characterized by volatility in the intraregional trade balances due to macroeconomic divergence (particularly, when instability and recession affects the largest economy, Brazil) and the divergent movements of the exchange rates. She discusses the reasons why a free trade area is a better option at present for Southern Cone countries than a customs union. Moreover, she answers the following questions: Do the Common Market of the South (MERCOSUR) and NAFTA represent divergent or convergent roads on the way to Western Hemisphere free trade? Does accession to NAFTA and the linkage of subregional integration agreements constitute an alternative or a complementary means to a Western Hemisphere Free Trade Agreement?

Raimundo Soto reviews the Chilean experience with structural reforms and discusses some of the most important implications for countries in the early stages of their own reform processes. He analyzes the main weaknesses of the current economic situation in Chile, the extent to which unilateral trade liberalization can overcome these limitations, and Chile's incentives to join trade agreements, such as MERCOSUR, NAFTA, and the Central American Common Market (CACM). He points out that in the Chilean case, trade is not the main incentive for joining a pact, as the reforms have already accomplished a high degree of integration into world markets; rather, nontrade factors—such as the reduction in the country's financial risk, prompt access to new technologies, and a defense against further protectionism in developed countries—appear to be more important determinants in the decision to join trade agreements.

Francisco E. Thoumi questions two of the explanations for the lack of manufacturing export growth in Colombia and the decline in total factor productivity in this sector in the 1980s that gave rise to trade liberalization policies. Mainstream economists, he argues, see the economic reforms as independent of the political and social ones and forecast an increase in the rate of GDP growth as a result of the economic reform implementations. The interpretation to which Thoumi adheres argues for deep institutional reforms to cope with the high level of violence and increased underground economy. The main problem is not that Colombia is a large and inefficient state, but rather, that it requires a deep transformation to become successfully proactive. Such reform, which transcends traditional economic policies, faces many obstacles—among which the most important is perhaps the illegal drug industry—that render policy success quite improbable.

IV. Trade Liberalization Beyond Frontiers

William Glade compares Mexico in relation to NAFTA and Central Europe in relation to the European Community. After analyzing the current and prospective trade of Mexico and Central Europe, Glade notes that a chief problem in the transition of Eastern Europe to trade liberalization is the vast amount of institution building yet to be accomplished to elicit the kind of enterprise behavior needed to raise productivity and income, to generate the human capital and entrepreneurial initiative, and to hone the skills needed by workers and consumers to make markets work. In contrast, over a period of 50 years of virtually unbroken growth, Mexico has carried out an extraordinary program of institution building. Indeed, the very rapidity and success with which the system was opened and restructured in the past few years, despite the crisis of the 1970–82 period and a huge foreign debt overhang, attests to the fundamental success in institution building of the state-led development program that went before.

Notes

1. Includes Antigua and Barbuda, Bahamas, Barbados, Belize, Dominica, Grenada, Guyana, Jamaica, Montserrat, St. Kitts and Nevis, St. Lucia, St. Vincent and the Grenadines, and Trinidad and Tobago.
2. The General System of Preferences, under which industrial countries gave developing countries privileged market access for a broad range of goods, was a way of implementing that objective.
3. An integrated regional market formed by Argentina, Brazil, Paraguay, and Uruguay.
4. Units of production and consumption in poor, rainfed lands.

References

Brooke, J. 1994. "The Hemisphere Summit Talks: Strictly Business." *New York Times*, December 12, A4.

CIEMEX-WEFA. 1995. *Mexican Letter* 13: 2. Cynwyd, Pennsylvania.

Dornbusch, R. 1992. "The Limit of Trade Policy Reforms in Developing Countries." *Journal of Economic Perspective* 6: 69–85.

Edwards, S. and M. Savastano. 1988. "Latin America's Intra-Regional Trade: Evolution and Future Prospects." NBER Working Paper 2738. Cambridge, Massachusetts: National Bureau of Economic Research.

Flam, Harry. 1992. "Product Market and 1992: Full Integration, Large Gains?" *Journal of Economic Perspective* 6: 7–30.

Golden, T. 1995. "More Mexican Anguish than Gratitude to U.S." *New York Times*, February 3, A4.

Hufbauer, G.C. and J.J. Schott. 1994. *Western Hemisphere Economic Integration*. Washington, D.C.: Institute for International Economics.

Krueger, A.O. 1980. *Trade and Employment in Developing Countries*, Vol. I. Chicago: University of Chicago Press.

Krueger, A.O. 1983. *Trade and Employment in Developing Countries: Synthesis and Conclusions*. Chicago: University of Chicago Press.

Krugman, P. and A. Venables. 1990. "Integration and the Competitiveness of Peripheral Industry." In C. Bliss and J. de Macedo, eds., *Unity with Diversity in the European Community*. Cambridge: Cambridge University Press.

Krugman, P.R. 1993. "The Narrow and Broad Arguments for Free Trade." *American Economic Review* 83: 362–366.

McCulloch, R. 1993. "The Optimality of Free Trade: Science or Religion?" *American Economic Review* 83: 367–371.

Melloan, G. 1995. "On Mexico, the U.S. Congress Just Doesn't Get It." *Wall Street Journal*, January 23, A17.

Nash, N.C. 1994. "Europe Seeks Latin Free Trade Ties." *New York Times*, December 7, C2.

———. 1995. "European Nations Abstain on Vote for Mexican Plan." *New York Times*, February 3, A1, A4.

Papageorgiou, D., A. Choksi, and M. Michaely. 1990. "Liberalizing Foreign Trade in Developing Countries: The Lessons of Experience." Washington, D.C.: World Bank.

Pollack, A. 1994. "U.S. Is Shifting Trade Emphasis Away from Japan." *New York Times*, November 4, C1, C2.

Rodrik, D. 1992. "The Limit of Trade Policy Reforms in Developing Countries." *Journal of Economic Perspective* 6: 87–105.

U.S. International Trade Commission. 1991. *The Likely Impact on the United States of a Free Trade Agreement with Mexico.* USITC Publication 2353. Washington, D.C.

Wonnacott, R.J. 1991. *Economics of Overlapping Free Trade Areas and the Mexican Challenge.* Toronto, Canada: Canadian-American Committee, C.D. Howe Institute.

Part I

Modeling NAFTA's Economic Effects

1

The Trinational Equation: Canada's Role in a North American Free Trade Area

Leonard Waverman

Introduction

With a population of 83 million people, Mexico is the eleventh largest nation in the world. The average income in Mexico is $2,100 U.S.; the minimum wage is one-fifth the Canadian or U.S. rates and the average wages far lower; unemployment rates range from 15 to 30 percent (no official statistics exist); and the foreign debt totaled $93 billion U.S. in 1990. Between 1930 and 1980, Mexico had far higher rates of gross national product (GNP) growth than Canada or the United States, but Mexican growth has stalled since 1981 and real wages fell some 50 percent through 1990.

Like Canada, Mexico has been involved in a war with the United States (1845–1848). Unlike Canada, Mexico lost half its territory—Texas, New Mexico, and California—to the United States and has been overrun by a succession of foreign powers. Mexico is an intensely nationalistic country and fear of dependence on the United States has been a major driving force behind policies.[1] Therefore, until the recent reforms begun in 1982, Mexico attempted to develop by limiting imports behind high protective walls, restricting foreign investment, relying on revenue from oil exports to pay for government expenditures, and concentrating largely on manufacturing for the domestic market.[2] However, despite its reluctance to be "dependent," Mexico shipped 65 percent of its exports to the United States in the mid–1980s, and two-thirds of Mexican imports came from the United States.

In 1982, the worldwide recession, the drop in oil demand, and the high and increasing interest payments on the huge foreign debt sent the Mexican economy into a tailspin. The two most recent Mexican administrations searched for means to reinstate growth in Mexico, reinvigorate the manufacturing sector, attract foreign investment to add to the inadequate domestic savings pool, reduce inflation (up to 160 percent per annum in 1987), and decrease the foreign debt. The de la Madrid administration

(1982–1988) brought Mexico into the General Agreement on Tariffs and Trade (GATT) in 1985 and began to liberalize trade and investment, deregulate, and privatize (in 1982, the Mexican government owned over 1,100 firms). With its ascension in 1988, the Salinas administration unilaterally liberalized trade and in-vestment at a speed and to a degree that is unprecedented in recent world history.

In 1990, Mexico proposed the negotiation of a Comprehensive Free Trade Agreement (FTA) with its once bitter opponent, the United States. Canada was soon added to the trilateral equation. For the United States, a trade pact with Mexico and former President Bush's Enterprise for the Americas Initiative (EAI) make geopolitical and economic sense. The U.S.-Canada border is the largest undefended border in the world and remains so because of the minimal flow of contraband, drugs, and illegal immigrants. The U.S.-Mexico border is also large and, despite efforts to stem illegal flows of goods and people, this border is quite porous. Economic growth in Mexico is seen as one way to reduce illegal flows (by increasing capital and income levels in Mexico), and a free trade agreement is a means to economic growth. The collapse of Mexican and other Latin American economies in the early 1980s also caused economic harm in the United States. The reduction in imports into Latin America substantially increased the U.S. trade deficit. Had Latin America and the Caribbean continued its import growth of the 1970s, the recent U.S. current account deficit would have been reduced by $40 billion.

Canadian officials and public originally appeared unsure of Canada's role in the North America Free Trade Agreement (NAFTA). This hesitation is natural. Canada has few geopolitical interests in Mexico and its economic interest appears tenuous. In 1992, Mexico-Canada trade was small—$2.8 billion in Canadian imports and $0.8 billion in Canadian exports—and Canadian investment in Mexico was, at $300 million, even smaller. *Given minimal trade and investment and Mexican wages of some $1.60 per hour, what is the value of a "trinational equation," and, specifically, why was Canada in the game at all?*

Originally, the Canadian government suggested that Canada should take part in trilateral negotiations as a defensive strategy to minimize losses in preferences in U.S. markets. This stance was probably unwise as a negotiating strategy and, more importantly, as a long-term view of the hemisphere. Canadians and Americans should welcome the ability to play an important and preferential role (after all, that is what a free trade area allows) in the building of Mexico. Such a role is not without its potential costs, both short term (Canadian trade diverted in the U.S. market to Mexico) and long term (potential investment diversion for both Canada and the United States). However, there are substantial potential benefits to the two northern countries. Economic growth in Mexico will be accompanied by an enormous appetite for imports, capital, technology, and know-how. The United States and Canada cannot ignore such an enormous opportunity. After all, despite its success, Japan was an underdeveloped country 25 years ago. Ten years ago no one thought of purchasing Korean goods. Mexico has the potential to be the North American tiger and, unlike Japan and Korea, is looking to North America to assist in and benefit from the transformation of the Mexican economy. It would be foolhardy to ignore the opportunity to take part in this transformation.

It must be remembered that low wages and low per capita income are the consequences of a lesser developed, i.e., lower productivity, country and not a cause of growth. While some Canadian and U.S. jobs will migrate to Mexico (as they have to Japan, Korea, Thailand, Malaysia, and other countries with which neither Canada nor the United States have trade pacts), low wages are not the key to world economic success. If they were, China, Romania, and Sub-Saharan Africa would be industrial leaders. Wages are low because labor is less productive. As productivity rises, so will wages.

Most importantly from the Canadian perspective, Canada will be affected whether or not it joins a free trade agreement with Mexico and the United States.[3] The United States and Mexico are free to negotiate any trade pact that benefits their citizens. Any such pact will have repercussions on Canada—*especially* if Canada attempts to remain outside such a pact. Canada cannot, nor should it, avoid the impacts of a more productive, more competitive Mexico, as it could not avoid the enormous growth in competitiveness of the Japanese economy, beginning in 1965, and the Korean economy, beginning in 1980. The worst possible scenario for Canada is to allow the United States to negotiate privileged access to the Mexican market, leaving Canadians on the sidelines. A U.S.-Mexico free trade agreement would lead to gain for the United States and Mexico and some trade diversion for Canada in U.S. markets. (Any improvement in Mexican competitiveness, whether it comes via a trade pact with the United States or superior domestic policies or increased investment in Mexico, would have such an impact.) However, there are clear gains from trade for Canada from increased market access between Mexico and Canada.

Canada will benefit because the far higher growth of the Mexican economy, resulting from secure access to North American markets, will generate a huge demand for foreign investment in Mexico and its corollary, a large current account deficit for Mexico. Canadians and Americans can provide the imports and the foreign investment Mexico requires if the equation is truly trilateral. To stay out of the agreement is to allow the United States privileged access to Mexico's potential. Therefore, the way was clear for Canada: negotiate for a tripartite free trade agreement in North America and welcome the clear opportunities and limited challenges that Mexico represents.

The United States, Canada, and Mexico

A Brief Description of the Three Economies

Table 1 reveals a number of characteristics of the U.S., Canadian, and Mexican economies. In 1988, U.S. and Canadian gross domestic products (GDPs) per capita were roughly nine times that of Mexico. Canadian population was 30 percent of Mexico's so that total Canadian GDP was roughly three times that of Mexico. Over the coming decade, Mexican population is expected to grow at double the rates of Canada and the United States, so by the year 2000 the Mexican population could be close to 100 million.

All three North American countries have a similar percentage of the present labor force engaged in manufacturing. The major differences in employment patterns are in the service sector and agriculture: the Mexican service sector employment is less than half that of the United States and Canada (as a percentage of employed persons) and Mexican agricultural workers represent eight to ten times their proportions of the work forces in Canada and the United States. Thus, while industrial output as a share of GDP is similar across the three countries, agriculture's share of GDP is much greater in Mexico than in the other two countries. The structure of industrial production is also different in the three countries, with Mexico producing proportionately fewer capital goods.

Labor compensation is markedly different (as it must be, given the data on GDP per capita): the average Mexican industrial wages of $1.57 per hour are one-ninth those in the rest of North

Table 1
Economic Characteristics: United States, Canada, and Mexico

Characteristic	United States	Canada	Mexico
Gross Domestic Product (GDP) per capita, 1988 (U.S.$)	19,678.00	18,747.00	2,116.00
Population mid-1988 (millions)	246.33	25.95	82.73
Population growth rate, 1982-1988 (percentage)	0.97	0.87	2.08
Population below 15 years old, 1987 (percentage)	21.50	21.40	41.60
Employment			
•number of employees, 1988 (millions)	118.00	12.40	7.40
•number in services (percentage)	69.60	69.80	31.30
•number in agriculture (percentage)	3.00	4.90	33.10
•number in industry (percentage)	27.40	25.30	28.10
Industrial production as percentage of GDP, 1987	30.00	35.00	34.00
Capital goods as percentage of industrial production, 1987	35.00	25.00	14.00
Labor compensation per industrial sector employee, 1988 (wages plus fringes)	$13.92	$13.58	$1.57
Per capita public expenditure on education	$1,126.00	$1,171.00	$59.00
Percentage of 20-24-year-olds enrolled in higher education, 1986	59.00	55.00	16.00
Productivity, GDP/employee, 1988	$42,161.00	$39,733.00	$7,935.00
Product quality (index: 0-100, with 100 being the best)	59.70	68.10	48.10
Gross domestic investment as percentage of GDP, 1986-1988	17.30	20.90	19.10
Expenditure on research and development (R & D) as a percentage of GDP, 1988	2.70	1.30	0.50
R & D personnel per 10,000 of the labor force, 1987	802.30	104.60	69.00

Source: IMD International, The World Competitiveness Report, Lausanne, Switzerland, 1990.

America. These lower wages reflect many things. Table 1 shows a lower skill level in Mexico, as measured by the percentage of the population aged 20–24 enrolled in higher education; enormously lower per capita expenditures on education in Mexico compared to the United States and Canada; and a far lower productivity in Mexico.[4] (GDP per employee is one-fifth that in the United States and Canada.[5])

Gross domestic investment as a percentage of GDP is higher in Canada and Mexico than in the United States. However, Mexico lags far behind Canada in its expenditures on research and development (and Canada lags badly behind the United States).

What emerges from this brief characterization is a picture of two relatively similar economies—those of the United States and Canada—and one economy—that of Mexico—quite different from the other two. These differences help determine the types of trade flows among the three countries.

Economists generally consider trade as being generated by

either differences in the "comparative advantage" of countries or through differences in product differentiation and through scale economies. The more dissimilar two economies are in terms of their endowments of factors (labor, land, capital, resources) and factor prices, the more should comparative advantage determine trade flows. The more similar two economies are in terms of their endowments of factors and factor prices, the more should trade be "intraindustry," flowing from specific advantages to individual firms (product differentiation and scale economies determine trade patterns).

Traditionally, the United States is viewed as rich in capital and human skills (engineering, scientific, research and development, etc.); Canada, in natural resources and human skills; and Mexico, in natural resources (agriculture, energy, some minerals) and unskilled labor. If based on comparative advantage then, trade among these three countries should involve the United States exporting the products of scientific and/or capital-rich industries to the other two; Canada exporting natural resources and the products of secondary manufacturing to the United States and Mexico; and Mexico exporting agricultural products and labor-intensive products to both Canada and the United States. Trade based instead on firms' advantages would involve intra-industry cross-shipments designed to broaden consumer choice and capture scale economies. Given the similarities between the United States and Canada, trade "should be" predominantly intraindustry and determined by firms' advantages. Given the enormous differences between Mexico and the other two North American countries, trade patterns between Mexico and the United States and Canada "should be" interindustry and based on comparative advantage.

Trade Flows

Table 2 provides a schematic overview of the trade flows among the three countries, as well their trade with the rest of the world (ROW). Exports are given in the rows; imports, in the columns. In 1992, the United States imported approximately $103 billion worth of goods and services from Canada, $33 billion from Mexico, and $416 billion from ROW, for a total of $553 billion. U.S. exports were $105 billion less than U.S. imports. U.S. exports to Canada were $79 billion; to Mexico, $41 billion; and to ROW, $328 billion. Canada had a current account surplus with the United States of $24 billion; Mexico, a trade deficit of $8 billion.

Table 2
North American Trade Flows, 1992
Trade Flows
(U.S. $ billions)

Imports	United States	Canada	Mexico	ROW	Trade total	Balance
Exports						
United States	—	79.29	40.6	327.51	447.40	-105.22
Canada	103.86	—	0.61	29.58	134.06	7.23
Mexico	32.62	2.21	—	7.87	42.70	-15.85
ROW	416.13	45.33	17.33			
Total	552.62	126.83	58.55			

Trade Flows, Exports and Imports, 1992
(percentages)

		United States	Canada	Mexico	ROW
United States:	exports to	—	17.7	9.1	73.2
	imports from	—	18.8	5.9	75.3
Canada:	exports to	77.5	—	0.5	22.1
	imports from	62.5	—	1.7	35.7
Mexico:	exports to	76.4	5.2	—	18.4
	imports from	69.3	1.1	—	29.6

ROW=rest of world.
Source: International Monetary Fund, Direction of Trade Statistics.

The lower half of table 2 shows trade flows as a percentage of total exports (and of total imports). In 1992, Canada received nearly 18 percent of U.S. exports, and Mexico took more than 9 percent of U.S. exports.

In overall trade, Mexico and Canada show similar patterns. In 1992 the United States took 76.4 percent of Mexican exports and 77.5 percent of Canadian exports. In that year the United States was the source of 69.3 percent of Mexican imports and 62.5 percent of Canadian imports. Canada and Mexico are nearly identically dependent on the United States as a market and as a source of imports. However, trade is at present a larger share of GDP for Canada than for Mexico.

Canada and Mexico represent, at this point in time, small markets for each other. Mexico is the destination for less than half of 1 percent of Canadian exports; Mexican exports represent nearly 2 percent of all Canadian imports. Since Mexican trade is so much smaller than Canadian trade, the Canadian market accounts for less than 5.2 percent of Mexican exports.

Several important points must be made before trade patterns are analyzed. First, Mexican trade liberalization had been in place for only four or five years and is clearly not complete, thus trade patterns with Mexico were (and still are) affected by past Mexican import protection and export promotion. Second, U.S. trade barriers (such as the Multifibre Agreement or the Voluntary Restraint Agreement) also distort trade with Mexico. Third, Canada-Mexico trade is so small that a new export/import deal could drastically affect the trade pattern. Fourth, it is impossible, in these categories, to distinguish high skill content, low skill content, high R&D content, or other components of product exports.[6] Finally, indirect exports from any country to another contained in goods re-exported to the third country cannot be measured.

In 1988/89, 47 percent of Canadian exports and 33 percent of Mexican exports to the United States consisted of resource or primary manufactured products (table 3). Nearly 60 percent of Canadian exports to Mexico were resource or primary manufactured products while nearly 70 percent of Mexican exports to Canada consisted of secondary manufactured products. Secondary manufacturing accounted for 72 percent of U.S. exports to Canada and Mexico.

The gross pattern that emerges is one of Canadian exports of resource and primary manufactured materials being exchanged for other primary materials, but mainly for secondary manufactured goods. This does not mean that Mexico is exporting more advanced goods than Canada. As noted, Mexican trade is distorted by trade barriers: its own and those of the United States. Thus, free trade with Mexico could increase primary or resource exports. In addition, Mexican exports of secondary manufactured goods need not (and do not) signify a highly skilled economy inasmuch as most of these exports represent goods with a high

Table 3
United States, Canada, and Mexico Trade Patterns, 1988–1989
(percentage of total trade)

Trading partners	Resources	Primary manufacturing	Machinery and transport equipment	Other secondary manufacturing
C/US	16.4	30.8	46.0	6.8
M/US	23.5	9.7	49.1	17.7
US/C	8.2	19.9	60.4	11.5
US/M	17.4	11.0	49.0	22.6
C/M	32.7	26.9	35.6	4.8
M/C	11.6	19.5	65.2	3.7

Note: C = Canada
US = United States
M = Mexico
Source: International Monetary Fund, Direction of Trade Statistics.

component of low-skilled assembly labor.[7] Thus, among the three countries, trade patterns are broadly consistent with the comparative advantage story.

In a further attempt to characterize trade between each pair of countries as predominantly "interindustry" (arising from specialization and comparative advantage) or "intraindustry" (arising from firms' advantages, economies of scale, and product differentiation), I calculated the adjusted Grubel-Lloyd (GL) index for each of the ten aggregate product categories.[8] The GL index is zero when trade is purely interindustry and unity when trade is totally intraindustry. The GL indexes for the three pairs of trade flows are given in table 4. Except for mineral fuels and other articles, trade between Canada and the United States in each of ten broad aggregates is *intraindustry,* with primary manufactured goods having the lowest GL index (0.786). Between Mexico and the United States (except for chemical products), trade in *manufactured* goods is also clearly *intraindustry,* while in *resource* products (except for food) trade is *interindustry. The GL indexes for Mexico-Canada trade show more interindustry trade than between Mexico and the United States or between Canada and the United States.* Resource trade between Mexico and Canada is clearly interindustry trade based on comparative advantage.

What do all these data show? We began by showing sharp differences between the Mexican economy, on one hand, and the Canadian and U.S. economies on the other. Trade data show a number of interesting patterns. The United States is clearly the crucial foreign market for both Canada and Mexico, accounting for two-thirds of each of those countries' trade. At a gross aggregate level, Mexico's trade pattern is not unlike Canada's, with almost half of both these countries' exports to the United States being machinery and transport equipment. A greater proportion of Mexican and Canadian exports to the United States are secondary manufactured goods, with Canada sending many more primary products to the United States than Mexico. Therefore, Canadian trade to the United States relies more on natural resource endowments and Mexican trade relies on its labor richness. Canadian trade with Mexico is a trade of Canadian primary products for Mexican manufactured goods.

Mexico's trade pattern reflects the exports of high labor component goods, exports reflecting the Mexican comparative advantage. The statistics make this trade appear intraindustry because the trade data ignore factor endowments and factor

Table 4
Adjusted Grubel-Lloyd Indexes, 1988, 1989

Canada-U.S. adjusted Grubel-Lloyd index, 1988

	Exports	Imports	Grubel-Lloyd index
food & live animals	3.28	3.20	0.954
beverages & tobacco	0.43	0.43	0.941
crude mat., ined., excluding fuel	1.03	0.91	0.997
mineral fuels, lubricants, etc.	8.58	1.38	0.306
oils & fats, animal & vegetable	0.08	0.07	0.992
chemicals & related products	3.38	3.55	0.917
manufactured goods by chief material	25.26	14.53	0.786
machinery and transport equipment	37.66	44.02	0.864
misc. manufactured articles	1.7	3.24	0.636
articles nes	0.53	1.52	0.473
Total	**81.93**	**72.85**	

Mexico-U.S. adjusted Grubel-Lloyd index, 1988

	Exports	Imports	Grubel-Lloyd index
food & live animals	1.97	1.52	0.977
beverages & tobacco	0.26	0	0
crude materials, ined., excluding fuel	0.37	1.46	0.340
mineral fuels, lubricants, etc.	3.31	0.46	0.294
oils & fats, animal & vegetable	0.08	0.14	0.632
chemicals & related products	0.72	1.83	0.482
manufactured goods by chief material	2.47	2.26	0.938
machinery and transport equipment	12.51	10.09	0.999
misc. manufactured articles	2.81	1.98	0.932
articles nes	1.00	0.86	0.969
Total	**25.50**	**20.6**	

Canada-Mexico adjusted Grubel-Lloyd index, 1989

	Exports	Imports	Grubel-Lloyd index
food & live animals	0.150	0.112	0.417
beverages & tobacco	0	0.015	0
crude materials, ined., excluding fuel	0.045	0.023	0.306
mineral fuels, lubricants, etc.	0	0.049	0
oils & fats, animal & vegetable	0.002	0	0
chemicals & related products	0.008	0.013	0.729
manufactured goods by chief material	0.162	0.332	0.840
machinery & transport equipment	0.214	1.111	0.706
misc. manufactured articles	0.004	0.042	0.425
articles nes	0.017	0.008	0.285
Total	**0.602**	**1.705**	

nes=not elsewhere specified
ined.=inedible

prices. However, the data described earlier in table 1 clearly demonstrate the highly labor-intensive nature of Mexico's relative factor endowments.

The Impacts of Free Trade Agreements

The interrelated effects of trade liberalization consist of several types of impacts, namely, the classical impacts of trade creation and trade diversion.[9] It is useful to briefly summarize these effects:

• Trade creation. Removing barriers to trade improves resource allocation by *trade creation*, which results in industry specialization. Through such international specialization, the resources of each country are devoted to the activity in which it has a comparative advantage. The stock of resources (land, labor, and capital) in each country produces more output when comparative advantage can be used. The potential for trade creation is particularly large when economies are dissimilar in their factor endowments.[10]
• Trade diversion. *Trade diversion* occurs in a bilateral or trilateral trade pact. The particular country with the new preferences can undersell other countries that must pay the tariff or face the barrier. Reductions in tariffs in the three countries for each other but not for other countries will allow trade to be diverted from outside North America to producers within North America.

The extent of trade diversion for Canada in U.S. markets following a Mexico-U.S. trade agreement is clearly an important issue, as it was for Mexico because of the Canada-U.S. Free Trade Agreement (CAFTA).[11] A reduction in the tariffs on Mexican goods entering the U.S. market reduces the price of these goods in U.S. markets both absolutely as well as relative to the price of Canadian goods.

A Mexico-U.S. Trade Agreement
I assume a broad Mexico-U.S. Free Trade Agreement (MUFTA), which would include across-the-board reciprocal tariff removal over time, plus some bilateral agreement on investment whereby existing Mexican stringent rules on foreign ownership would be loosened for U.S. firms. Thus, Mexican firms would be given equal preferential access in U.S. markets with Canadian firms, as well as with all other countries/firms that already receive preferential access to the U.S. market through Most Favored Nation (MFN) or Generalized System of Preferences (GSP) tariffs. In addition, U.S. firms would gain preferential access to Mexican domestic markets over all other producers, including Canada.

Economists have cranked up a wide variety of models—computable general equilibrium (CGE), macro, and "back of the envelope" models—to estimate the gains to the United States and Mexico from a MUFTA.[12] Hufbauer and Schott (1992) summarize these studies

Table 5
Alternative Projections of Changes in Trade Levels, Employment, and Wage Rates in the United States and Mexico as a Result of NAFTAa
(billions of dollars, except where noted)

	IIE	Almon[b]	KPMG[c]	Berkeley[d]	Baylor[e]	Michigan-Tufts[f]	El Colegio[g]
U.S. exports to Mexico	6.7	8.5e	1.2	2.3	6.9	4.2	3.4
Mexican exports to U.S.	7.7	2.7e	3.9	2.5	5.1	3.5	1.3
U.S. net exports to ROW	0.0	0.2e	1.6	0.2	n.a.	-1.0	n.a.
Mexican net exports to ROW	-3.0	3.1e	1.3	-0.2	n.a.	0.5	-1.3
U.S. trade balance	9.0	6.0	-1.1	0.0	1.8	-0.3	2.1
Mexican trade balance	-12.0	-2.70	4.0	0.0	-1.8	-0.2	0.0
U.S. employment (thousands of workers)	130.0	44.0f	0.0	-234.0	n.a.	0.0	0.0
Mexican employment (thousands of workers)	609.0	-158.0f	1,464.0	273.0	n.a.	0.0	0.0
U.S. wage rate (percentage change)	0.0	0.02	0.03	0.4g	0.01	0.1	n.a.
Mexican wage rate (percentage change)	8.7	n.a.	0.0	2.27g	n.a.	2.9	16.0

ROW=rest of world
n.a.=not estimated or not available

a. The econometric and computable general equilibrium (CGE) models (all except the IIE model) generally assume elimination of tariffs and total or partial elimination of nontariff barriers. However, the Baylor model only eliminates tariffs. The IIE historic models assume elimination of all trade barriers and continuation of major policy reforms, including liberalization of Mexican energy policy. The econometric and CGE models usually do not incorporate the effects of policy reforms, outside of trade liberalization. The dollar figures are expressed in terms of 1988 or 1989 price levels. The Berkeley, Michigan-Tufts, and El Colegio models assume fixed levels of employment and hence generate relatively large wage gains in Mexico. The wage gain in the IIE model reflects real appreciation of the peso.

b. The trade figures in the Almon report are based on 1977 price levels. They were adjusted to 1988 price levels by applying a multiple of 1.70 (based on the U.S. producer price index for industrial commodities). The employment figures in the Almon model are for the year 1995.

c. The KPMG model summarized here assumes that the FTA spurs an additional $25 billion of investment in Mexico. The model is specified so that the change in the U.S. employment level and the change in the Mexican wage rate are both zero.

d. The Berkeley model summarized here is described as the pro-competitive trade liberalization model. It reflects reduced distortions in U.S. and (especially) Mexican capital allocation, together with complete trade liberalization. The wage rate figures in the Berkeley model are weighted averages for various skill categories. The decline in U.S. employment largely reflects a return flow of illegal immigrants to Mexico.

e. The percentage change figures in the Baylor study are applied to 1989 trade flows to produce these estimates.

f. The Michigan-Tufts results summarized here are roughly calculated as the difference between the reported NAFTA results with investment liberalization that leads to a 10 percent increase in Mexico's capital stock and the Canada-U.S. FTA results. The NAFTA results in the Michigan-Tufts model reflect a partial rather than a total relaxation of agricultural and textile nontariff barriers.

g. The El Colegio results summarized are from Version Three, which specifies zero change in Mexican employment, but allows the Mexican capital stock to increase.

and add their own. Table 5, taken from Hufbauer and Schott, summarizes the main results of these studies. All agree that the Mexican current account will increase (the zero entries are from models that assume equilibrium on the trade side) and that the U.S. current account deficit will decrease. Of course, there is disagreement as to the magnitude of trade growth. The most optimistic scenario, that of Hufbauer and Schott, is far outside the other projections, but it is, in my view, the most realistic because it is not simply model driven but is reconciled with the experience of other developing countries, including Spain. Hufbauer and Schott translate these changes in trade flows into jobs by using the average employee per dollar of U.S. exports from 1986 and assuming that the average employee growth per dollar of exports is six times as great in Mexico. Clearly, the "leaner and meaner" U.S. economy of 1995 (the year for these projections) will be far different from that of 1986. Thus, I think these job gains are magnified.

Hufbauer and Schott show no impact on wages, stating that these 130,000 additional jobs are "an insignificant proportion of total U.S. employment, and we assume that there is no impact on overall U.S. real wage rates." This net overall Hufbauer and Schott job gain statistic ignores *interindustry and intraindustry* employment changes where wage effects would occur.[13] The Michigan-Tufts model quoted in Hufbauer and Schott shows U.S. production falling in agriculture, glass products, nonferrous metals, electrical machinery, transport equipment, mining, and utilities. Moreover, Mexico ships products of its relatively rich endowment of unskilled labor north, thus Brown et al. (1992) state "To the

---

Sources: The IIE historical model is described in this chapter. KPMG CGE model: KPMG Peat Marwick, Economic Policy Group, The Effects of a Free Trade Agreement Between the U.S. and Mexico (Washington: KPMG Peat Marwick, May 1991), tables 21-30. Almon econometric model: Interindustry Economic Research Fund, Industrial Effects of a Free Trade Agreement between Mexico and the USA (Washington: U.S. Department of Labor, September 1990), 3, VII-A-9, IX-A-1. Berkeley CGE model: Raul Hinojosa-Ojeda and Sherman Robinson, Alternative Scenarios of U.S.-Mexico Integration: A Computable General Equilibrium Approach (Berkeley: University of California, Division of Agricultural and Resource Economics, 1991), tables 1, 5, 7, and 8. Baylor CGE model: Roy G. Boyd, Kerry Krutilla, and Joseph A. McKinney, The Impact of Tariff Liberalization Between the United States and Mexico: A General Equilibrium Analysis (Waco, Texas: Baylor University, Hankamer School of Business, 1991), 13 and table 3. Michigan-Tufts econometric model: Drusilla K. Brown, Alan V. Deardorff, and Robert M. Stern, A North American Free Trade Agreement: Analytical Issues and Computational Assessment (Ann Arbor, MI: University of Michigan and Medford, MA: Tufts University, 27-28 June 1991), table 4. El Colegio de Mexico CGE model: Horacio E. Sobarzo, A General Equilibrium Analysis of the Gains from Trade for the Mexican Economy of a North American Free Trade Agreement (Mexico City: El Colegio de Mexico, June 1991), table 7.

Source: Reproduced form G.C. Hufbauer and J.J. Schott, North American Free Trade (Institute for International Economics,) 1992, pp. 58, 59.

extent that intersectoral labour reallocation is substantial, the subsequent fall in wages in the United States, particularly of unskilled labour, is likely to aggravate the already growing income disparity between skilled and unskilled workers." (p. 13). Thus, dislocation will occur and we should not ignore those who bear the adjustment costs in a trade pact that raises overall GNP.

While the United States and Mexico enjoy real gains from a free trade agreement with only some distributional issues to examine, what of Canada? Is Canada better off out of or in the trilateral equation?

Trade Effects of a MUFTA on Canadian Exports to the United States and Mexico

A set of estimates of potential short-run trade diversion, as well as estimates of trade creation for Canada following a MUFTA, can be made using values calculated by William Cline (1989). Cline estimates export equations for a number of developed and developing countries, including Canada, the United States, and Mexico. The export equations are of the form:

$$\ln q_{ijt} = a_{ij} + \beta_{ij} (\ln Y_{jt}) + g_{ij} (\Sigma_k w_k \ln[P_{i,k} / P_{j,k}]) + \partial_{ij} (\Sigma_k w_k \ln[P_{i,k} / P_{j,k}])$$

$\beta_{ij}=$ *income elasticity;* elasticity of the demand for exports from
    country i with respect to changes in the income of country
    j (Y_j);
$g_{ij}=$ *direct price elasticity of demand;* elasticity of the demand for
    exports from country i to country j with respect to a change
    in the price of i relative to the price of (P_{ij});
$\partial_{ij}=$ *cross-price elasticity of demand;* elasticity of the demand for
    exports from county i to country j with respect to a change in
    the price of i relative to the price of all competitive foreign
    suppliers to j (not including j itself).[14]

From Cline's data and results, I have calculated the relevant elasticities for the United States, Canada, and Mexico, aggregating all other countries into rest of the world (ROW).

These elasticities tell the following story, concentrating on the short-run static responsible to a tariff reduction. It is not the whole story for it ignores the dynamics of Mexican growth. Let us assume a 1 percent fall in Mexican prices relative to both U.S. and Canadian producers' prices in the U.S. market due to the signing of a Mexico-U.S. Free Trade Agreement. (This choice of 1 percent is simply to point out directions of impacts; below I particularize the values to reflect potential tariff reductions.) A reduction of 1 percent in the price of Mexican exports to the United States will have direct price effects as follows, given Cline's calculated elasticities:

a. A reduction in the relative price of Mexican exports to the United States will increase *direct* Mexican exports to the United States by 1.442 percent. This increase in Mexican exports comes about through an expansion of U.S. demand and a contraction of U.S. production.

b. Mexican exports will increase by 0.536 percent through *diverting* trade from all other exporters in the U.S. market. In 1988, Canadian exports were 18.3 percent of U.S. imports (aside from Mexico), so the trade diversion in favor of Mexico at the expense of Canada is 0.536 x 0.183 or 0.098 percent for every 1 percent fall in Mexican prices relative to Canadian prices. If Mexican goods actually compete more with Canadian goods than ROW goods in U.S. markets then the trade diversion effects on Canada are greater than this calculated elasticity (0.098).

This 1 percent reduction in the price of Mexican exports to the United States will, however, alter U.S. welfare and incomes and have the following effects:

c. Three opposing effects on U.S. welfare and GNP are created by an increase in Mexican exports to the United States following a decrease in the price of Mexican exports to the United States. First, U.S. consumers are better off because they now have cheaper goods. Second, U.S. producers are worse off to the extent that the increased competition from Mexican producers generates unused resources in the United States. Over time, as these resources are reallocated (specialization and trade creation), producers' incomes rise again. Third, if the increase in Mexican exports is large enough and Mexican production is characterized by different factor endowments than those in the United States, then the returns to labor and capital are altered in the United States. Considering Mexico as labor rich, increased Mexican exports to the United States would be high in labor content and thus tend to lower U.S.

wage rates in certain sectors.

As Mexican production increases, incomes in Mexico increase, leading to the following effects:

d. As Mexican incomes increase, imports are demanded, thus generating increases in production in the United States (and other countries). Large income increases in Mexico and large import expenditures could mitigate the production losses in the United States (shown in a. and c. above).

As a result of changes in U.S. and Mexican income, induced effects on Canadian welfare are generated *even though Canada was not a party to this U.S.-Mexico trade agreement.* These induced effects are in addition to trade diversion effects in U.S. markets.

Therefore, besides the direct trade diversion losses resulting from lower priced Mexican exports to the United States (b. above), Canada's producers are affected in two other ways. First, as income (GNP) and returns to labor and capital in the United States alter, Canadian exports to the United States are indirectly affected. Second, as Mexican exports increase, income (GNP) in Mexico increases and returns to labor and capital alter (wages rise relative to the return to capital). As a result, Canadian exports to Mexico increase.

To estimate realistic potential impacts of a MUFTA, the prices of Mexican exports in the U.S. market were lowered relative to all competitors, including Canada, by 5 percent (an estimate of the trade-weighted tariff on Mexican goods into U.S. markets), using the Cline estimates as a guide to potential short-run impacts. The direct price elasticity is −1.442, therefore Mexican exports increase 7.21 percent (−0.05 x −1.442) or by $1.5 billion (7.2 percent of $20.6 billion 1988 Mexican exports to the United States, adjusted for maquiladora output). We assume that U.S. GNP falls by $1 billion as a result of these increased Mexican exports, after accounting for the increased U.S. exports to Mexico resulting from income growth (see below).

The short-run impacts on Canada then are:

a. *Direct trade diversion.* A 5 percent decrease in Mexican prices in U.S. markets generates a further 2.68 percent increase in Mexican exports to the United States at the expense of all other countries. 2.68 percent of 1988 Mexican exports to the United States is $0.55 billion; Canada represents 18.3 percent of U.S. imports (aside from Mexico). Canadian direct trade diversion losses in the United States are estimated at $100 million.

  b. *Induced export losses due to lower U.S. income.* If U.S. GNP falls $1 billion or 0.0002 percent, through U.S. income elasticity for imports, U.S. imports from Canada fall 0.00004 percent, or $28 million.

  c. *Induced export gains through higher Mexican income.* Mexican exports increase by a total of $2 billion when export prices fall 5 percent because of a MUFTA.[15] Assume that exports represent income gains to Mexico as the resources employed in export activity were previously unemployed. Then Mexican income (GNP) increases by 1.2 percent because of these new exports. The income elasticity for Canadian goods into Mexico is estimated by Cline to be 0.443. Therefore, Canadian exports increase by 0.5 percent, or by $3 million.[16] U.S. exports to Mexico increase by 2.36 percent, or by $486 million, offsetting 24 percent of the initial Mexican export increase to the United States.

To this point, I have considered a one-sided deal—the price of Mexican exports fall by 5 percent in U.S. markets. Now consider the other side of a MUFTA where *U.S. prices fall 15 percent in Mexican markets* (the average trade-weighted Mexican tariff is assumed to be 12.6 percent plus surcharges).

As a result of this price decrease in Mexican markets, U.S. direct exports to Mexico increase by 5.7 percent (elasticity of 0.381 times the 15 percent price decrease), or by $1.17 billion. The impact of these increased U.S. exports on Canadian exports is a loss of 3.5 percent (cross-price elasticity of 0.236 between the United States and ROW times the 15 percent relative price decrease for U.S. goods) or a loss of $21 million in Canadian exports to Mexico (trade diversion losses for Canada in the Mexican market due to a MUFTA).

The impacts of a MUFTA do not end here. Consider how a MUFTA enables Mexican producers to penetrate Canadian markets.

Trade Effects of a MUFTA in Canadian Markets

Trade diversion in U.S. markets occurs against Canadian producers when there is a Mexico-U.S. trade agreement and Canada is on the sidelines; thus, trade diversion does not require Canada to be a direct party to the agreement. However, an agreement, which directly excluded Canada as treaty participant, would affect Canadian producers in the Canadian domestic market as well. The reason is simple: as Mexican exporters expand in the U.S. market, they gain sales, experience, scale economies—elements allowing them to increase sales in Canada, even if Canada was not part of the agreement.

Mexico and Canada are not presently significant traders with each other (table 2). However, the composition of Mexican exports to Canada is changing. In 1981, oil accounted for 89 percent of Mexico's exports to Canada; in 1989, 5 percent. In 1989, machinery and transport equipment represented 70 percent of Mexican exports to Canada. Between 1982 and 1989, textile exports from Mexico to Canada expanded by 600 percent (but to only $35 million), apparel exports increased 400 percent (but to only $4 million), and automotive equipment expanded 350 percent to $299 million.

The increased specialization in the Mexican economy, the reductions in costs due to scale economies, the efficiency-enhancing dynamic aspects following a Mexico-U.S. trade agreement will make Mexican industry greater competitors in Canadian markets. This is good: lower prices in Canada increase consumer welfare. But will Mexican industries compete in Canada with Canadian firms producing in Canada or with foreign firms importing into Canada? If Mexican firms compete better with foreign importers, Canadian welfare clearly rises. If Mexican firms compete more with Canadian domestic producers, Canada has to bear the transitional costs as these domestic firms adjust to new specialization and trade creation.

In the short run, it is unlikely that far greater competition in the Canadian market with Canadian produced goods would occur following a MUFTA inasmuch as some 80 percent of Mexican goods already enter duty-free or under the GSP tariff. In addition, many other Mexican goods (textiles, apparel, footwear) compete primarily with imported goods. However, without any new trade deal in North America, Mexican goods would continue to grow in Canadian markets. A trade pact between Mexico and the United States would have augmented this growth, but not enormously.

The point is that as a result of a bilateral Mexico-U.S. trade agreement—an agreement that directly excluded Canada-Mexico bilateral trade concessions—Mexico would become a more substantial competitor in some Canadian markets. However, other industries in other countries become more or less competitive in

Canadian markets all the time so that the changes in Mexico should not come as a great shock to Canada. However, trade pacts are not like changing technology: pacts are under government control. As I show below, a true trilateral agreement is better for Canada.

NAFTA: A Tripartite Agreement

In a tripartite agreement, I assume there would be a core agreement providing for movement of core goods, services, and capital across the three countries. This does not mean that the three countries would have identical banking laws or investment laws but that each would offer the other two, over time, duty-free shipment of goods plus national treatment in other areas (see Lipsey 1990). Again, markets must be examined in the United States, Canada, and Mexico. Remember that all three of these markets for Canada were affected by a MUFTA that did not include Canada. Now we are assuming an agreement where Canada is a direct equal partner.

We begin with an examination of the U.S. market. But that examination has already been made inasmuch as a NAFTA and a MUFTA yield identical impacts for Canada in the U.S. market. Whatever preferences Mexico achieves in the U.S. market from a MUFTA, no additional gains are made in a NAFTA.

Trade diversion for Canada in U.S. markets is identical whether the agreement is U.S.-Mexico or includes Canada. Therefore, the costs and benefits of a tripartite agreement, like NAFTA, can ignore trade diversion in the United States and concentrate on the differential impacts for Canada in the Mexican and Canadian markets arising from a tripartite agreement as compared to a U.S.-Mexico bilateral pact.

The incremental costs to Canada of a tripartite agreement relate therefore to the incremental penetration of Canadian markets due to the lowering of Canadian tariffs to Mexican industry. The benefit to Canada is the preferential access gained to Mexican markets. The trade-weighted average tariff against Canada in Mexico is far greater than the preferential tariff already facing most Mexican goods in Canadian markets. Moreover, as Mexican goods can be embodied into U.S. goods and pass across the Canadian border as long as the rules of origin of the Canada-U.S. Free Trade Agreement are met, MUFTA provides some duty-free access by Mexico to Canada. Therefore, a tripartite agreement yields greater potential incremental benefits to Canada than those available to Mexico—incremental meaning after the impact of a

Mexico-U.S.agreement is considered. When the potential for preferential access to investment in Mexico for Canada following a NAFTA is added, a tripartite agreement maximizes Canadian benefits and a MUFTA minimizes these benefits.
Let me not oversell the story. Mexican duty-free access to U.S. markets will involve costs for Canada. These costs can be overcome by benefits only if the agreement is tripartite and only if Canadians aggressively court Mexican trade and investment needs. Insofar as Canadian firms can already access Mexico through their U.S. operations, then the incremental benefits of a tripartite agreement for Canada are diminished.

We can provide estimates of the incremental short-run costs and benefits of NAFTA on Canada by using Cline's estimates and elasticities. We add to the earlier calculations *direct* impacts on Canadian markets due to a relative decrease in Mexican imports and *direct* increased Canadian exports to Mexico due to lower Canadian prices in Mexican markets.

In Canadian markets, a fall of 5 percent in the price of Mexican exports would directly increase Mexican exports to Canada by 14.8 percent (the elasticity is 2.96), or by $250 million (0.148 times $1.6 billion). Mexican exports to Canada also increase at the expense of the ROW by 2.6 percent, or by $43 million. A 15 percent decrease in the price of Canadian exports to Mexico increases Canadian exports 15.39 percent, or $93 million. Canadian exports to Mexico also increase at the expense of ROW exporters by 12.6 percent, or by $76 million. Because Mexican income rises by $293 million (the sum of the new Mexican exports), Canadian exports rise through the Mexican income import elasticity by another $1 million (table 6).

Cline's model assumes that the supply of exports from any country is perfectly elastic (see Cline 1989). Domestic supply is not, however, perfectly elastic. If it were, imports would be zero or supply all domestic consumption. The model is as shown in figure 1, where S_{MEX} is the perfectly elastic supply of exports from Mexico to Canada, D is downstream demand (in Canada or the United States) and S_{DOM} the supply of domestic Canadian producers. Domestic production is OD and exports from Mexico are DM.

A fall in the price of Mexican exports in Canada has two effects. Total demand increases to N, domestic production decreases to S. Therefore, the increase in Mexican exports to Canada is not totally at the expense of domestic producers. The division of the increased exports between gains to consumers and losses to

Table 6 MUFTA and NAFTA: Hypothetical Annual Impacts on Canada*	MUFTA (millions $U.S.)	NAFTA (millions $U.S.)
Static		
1. Trade diversion losses for Canada in U.S. markets	-100	-100
2. Indirect trade changes due to U.S. income changes	-28	-28
3. Direct export gains for Canada in Mexican markets	0	93
4. Trade diversion losses for Canada in Mexican markets	-21	0
5. Trade diversion gains for Canada in Mexican markets	0	76
6. Indirect trade changes due to Mexican income changes	3	4
7. Canadian production losses due to increased Mexican exports to Canada	0	-125
	-146	-80
Dynamic income gains**		
8. Income gains	120	420
Incremental gains of NAFTA versus MUFTA	366	

* Based on the assumption that changes in exports are a measure of gains, ignores consumers surplus gains in Canada, etc.
** Calculated only as increased exports resulting from increased current account deficit in Mexico, does not involve recalculating items 1-7.

domestic producers is a function of the elasticities of domestic demand and domestic supply; the greater the elasticity of domestic demand (in absolute terms) and the lower the elasticity of domestic supply, the lower are losses to domestic producers.

Cline does not estimate the price elasticity of domestic consumption or domestic supply. In the short run, the elasticity of domestic production is likely low. First, for goods that have no or little domestic production (if trade is due to "comparative advantage"), no domestic supply response occurs. Second, for manufactured goods, domestic firms have existing plants in place and will reduce production only if the new price falls below average variable costs of production.

For Canada I assume the aggregate price elasticity of consumption to be -1.0 and the aggregate supply elasticity of manufactures to be 1.0. Therefore, a 5 percent decrease in the price of Mexican imports that produces a 14.89 percent increase in Mexican exports to Canada results in a 7.4 percent increase in domestic consumption and a 7.4 percent decrease in domestic production. Thus, the direct production loss in Canada due to lower Mexican prices that result from NAFTA is $125 million (table 6).

The Impacts of Mexican Growth
To this point a standard, static, short-run analysis of the impacts

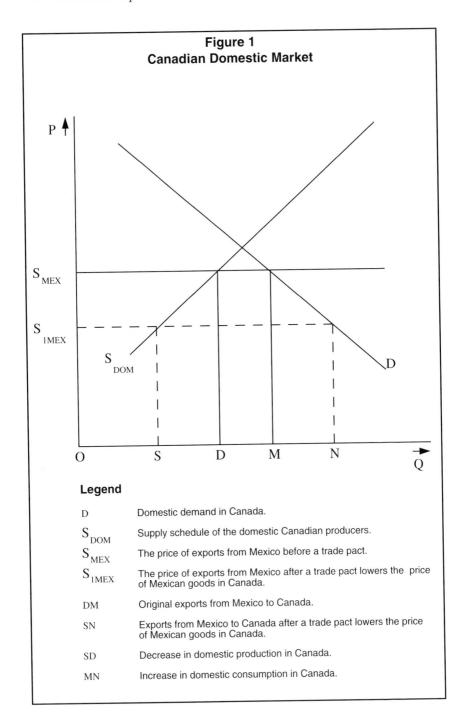

Figure 1
Canadian Domestic Market

Legend

D	Domestic demand in Canada.
S_{DOM}	Supply schedule of the domestic Canadian producers.
S_{MEX}	The price of exports from Mexico before a trade pact.
S_{1MEX}	The price of exports from Mexico after a trade pact lowers the price of Mexican goods in Canada.
DM	Original exports from Mexico to Canada.
SN	Exports from Mexico to Canada after a trade pact lowers the price of Mexican goods in Canada.
SD	Decrease in domestic production in Canada.
MN	Increase in domestic consumption in Canada.

of Mexican trade liberalization on Canada has been used. Tariffs have been lowered and the nature of the response examined at the margin.

Mexico is not contemplating a fundamental shift in the orientation of its society in order to have marginal effects on the economy's performance. Mexican trade and investment liberalization is intended to put the economy on a different growth path.

As Mexico begins to realize the specialization, trade creation, and productivity gains as its economy is restructured, a number of constraints will appear: a lack of domestic savings, a lack of capital goods, a lack of technology. Therefore, as Mexican growth accelerates, Mexico will begin to import foreign investment in increasing quantities and correspondingly run a deficit on its current account, reflecting the imports of goods and services required to restructure the economy.

It is common for developing countries to experience large inflows of foreign capital and large current account defaults as growth accelerates. The experience of Spain is particularly relevant. Not only did Spanish imports jump, as did foreign direct investment (to U.S. $18 billion in 1988), after Spain joined the European Community (EC), but the composition of imports shifted to its common market partners.

How large will this market expansion be? Though its population is one-fourth that of Mexico's, Spain is more developed and in better financial shape. Rogelio Ramirez de la O (1990) has estimated the growth in Mexican income, imports, exports, and the current account deficit assuming a NAFTA. He shows imports increasing from $27 billion (U.S.) in 1990 to $69 billion five years after an agreement, with an increase in net imports of goods of $16 billion and an increase in the trade deficit of $6 billion.

Canada's share of Mexican imports is now 3.3 percent, so, other things being equal, Canadian exports to Mexico could grow by $198 million (3.3 percent of $6 billion). It is unreasonable, however, to expect Canadian exports to Mexico to grow at that rate under a MUFTA or under a NAFTA. Under a MUFTA, U.S. firms gain clear preferences over Canadian firms. Therefore, I assume that the Canadian share of Mexican incremental imports would fall, say, to half or so the calculated increase. With NAFTA, the Canadian market share of imports into Mexico increases—this was calculated earlier as trade diversion relative to ROW and represents roughly a 30 percent gain in market share (to 4.2 percent of Mexican imports). However, given investment and trade preferences and the dynamic nature of the changing Mexican economy, it is not unreasonable to expect Canada to double its market share to 8 percent of the incremental Mexican imports—or $480 million U.S.[17] I consider this a most conservative assumption. (Remember the great annual growth in EC exports to Spain.) The value of these incremental exports are given below.

Incremental Impacts on Canadian Exports of
Accelerated Growth in Mexico
(millions $U.S.)

MUFTA	NAFTA
+120	+480

Longer Term Impacts—Investment
The most significant aspect of a MUFTA, or a NAFTA, would be the longer term investment consequences. As plants wear out and new investments are needed, investors will increasingly examine Mexico as a logical place for longer term investments. These investments are the key to the success of the trade initiatives for Mexico. If the investments do not occur, Mexico will not be increasingly integrated into the rest of North America.

Where will these investments come from? These investment decisions will be, first, new investments not at the expense of other countries; second, investments that would have occurred in Canada and the United States; third, investments that would have taken place outside North America. The calculations made above suggest net gains to the United States and Canada from increased trade with Mexico, therefore, net investment in the United States and Canada rises and does not fall under a North American free trade agreement. The growth rate of Mexican GNP and the Mexican current account deficit have favorable spillovers, on balance, to the country's northern neighbors.

However, wouldn't investment be even greater if Mexico was not there to divert capital from Canada and the United States? Consider the auto sector, the key sector in the minds of many Americans and Canadians, especially auto assembly and auto parts.

In 1989, Mexican motor vehicle production assembly was 640,000 units, of which 440,000 were passenger cars. By way of comparison, U.S. and Canadian automobile production in 1989 was 7.068 and 1.007 million cars, respectively. Mexican production is less than half that of Brazil and Korea and one-quarter that of Spain. Both Spain and Brazil have had the capacity to produce 1 million cars per year since 1980; Brazilian output has been stagnant, while Spanish output has increased by 80 percent since 1980. Korea produced 123,000 vehicles in 1980 and nearly ten times that number in 1989. Mexican motor vehicle production, however, fell by 50 percent between 1981 and 1983 due to the severe domestic macroeconomic crisis. Mexican exports of motor vehicles were insignificant before 1985 (and only 58,000 units in 1985). Mexico now exports close to 200,000 motor vehicles annually to the United States, one-third of Canada's motor vehicle exports to the United States.

Actual planned assembly capacity, to be on stream in Mexico by the end of 1993, will be some 1.1 million cars, up from the present 600,000. This figure includes only the announced expansion plans of Nissan, Volkswagen, Ford, and General Motors. Womack et al. (1990) lists another 900,000 1989 autos and pickup trucks sold in the United States and Canada, labeling these as candidates for Mexican production. These are all small cars presently produced not in North America, but primarily in Japan and Korea.

These 900,000 potential additions and actual planned additions of 500,000 cars per year to Mexican assembly are all small cars or small pickup trucks. Assuming that by 1993 1.4 million new cars and pickup trucks will be assembled in Mexico, what does this mean for the United States and Canada?

Womack et al. (1990) estimated a 1992 assembly capacity in the United States and Canada of 15.1 million autos and pickups, of which Japanese transplant capacity would be 2.5 million. An addition of 1.4 million auto assembly units in Mexico adds 9 percent to North American capacity and 50 percent to foreign transplant capacity in North America (1.3 million added to 2.6 million). What percentage of this incremental 1.4 million capacity would have occurred in the United States or Canada? Womack is clear on this point—*none* of the 900,000 "candidate" car production for Mexico would be produced in the United States or Canada. Instead, this production would remain in Asia.

Of the actual 500,000 planned capacity additions on stream in Mexico, 200,000 are by Nissan and 150,000 by Volkswagen. Volkswagen exited the U.S. assembly market in 1985 and is not considering reentry. Nissan, the first Japanese firm to produce in the United States, has a 265,000 car/year plant in Smyrna, Tennessee, which is planned to expand to 400,000 cars/year. Therefore, it is safe to assume that some—say, 300,000—of the 500,000 planned capacity additions in Mexico could have come to the United States or Canada.

This exercise in calculating "investment diversion" is simplistic because it ignores the potential for domestic car sales in Mexico. In 1989, 455,000 vehicles were sold in the domestic Mexican market. Of these, 274,000 were passenger cars. In Canada in 1989, car sales were 975,000 (truck sales were another 480,000) on a population base of 26 million. If Mexican domestic car sales grew to one-quarter the Canadian per capita value (or one per 70 persons), 740,000 cars could be sold in Mexico. The Automotive Parts Manufacturers' Association (APMA) (1990) estimated that the 1992 car sales in Mexico could be some 400,000. Economic growth in Mexico could make the actual planned domestic capacity of some 1.1 million cars by 1992, used mainly for the domestic market in the mid- to late 1990s.

Table 7 presents data on U.S. imports of automotive parts from Canada, Japan, and Mexico for 1985 and 1989. Total imports from each country are shown as well as their disaggregation into sixteen categories of car parts and a large category of "other"

Table 7
U.S. Automotive Parts Imports
from Canada, Japan, and Mexico, 1985 and 1989
(millions of dollars)

Parts	1985			1989		
	Canada	Japan	Mexico	Canada	Japan	Mexico
Gas engine	1,265	417	205	704	1,680 J	659
Chassis	589	21	—	644	32 J	—
Transmission	686	252	22	402	1,632 J	13
Brakes and parts	369	67	40	582	301 J	65
Auto furniture	453	62	93	510	113	294 M
Gas engine parts	340	141	29	414	366 J	61
Auto tires	250	208	3	384	380	20
Bumpers	181	41	—	369	101	—
Truck and bus tires	181	259	—	170	340	26
Lock and hinges	172	44	3	169	169	13
Wheels	200	71	3	231	147	17
Springs	137	17	37	169	23	38
Mufflers and tailpipes	89	30	3	73	113	99
Ignition wiring sets	73	31	384	68	48	918 M
Bodies	110	106	1	132	406 J	20
Radiators	98	23	3	103	17	43
Other components	4,074	2,848	963	4,892	5,812 J	1,999 M
Total	**9,267**	**4,638**	**1,789**	**10,016**	**11,680**	**4,285**

M: substantial change Mexican exports from 1985 to 1989
J: substantial change Japanese exports from 1985 to 1989

Source: Booz, Allen & Hamilton, "Automotive Parts International," 1990.

components. In 1985, U.S. automotive parts (hereafter labeled "parts") imports were $9.26 billion from Canada, $4.63 billion from Japan, and $2.3 billion from Mexico. From 1985 to 1989, U.S. parts imports from Japan had climbed 150 percent; from Mexico, 80 percent; and from Canada, 8 percent.

These growths in imports are due to two factors: a real change in the number of units imported and a change in the nominal value of imports due to exchange rate fluctuations. Between 1985 and 1989, the U.S. dollar fell 15.3 percent in relation to the Canadian dollar and 58 percent relative to the yen, but increased ninefold relative to the peso. Therefore, in *real* terms, between 1985 and 1989, imports of automotive parts to the United States from Canada fell by 7 percent, while from Japan they increased by 91 percent. It is difficult to translate the nominal U.S. imports from Mexico into real (aside from exchange rate) terms. The ninefold devaluation of the peso does not signify a ninefold drop in real imports from Mexico because many of the components and capital used in the construction of Mexican auto parts would have been imported from the United States.

A "real" shift has occurred. The rapid increase in auto parts imports from Japan can be explained by the new transplant capacity in the United States and the desire by Japanese assemblers to use component suppliers known and trusted. This brought about a substantial increase in imports from Japan of engines, transmissions, brakes and parts, and car bodies. As the Japanese move (or are forced) to include more North American content, these imports should diminish.

U.S. imports of automotive parts from Mexico also grew substantially, especially in auto furniture, ignition wiring sets (GM produces all its ignition wiring sets in Mexico), and "other" components.

After accounting for exchange rate effects, imports of auto parts—especially engines and transmissions—from Canada to the United States decreased. The decline in Canadian exports of engines and transmissions is not due to an increase in Mexican exports of those two major parts (since Mexican exports of these two components did not increase).

Booz, Allen & Hamilton Inc. (BAH) (1990) examine the changing nature of the parts market in the United States. Parts are characterized by the degree of technology required and vary from standard products (such as forgings and fasteners), to parts produced to a design generated by an assembler (stampings), to parts developed in conjunction between the parts supplier and the assembler (plastics and rubber components), and to parts designed entirely by the parts producer (sophisticated components). These parts are being sourced in a quickly changing industry where increased competition puts pressures on prices and quality. Changes to the production technology, to the kanban and just-in-time processes affect logistics. These pressures affect the parts industry. For lower technology, standardized parts that are bought in bulk and placed in inventory, the delivered price is crucial. For other, higher technology components, where parts producers and assemblers are working together on the design, quality is crucial and logistics are important as the parts are shipped just-in-time to be assembled into an automobile.

Occurring at the same time that Mexico is liberalizing its trade and investment rules, these pressures—competitive, technological, logistical—are thus placed on the U.S. and Canadian auto parts industry. These pressures are not, however, "because of" cheap Mexican labor but because of the changing structure of the world automotive market.

Mexico, being closest to the assemblers' North American locations, is the country best able to take advantage of opportunities in the United States and Canada. But Mexico is not alone: South Korea, Brazil, and Taiwan have also substantially increased their exports of automotive parts to the United States. "Mexico . . . is world competitive for winning harnesses, radios, hand sewn leather seat covers, etc." (BAH, p. II-10) and "was lower cost than the USA in assembly, engines, pistons, aluminum castings, wheels, glass, leaf springs and seats" (BAH, A-2). A survey by BAH, however, indicated that proximity to customers (within 500 miles) was more important than labor costs as the just-in-time system required certain delivery and close proximity for problem solving.

Mexican auto parts plants clearly have an advantage in labor costs, which make up 10–30 percent of the costs of a "typical North American part" (BAH, p. II-10), but are far from Canadian and U.S. assembly plants and are constrained by a domestically owned high-cost and inefficient land transportation system.[18]

Therefore, auto parts plants that require a high labor content will continue to exit from Canada and the United States. This exit has little to do with free trade (or, as some have suggested, with the U.S.-Canada Free Trade Agreement). These firms have shift-ed to Mexico as a result of a de facto free trade in automotive parts in North America. The shifts are, as indicated, part of the global trend to outsourcing. Will a bilateral or trilateral North American trade pact greatly accelerate this flow, leading to large investment diversion for Canada?

Insofar as a NAFTA decreases uncertainty for investment in Mexico, additional parts plants would shift to Mexico. However, the process is limited by the location of most existing assembly plants in the northeastern United States/Canada. In the long run, the locations of these plants are essential to the investment diversion story. If, as Womack argues (and I agree), Mexico will become the site of small car assembly presently undertaken in Asia, the investment diversion is at the expense of Asia, not North America. Moreover, the remaining assembly plants in Canada and the United States are largely new or refurbished state-of-the-art plants with long expected lifetimes. Pressures to move these plants will occur, if at all, ten years from now.

Summary

The analysis presented here suggests that a trade agreement between the United States and Mexico will generate real gains for those two nations but will lead to some trade diversion for Canada in U.S. markets and to some new penetration of Mexican goods into Canadian markets. If the United States alone had negotiated a trade pact with Mexico, Canada would have been affected. A Mexico-U.S. free trade agreement provides some costs and few benefits to Canada. The only benefits are the spillovers from Mexican accelerated growth that is not diverted to the preferential access of the United States. It is only with a true North American agreement that both Canada and the United States can receive the real benefits of free trade. While Mexican trade liberalization since 1986 has been enormous, the nominal trade-weighted tariff rate is still high, skewed heavily toward end products, and compounded by significant transitory surcharges. Foreign investment, while fundamentally liberalized, still has significant roadblocks. Preferences in the Mexican market would be important.

Won't NAFTA, however, involve competing with $1.60 cent per hour labor? As noted, if cheap labor was the key to industrialization, Mexico, China, Romania, and Sub-Saharan Africa would be industrialized and world leaders in manufacturing exports. As Michael Porter states in the *Competitive Advantage of Nations*, it is *productivity*, not just cost, that is crucial. Americans and Canadians cannot undertake all economic activities. We must rely on what we can do at a "comparative advantage" and negotiate for our firms the market access required.

The calculations contained in this paper suggest that Canada would have sustained small losses due to a Mexico-United States free trade agreement. A tripartite agreement provides incremental gains for Canada, as detailed in table 6. This table suggests that there are incremental gains to Canada in NAFTA. Canadians bear "the pain" in MUFTA, but capture benefits in NAFTA. The table is hypothetical because it is based on past elasticities, estimates of tariffs, and guesses of income changes in Mexico and the United States generated by the trade pacts. The table is also conservative in two ways. First, it underestimates the degree to which Mexican industry and entrepreneurs will be invigorated by free trade. Second, it is based on an ancient mercantilist view that increases can be measured by gains in exports. It therefore assumes no change in consumers surplus and that a decline in exports means that resources are unused.

The "trinational equation" equals clear gains for all three countries. However, there will be winners and losers, and attention must be directed toward helping losers adjust to change. The changes wrought by NAFTA in the United States and Canada are small compared to the changes caused by all the forces of global restructuring. Thus, learning to adjust to change is not a lesson that Mexico alone brings north.

Notes

1. For example, President Echeverria (1970–1976) decided to hold oil exports to the United States to a maximum of 50 percent of Mexican output in order to minimize this dependence. Two points are important. First, supplying a neighbor with resources may increase that neighbor's dependence, not one's own. Second, these policies have an echo in Canada. In 1967, Prime Minister Lester B. Pearson originally vetoed the additional capacity for the Great Lakes Transmission Company (natural gas) because the proposed line went through the United States.

2. Some of these policies will be familiar to Canadian readers, although Canadian policies were never as protectionist as those of Mexico.

3. Some have argued that the Canada-U.S. Free Trade Agreement (CAFTA) drags Canada into these discussions. However, without the existence of CAFTA, negotiations between the United States and Mexico could have put Canada in a worse situation. Mexico wants preferences at least equal to those of Canada in the U.S. market. Without CAFTA, Mexico would have been negotiating treatment preferential to what Canada has in U.S. markets. Therefore, those observers who argue that Canada has been led into the Mexico trap because of CAFTA are quite wrong.

4. Labor productivity is a biased measure of true productivity because it ignores the other factors of production. In particular, Mexico uses higher labor-capital technologies than the United States or Canada.

5. On average, labor in Mexico earns one-tenth of labor in Canada, yet Mexican labor is one-fifth as productive as Canadian labor. Labor in Mexico earns far less as a percentage of GNP than does Canadian (or U.S). labor. The returns to capital are unusually high (as one referee of this paper stated). Several explanations hold. First, these data for an economy such as Mexico's are suspect: the averages may be wrong and the average masks an enormous range of differences. Second, capital goods industry has been enormously protected and earns rents. Increased competition should reduce these rents. Third, as noted in table 1, labor force participation rates are very low in Mexico. With Mexican growth, the share of labor will increase.

6. Magun (1993) examines the structure of trade in a different way by measuring "revealed comparative advantage" (a greater share of a particular product's exports than for overall exports). Magun finds "the Mexican comparative advantage is significantly different from that of Canada" (p. 15).

7. Mexico has made enormous strides in recent years in raising the skill level of employees and producing more complex quality products.

8. The adjusted Grubel-Lloyd index is calculated as

$$GL_{ijk} = 1 - \frac{\dfrac{X_{ijk}}{X_{ij}} - \dfrac{M_{ijk}}{M_{ij}}}{\dfrac{X_{ijk}}{X_{ij}} + \dfrac{M_{ijk}}{M_{ij}}}$$

where X_{ijk} and M_{ijk} denote, respectively, the exports from country i to country j and the imports in country i from country j, in industry k. X_{ij} and M_{ij} denote the total manufacturing exports and imports between countries i and j. In any given industry k, this index will be equal to one, when exports and imports (as a percentage of total exports and imports) are equal and zero (intraindustry) when trade is unilateral.

9. Other sets of impacts—difficult to quantify—are not discussed here: the impacts that greater trade will have on competition and the scale economies of Mexican industry and the "dynamic" effect that liberalization will have on Mexican entrepreneurs and the country.

10. See Damien Neven (1990) for a discussion of the impact of Europe 1992 on the trade patterns of various EC member countries.

11. I ignore "terms of trade effects." Lowering tariffs changes the "terms of trade" or the real exchange rate between imports and exports. The magnitude of the terms of trade effect (or even its sign) depends on the assumptions one makes about how a country's exports or imports affect the price in the other country. Traditionally, the assumption is made that Canada is a price taker and cannot affect world prices for products, i.e., Canada imports from the United States at the U.S. price (plus tariff) and exports to the United States at the world price (U.S. customers pay the world price plus the U.S. tariff). A similar assumption could well be made for Mexi-

can trade, i.e., increased Mexican trade with the United States and/ or Canada will not affect the world or market price in Canada or the United States.

12. Some of these models include Canada, but the results for the United States and Mexico are largely the same whether Canada is included or not.

13. Hufbauer and Schott do recognize this issue but only in the context (see pp. 127, 128) of their discussion of the transitional problem of job dislocation.

14. These elasticity estimates are different from those calculated by Shiells in the following ways. First, Shiells calculates elasticities for specific products; Cline, for the entire export basket of a country. Second, Shiells aggregates countries into two groups, developed and undeveloped; Cline estimates elasticities particular to a country. Finally, the estimation period and methodology differ.

15. The reader may be surprised by this relatively small decrease in Mexican exports to the United States as a result of MUFTA. The Cline elasticities are underestimates of the effects of trade liberalization on the Mexican economy.

16. This estimated income elasticity is low.

17. In an earlier work (Waverman 1991), I calculated a higher growth dividend based on Mexican growth in net goods and services imports, but here I use only net goods trade. Hufbauer and Schott use other assumptions and come out with similar totals.

18. It is in overall Mexican interests to modernize this system, and intense U.S. pressure for cross-border competition will likely occur in negotiations.

References

Automotive Parts Manufacturers' Association (1990), "The Mexican Auto Industry: A Competitor for the 1990's," mimeo, Toronto, September.

Balassa, Bela (1990), "Economic Prospects and Policies in Mexico," *Journal of the North American Economics and Finance Association,* September.

Booz, Allen & Hamilton Inc. (1990), "A Comparative Study of the Cost Competitiveness of the Automotive Parts Manufacturing Industry in North America," mimeo, Toronto, March.

Brown, Drusilla K., Alan V. Deardorff and Robert M. Stern (1992), "A North American Free Trade Agreement: Analytical Issues and a Computational Assessment," *The World Economy,* Volume 15, Number 1, pp. 11–30.

Bueno, Gerardo M. (1990), "Trade and Development Policy in Mexico in the Context of North American Economic Relations," *Journal of the North American Economics and Finance Association,* September.

Canada, Department of Finance (1986), *The Canada-U.S. Free Trade Agreement: An Economic Perspective,* Ottawa.

Cline, William R. (1989), *United States External Adjustment and the World Economy,* Washington: Institute for International Economics, March.

Cox, David and Richard G. Harris (1980), "A Quantitative Assessment of the Economic Impact on Canada of Sectoral Free Trade with the United States," *Canadian Journal of Economics,* August.

Dornbusch, Rudiger (1990), "U.S.-Mexican Trade Relations," testimony before the Subcommittee on Trade, Committee on Ways and Means, U.S. House of Representatives, June 14.

Government of Mexico, HACIENDA (1990), "The Renegotiation of Mexico's Eternal Debt," mimeo, Mexico City, February 4.

Gregory, Peter (1986), *The Myth of Market Failure: Employment and the Labor Market in Mexico,* Baltimore: Johns Hopkins Press for the World Bank.

Harris, Richard G. (1987), "Comments on Brown and Stern" in Robert M. Stern et al., *Perspectives on a U.S.-Canadian Free Trade Agreement*, Ottawa: Institute for Research on Public Policy.

Harris, Richard G. and David Cox (1984), *Trade Industrial Policy and Canadian Manufacturing*, Ontario Economic Council, Toronto.

Hart, Michael (1990), "A Mexico-Canada-United States Free Trade Agreement: The Strategic Implications for Canada," mimeo, Ottawa, May.

Helleiner, Gerald K. (1990), "Considering a U.S.-Mexican Free Trade Area," paper prepared for a conference on "Mexico's Trade Options in the Changing International Economy," Universidad Technologica de Mexico, Mexico City, June 11–15.

Hufbauer, G.C. and J.J. Schott (1992), *North American Free Trade*, Institute for International Economics, Washington, D.C.

Lipsey, Richard G. (1989), "Innis Lecture: Unsettled Issues in the Great Free Trade Debate," *Canadian Journal of Economics*, February.

———. (1990), "Canada at the U.S. Mexico Free Trade Dance: Wallflower or Partner?" C.D. Howe Institute, Commentary, Toronto.

Lipsey, Richard G. and Murray G. Smith (1985), *Taking The Initiative: Canada's Trade Options in a Turbulent World*, C.D. Howe Institute, Toronto.

Magun, Sunder (1993), in Mario F. Bognanno and Kathryn J. Ready (eds.), *North American Free Trade Agreement*, Westport, Connecticut: Praeger.

Markusen, James R. (1985), "Canadian Gains From Trade in the Presence of Scale Economies and Imperfect Competition," in John Whalley and Roderick Hill (eds.), *Canada-United States Free Trade*, Volume 11 in a series of studies commissioned for the Royal Commission on the Economic Union and Development Prospects for Canada, Ottawa.

Neven, Damien J. (1990), "EEC Integration Towards 1992: Some Distributional Issues," *Economic Policy*, April.

Ramirez de la 0, Rogelio (1990), "Mexico-U.S. Free Trade Talks: Why Canada Should Get Involved," Royal Bank of Canada, ECONOSCOPE.

Reynolds, Clark W. (1990), "Dynamic Comparative Advantage: Some Implications for Trade Policy in North America," *Journal of the North American Economics and Finance Association,* September.

Sawyer, John A. (1990), "Foreign Trade and the Changing Industrial Structure of Canada, 1961–1985," Ontario Centre for International Business, Working Paper Series, Toronto, April.

Shiells, Clinton R. (1985), *A Disaggregated Empirical Analysis of U.S. Import Demand, 1962–1981,* Ph.D. dissertation, The University of Michigan, Ann Arbor, Michigan.

Waverman, Leonard (1991), "Free Trade with Mexico: A Canadian Perspective," mimeo, University of Toronto.

Weintraub, Sidney (1988), *Mexican Trade Policy and the North American Community,* Volume X, Number 14, Significant Issue Series, Centre for Strategic and International Studies, Washington.

————. (1989), "The Impact of the U.S.-Canada Free Trade Agreement on Mexico," paper prepared for "The Future of the U.S.-Canadian Free Trade Agreement," Study Group of the Council on Foreign Relations, mimeo, New York.

Whalley, John (1990), "Now That the Deal is Over: Canadian Trade Policy Options in the 1990's," *Canadian Public Policy,* June.

Wigle, Randall (1988), "General Equilibrium Evaluation of Canada-U.S. Trade Liberalization in a Global Context," *Canadian Journal of Economics.*

Womack, James P., Daniel T. Jones and Daniel Roos (1990), *The Machine That Changed the World,* Rawson Associates Limited.

Wonnacott, Ronald (1990), "Canada and the U.S.-Mexican Free Trade Negotiations," paper prepared for a conference entitled "Mexico's Trade Options in the Changing International Economy," Universidad Technologica de Mexico, Mexico City, June 11–15.

2

Assessing the Effects of NAFTA: Economywide Models of North American Trade Liberalization

Joseph F. Francois

Introduction

The North American Free Trade Agreement (NAFTA) has been the subject of protracted public debate. While the agreement was announced in August 1992, the public debate on NAFTA in the United States began much earlier. In May 1991, the U.S. Congress extended the President's authority to negotiate trade agreements under "fast-track" authority.[1] However, the extension was granted only after an acrimonious series of exchanges on the likely economic effects of NAFTA.

The attention devoted to NAFTA in the United States has been much greater than that which accompanied the Canadian Free Trade Agreement (CAFTA). This is due, in part, to the expressed concerns of organized labor and others about the effects of NAFTA on U.S. wage rates. Economic recession also served to focus public attention more directly onto economic issues. Regardless of the motivation for a heightened public interest, economywide models of NAFTA featured prominently in the resulting public discourse on the economic effects of NAFTA. In a sense, the policy debate represented a coming-of-age for this type of economic policy analysis in the United States.

One of the more heated elements of the general fast-track reauthorization debate concerned computable general equilibrium (CGE) assessments of wage effects. In one of the first assessments of the proposed U.S.-Mexico Free Trade Agreement, the U.S. International Trade Commission (ITC, 1991) reported that NAFTA might result in a slight depression or a slight increase in average wage levels for unskilled labor. However, regardless of decreases or increases, the effects on average wage rates were projected to be very small. Later public clarifications defined "slight" as, essentially, indistinguishable from zero (ranging from –0.002 to + 0.01 percent of annual earnings per worker per year).[2] Notwithstanding the order of magnitude of these effects, a lively and emotional debate ensued as part of the overall fast-track reauthorization process. For some parties, the order of magnitude was not as important as whether wages increased or decreased. Still others explained in testimony that the ITC's "slight" really meant "massive," and that "unskilled" really covered 60 percent of the U.S. workforce. Hinojosa and Robinson (1991) later reported wage changes for unskilled U.S. labor that were larger than the ITC estimates, though generally positive, in the range of –0.1 to 1.8 percent of annual earnings per year. Within this range, unskilled urban labor wage rates fell in only one of four free trade agreement (FTA) implementation scenarios examined. The Hinojosa and Robinson results were added to the arsenal of estimates cited by both sides prior to the fast-track vote. In some quarters, the one set of estimates (out of four) showing unskilled wages falling was drawn on as the definitive assessment of likely economywide effects.

During the fast-track debate, the U.S. administration cited three major economic analyses of NAFTA: the INFORUM-CIMAT (1990) study, also known as the Almon study; the KPMG Peat Marwick study (1991); and the 1991 ITC study.[3] The Almon study employed two separate macroeconomic forecasting models, for Mexico and the United States, and linked them through the bilateral trade equations. The Peat Marwick project constructed a CGE model of Mexico and the United States. The ITC report was qualitative rather than quantitative, but drew upon a three-sector, two-country general equilibrium model to assess wage and migration effects, as well as partial equilibrium models of particular industrial sectors.

In addition to citing these three studies, the Bush administration pledged, prior to fast-track approval, to draw on new economic analyses of NAFTA as they became available. Accordingly, U.S. Trade Representative Carla Hills requested that the ITC hold a public symposium, at which researchers involved in economywide analyses of NAFTA would present papers outlining their methods and findings. The symposium was held at the ITC in February 1992. In general, the papers presented at the ITC symposium found that NAFTA held potential benefits for all three parties involved, that the dynamic gains from NAFTA would far outweigh the static gains, and that real wages of U.S. workers would rise, albeit slightly.

This chapter provides an overview of economywide models of NAFTA. It first offers a brief discussion of the structure of the NAFTA economies and the implications of these issues for the modeling exercise. This is followed by a discussion of actual economywide models of NAFTA. Finally, the results of these modeling efforts are examined in light of the structure of the actual agreement.

The North American Economies

An Overview

NAFTA represents a step toward the economic integration of countries with widely disparate income levels. In contrast, CAFTA furthered the integration of very similar economies. Mexico is a relatively labor-abundant country when compared with its North American neighbors. Wage rates are relatively low, and a large stock of labor is employed in inefficient agricultural production. The Mexican economy is also much smaller when compared to the combined CAFTA market.

Figures 1 through 3 present some basic macroeconomic indicators for 1990 for the North American economies. In 1990, the real Gross Domestic Product (GDP) in Mexico was $236 billion, or $2,680 per capita. On a per capita basis, U.S. real per capita income levels were almost 10 times larger, at $21,800. Overall, the U.S. economy is almost 20 times larger than the Mexican economy, on a real GDP basis. In 1990, U.S. GDP was valued at $5,465 billion. (See figure 1.) These simple relationships lie at the root of the findings of practically all of the economywide studies of NAFTA. The relative size of the combined CAFTA economies and the Mexican economy imply that most of the pressure for adjustment will be on the Mexican side of the border. At the same time, relative income and wage levels imply greater adjustment in wage rates than that which has accompanied CAFTA. Of these two factors (relative scale and factor endowments), the dominant one in assessing the immediate- to medium-term impact of NAFTA proves to be country size. As will be discussed later in this chapter, in practically all of the static economywide studies, adjustment pressures are focused on Mexico. Even for unskilled labor, the impact of closer integration of the Mexican economy with one many times its size is, not surprisingly, concentrated on the smaller economy.

Because of the disparity in wage rates, some of the greatest concerns about NAFTA have been raised by organized labor interests. The effect of NAFTA on U.S. wages, especially for low wage workers, should be greater than that of CAFTA. Trade theory suggests that U.S. wages may fall in response to NAFTA, both in absolute terms and relative to the rental fee on capital services. The actual effect is an empirical question and depends on a number of factors, including the potential complementarity of U.S.-Mexican

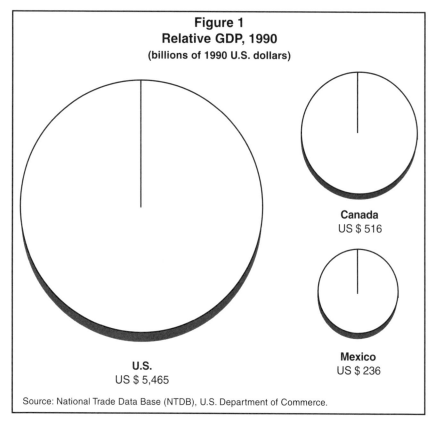

Figure 1
Relative GDP, 1990
(billions of 1990 U.S. dollars)

Canada
US $ 516

U.S.
US $ 5,465

Mexico
US $ 236

Source: National Trade Data Base (NTDB), U.S. Department of Commerce.

production, effects related to third country trade, and the structure of production.[4] While Mexico is certainly a lower wage country, this is not due solely to the availability of private capital. Current wage differences are due to a number of additional, interrelated factors, including education, productivity, and the quality of infrastructure. To highlight such differences, figure 2 illustrates the current disparity in the level of development of transportation infrastructure in the three countries. Such disparities are at least as striking as wage differences and at least as important. They imply that capital flows or trade alone simply cannot lead to an equalization of wage rates.

The dynamic structure of the North American economies is also important. While the United States and Canada are larger, the Mexican economy has recently been the most dynamic and, in general, the fastest growing. Figure 3 illustrates these patterns for 1990. As of 1990, population growth was 2.2 percent per year in Mexico, compared to 0.8 percent in the United States and 1.1 percent in

Canada. Mexico's population is relatively young, with a dependency ratio (measured as nonworking population per worker) of 0.69, compared to 0.51 in the United States and 0.48 in Canada. Real GDP growth was 3.9 percent in Mexico, 1.0 percent in the United States, and 0.9 percent in Canada in 1990. On a per capita basis, the growth rate was 1.1 percent in Mexico, compared to 0.2 percent in the United States and –0.2 percent in Canada.

Trade patterns reflect both the relative scale of the NAFTA economies and the extent to which integration has already taken place. The United States is Mexico's most important trading partner, accounting for over 70 percent of Mexican exports and imports in 1989. At the same time, from a U.S. perspective, Mexico ranks behind Canada and Japan, with 6 percent of U.S. imports and 7 percent of exports in 1989. With regard to Canada, its trade with the United States in 1989 amounted to $163 billion, while Canadian trade with Mexico accounted for only $2 billion of imports and exports.

The extent to which integration has already taken place, espe-

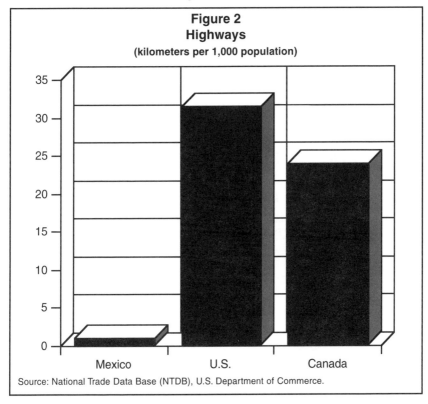

Figure 2
Highways
(kilometers per 1,000 population)

Source: National Trade Data Base (NTDB), U.S. Department of Commerce.

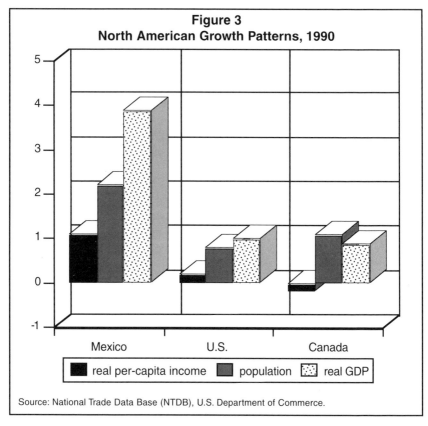

Figure 3
North American Growth Patterns, 1990

Source: National Trade Data Base (NTDB), U.S. Department of Commerce.

cially under CAFTA, the U.S.-Canada auto pact, and the offshore assembly provisions of the U.S. tariff code, is reflected in the current level of intraindustry trade and shared production arrangements. To illustrate the importance of such trade, table 1 presents U.S. imports of automobiles and auto parts for 1990 under Harmonized Tariff Schedule (HTS) tariff subheadings 9802.00.60 and 9802.00.80, which provide for production sharing. Canadian imports of these products would enter duty free anyway under the Automotive Products Trade Act (APTA). However, the extension of a customs user fee, first imposed in 1986, motivates the importers of duty-free vehicles and parts from Canada to declare eligibility under 9802.00.80. According to customs data, $19.5 billion dollars worth of automobiles and parts entered the United States from Canada in 1990 under the production sharing headings. Of the imports from Canada, about $7.2 billion represented U.S. components, a 36 percent value share. In the case of Mexico, $3.9 billion was imported under these provision headings, with a U.S. components value share of 47 percent. To a large extent, the pattern of U.S. trade in automobiles and auto parts with Mexico already reflects relative labor cost differences. The primary change under NAFTA may be expanded access to a growing Mexican auto and truck market for U.S. producers.

Another important factor in the case of autos is the existence of scale economies. Industries with fixed costs, such as the auto industry, can produce at lower cost per unit if the scale of production is increased. Trade theory suggests that trade barriers may support too large a number of product varieties, each of which is produced at too low a volume. This is arguably the case, for example, for the portion of the Mexican auto industry located near Mexico City. Roland-Holst et al. (1992) offer evidence that, due in part to relatively low production volumes, Mexican production costs for domestic consumption are substantially higher than comparable costs in the United States and Canada. Trade liberalization may lead to economic gains through rationalization of the domestic industry. These rationalization gains, whereby inefficient plants are closed and remaining plants

Table 1
U.S. Imports of Automobiles and Auto Parts Under
HTS Subheadings 9802.00.60 and 9802.00.80, 1990
(thousands of dollars)

	Total value	Duty-free value	Dutiable value
Canada			
9802.00.80			
internal combustion engines and parts	964,292	97,488	866,804
motor vehicles	17,275,016	6,739,643	10,535,374
motor vehicle parts	1,270,130	330,826	939,304
9820.00.60			
internal combustion engines and parts	3,860	1,910	1,950
motor vehicle parts	1,219	564	655
Total	**19,514,517**	**7,170,431**	**12,344,087**
Mexico			
9802.00.80			
internal combustion engines and parts	279,137	97,268	181,869
motor vehicles	2,602,160	1,061,650	1,540,510
motor vehicle parts	1,049,637	677,692	371,946
9820.00.60			
internal combustion engines and parts	9,312	7,333	1,979
motor vehicle parts	21,828	7,345	4,483
Total	**3,962,074**	**1,861,288**	**2,100,787**

Source: Product Sharing: U.S. Imports Under Harmonized Tariff Schedule Subheadings 9802.60 and 9802.80, 1987-1990, USITC publication 2469, December 1991.

operate at more efficient levels, may be an important part of the effects of NAFTA, especially for Mexico.

The Models

Some Background

Before discussing how the results of the various models of NAFTA differ, it may be useful to discuss first some of the basic structural characteristics common to most of the models. CGE models are firmly rooted in microeconomic theory. They use the structure of the economy in a single year, referred to as the benchmark, as a basis for policy experiments. However, estimates of actual behavioral relationships in the model are usually based on an empirical analysis of time-series data.[5]

A distinction can be drawn between static and dynamic CGE models. Static models focus on the economy in a single benchmark or base year and employ data on trade, interindustry transactions, and consumption patterns for that year. Trade liberalization experiments alter the level of tariffs and other trade restraints, solving for prices and quantities that would prevail in the base year if everything had been the same except for the level of trade restrictions. The results of this comparative static experiment tell us what an economy with the base year structure would look like, in equilibrium, given the trade policy changes and general equilibrium constraints.

Within the set of static models, a distinction can be drawn between models that assume constant returns to scale and models that assume increasing returns to scale. If there are increasing returns to scale, trade liberalization may induce inefficient firms to exit and push remaining firms down their average cost curves. This can be an important source of gains from trade, in addition to the standard gains arising from differences in factor proportions. For similar countries (such as the European Community), this type of effect may account for a very large share of static gains. It is usually presumed that CGE models of NAFTA that incorporate imperfect competition (increasing returns to scale) will capture important gains from trade liberalization precluded by models that assume perfect competition (constant returns to scale).

In models with increasing returns, some form of imperfect competition is assumed. Various NAFTA models employ the following types of imperfect competition: Bertrand, Cournot, contestable markets, Eastman-Stykolt, and monopolistic competition hypotheses.

Under most of these forms of imperfect competition, it is possible to hold the number of firms in the market fixed or, alternatively, to allow costless entry and exit. The form of imperfect competition chosen and whether or not there is free entry and exit affects the simulation results in a complex manner. In dynamic models, an entire time path is constructed from data on levels and growth rates for variables in a single year. The dynamic model is used to simulate what prices and quantities would be in the future, say 1992–2000, given the data and assuming that some variables are not determined within the model. In general, the current generation of static and dynamic CGE models does not deal adequately with monetary policy issues. Instead, the evolution of monetary and fiscal policy are typically assumed to be determined outside the model (i.e., the money stock and government budget deficit are exogenous). The model is solved again for the new equilibrium values, given proposed trade policy changes. This process yields a second time path for prices and quantities. The difference between these two paths of prices and quantities is interpreted as the incremental effect of the tariff changes.

Within dynamic models, a distinction can be drawn between level effects and growth effects.[6] A tariff reduction on capital goods imports, for example, will lead to increased investment and a larger capital stock. In itself, however, the tariff decrease will only lead to an increase in the level of output per worker. While this leads to a temporary increase in growth rates, it does not lead to a permanent acceleration in the rate of economic growth. Potential sources of economic growth include population growth and technical change. The rate of technical change may either be specified outside the model (i.e., exogenously) or may be determined within the model (i.e., endogenously). In the endogenous growth literature, sources of endogenous technical change include human capital accumulation, learning-by-doing, specialized inputs, or research and development. If technical change is endogenous, it is theoretically possible for trade liberalization to increase the rate of economic growth. Thus, endogenous growth models are needed to capture dynamic gains from trade liberalization. It is widely believed that these dynamic gains may greatly exceed the gains from trade in static models.[7]

Model Structure
Table 2 summarizes some of the main structural features of the NAFTA CGE models. The table is divided into static models and

dynamic models. Some of these models were structured to emphasize the impact of a NAFTA on one or two sectors. In particular,

Table 2
CGE Model Structures

Static models	Countries	Sectors	Base year/ time path	Market[1] structure	Experiment[1]	Focus sectors
Bachrach & Mizrahi	Canada, Mexico, U.S.	44	1988	CRS	Tariffs NTBs	
Brown et al.	Canada, Mexico, U.S.	29	1989	IRS	Tariffs	
Harris & Cox	Canada	19	1989	IRS	Tariffs	
Hunter et al.	Canada, Mexico, U.S.	2	1988	IRS with multinationals	Tariffs	Autos
Robinson et al.	Mexico, U.S.	11	1988	CRS	Tariffs NTBs	Agriculture
Roland-Holst et al.	Canada, Mexico, U.S.	26	1988	CRS IRS	Tariff NTBs	
Sobarzo	Mexico	27	1985	IRS	Tariffs	
Trela & Whalley	Canada, Mexico, U.S.	5, 3	1986	CRS	Tariffs NTBs	Steel textiles

Dynamic models	Countries	Sectors	Base year/ time path	Source of growth	Experiment	Focus sectors
Levy & van Wijnbergen	Mexico	7	1991/ 2000	Exogenous	Tariffs	Agriculture
				Hicks-Neutral technical progress	Other[2]	
				Exogenous capital stock and population growth		
McCleery	Mexico, U.S.	2	1991/ 2000	Exogenous population growth		
				Technical progress dependent on output of capital goods		
Young & Romero	Mexico	12	1992/ 2000	Exogenous population growth	Tariffs	

[1]IRS denotes increasing returns to scale specifications. These include, in various models, scale economies with average cost pricing (contestable markets), Cournot pricing, and Bertrand pricing. CRS denotes constant returns to scale. NTBs denote nontariff barriers.

[2]Levy and van Wijnbergen examine liberalization of domestic and trade-related agricultural policies.

Hunter et al. focus primarily on North American autos, Levy and van Wijnbergen concentrate on agriculture, while Trela and Whalley focus on textiles and steel. In these models, trade liberalization in the rest of the economy under NAFTA is modeled, to a greater or lesser degree, in a stylized fashion. The country focus of these models varies as well. For example, the Harris and Cox model and Sobarzo model focus on Canada and Mexico, respectively. These models miss some feedback effects between countries but do greater justice to the country being modeled than multicountry models. Finally, the largest three-country, multisector models are those of Bachrach and Mizrahi, Brown et al., and Roland-Holst et al.

Most of these models assume some degree of product differentiation, either at a country level or at a firm level. Country-level product differentiation is commonly referred to as the Armington assumption. Depending on entry and exit assumptions, firm-level product differentiation can prove operationally similar, if not identical, to Armington structures. In such models, imports are imperfect substitutes for domestic products. Such a structure fits well with the empirical reality of two-way trade within product categories.[8] The exceptions are the Trela and Whalley model and the Young and Romero model. Both assume that imports are perfect substitutes for domestic products. This structure implies more direct competition between imports and domestic products and hence more direct (and larger) wage and output effects from trade liberalization.

The general equilibrium resource constraints in CGE models involve labor markets, capital markets, and related exchange rates. The static models adopt a variety of closure rules with respect to these markets. With regard to labor markets, in some models it is assumed that each country's endowment of labor is fixed. Wages adjust to clear the labor market. Alternatively, in some models wages are fixed and aggregate employment adjusts to clear the labor market. In almost all of the static models, it is assumed that labor is homogeneous, perfectly mobile between sectors within a country, and immobile internationally. The Robinson et al. paper allows for different types of labor and for international labor migration.[9] This segmentation of the labor market makes necessary additional labor-related constraints. In their model, there is enough migration to fix the rural/urban-unskilled wage differential within Mexico and the rural/rural and urban-unskilled/urban-unskilled wage differentials between Mexico and the United States (expressed in a common currency). An implication of this closure rule is that exchange rate changes lead to international labor migration.

With regard to the foreign investment effects of NAFTA, most of the models follow approaches that are best described as ad hoc. Some fix the rental fee on capital services, thereby allowing for imports of capital, while others fix the aggregate capital stock, thereby allowing the rental fee on capital to adjust. If the aggregate capital stock is assumed to be determined outside the model, i.e., exogenously, then it is possible to combine an exogenous increase in the aggregate capital stock with a trade liberalization experiment. The only modeling team to model the effect of trade liberalization on firms' investment decisions is Young and Romero.

Different approaches are also taken with regard to exchange rates. The exchange rate can be fixed, with the trade balance to adjust to restore equilibrium in the foreign exchange market. Alternatively, the trade balance can be fixed, with the exchange rate to adjust to clear the foreign exchange market. In most models, the trade balance is fixed and the exchange rate adjusts. As in the case of capital markets, both approaches taken with regard to exchange rates are best described as ad hoc. Ideally, both the current and capital account would be determined within the model, with the trade balance and the exchange rate jointly determined.[10] Available CGE assessments of investment effects are, for this reason, somewhat unsatisfying.

Results

Aggregate results—of real GDP, average wages, employment, return to capital, and national welfare—from various NAFTA models are presented in table 3. Given the variety of CGE model structures employed to assess NAFTA, there is a surprising degree of unanimity regarding the aggregate implications for Canada, Mexico, and the United States. All three countries are expected to gain from NAFTA, with the benefits for Mexico generally exceeding those for its North American neighbors. Overall, these studies uniformly demonstrate that all three countries would benefit from NAFTA, as shown by increases in welfare and real GDP. In those models that measure welfare in terms of equivalent variation as a percentage of GDP, the Mexican increase ranges from 0.11 to 5 percent with the implementation of NAFTA. The U.S. welfare increase ranges from 0.07 to 2.55 percent of GDP. The Mexican real GDP increase ranges from 0.01 to 11.39 percent while the U.S. real GDP increase ranges from –0.005 to +2.07 percent. As a group, the estimated effects on U.S. GDP are clustered around zero. Most studies show smaller gains for Canada than for Mexico, with welfare changes ranging

	Real GDP	National welfare[1]	Average wages	Employment	Return to capital
Table 3 — CGE Model Results (percentage changes)					
Canada					
Brown et al.	**	0.7	0.4 – 0.5	**	0.4 – 0.5
Harris & Cox	0.12	0.03	0.04	**	**
Hunter et al.	-0.01 – 0.01	**	**	**	**
Roland-Holst et al.	0.38 – 10.57	0.24 – 6.75	**	0.61 – 11.02	0.94 – 20.74
Trela & Whalley	-0.00 – -0.01	**	**	**	**
Mexico					
Bachrach & Mizrahi	0.32 – 4.64	**	**	0.85 – 6.60	0.60
Brown et al.	**	1.6 – 5.0	0.7 – 9.3	**	0.6 – 3.3
Hunter et al.	0.09 – 0.73	**	**	**	**
Levy & van Wijnbergen	16.9 – 21.99[2]	**	**	**	**
McCleery	0.01 – 11.39[3]	**	**	**	**
Robinson et al.	0.27	**	**[4]	**	1.1
Roland-Holst et al.	0.13 – 3.38	0.11 – 3.29	..	0.33 – 2.40	0.45 – 6.57
Sobarzo	1.7 – 8.0	2.0 – 2.4	16.2	5.1 – 5.8	6.2 – 6.6
Trela & Whalley	**	1.2 – 1.6	**	**	**
Young & Romero	2.6 – 8.1[5]	**	**	**	-25.00
United States					
Bachrach & Mizrahi	0.02 – 0.04	**	0.02 – 0.03	**	0.3 – 0.7
Brown et al.	**	0.1 – 0.3	0.2 – 0.2	**	0.2 – 0.2
Hunter et al.	-0.005 – 0.001	**	**	**	**
McCleery	0.22 – 0.51	**	**	**	**
Robinson et al.	0.23	**	**	**	0.1
Roland-Holst et al.	0.06 – 2.07	0.07 – 2.55	**	0.08 – 2.47	0.1 – 3.4
Trela & Whalley	0.01 – 0.01	**	**	**	**

Note: ** means values are not reported, not estimated, or held constant.
-0.00 denotes negative, but indiscernible, effects.
[1]Welfare is measured as equivalent variation, measured as a percentage of GDP.
[2]These values represent the present value of increases through 2000, as a percentage of 1990 GDP.
[3]These values represent the percentage increase in baseline GDP in the year 2000.
[4]Wage effects vary by class of worker.
[5]These values represent an increase over steady-rate values.

from 0.03 to 6.75 percent and changes in real GDP ranging from 0.0 to +10.57 percent.

Many of the models are applied in a set of liberalization experiments, ranging from tariff liberalization alone to tariffs and nontariff barriers (NTBs). Other scenarios involve possible cross-border investment flows. With tariff liberalization alone, increases in Mexican real GDP range from 0.0 to +1.9 percent, while increases in U.S. real GDP range from 0.02 to 0.11 percent. Within these ranges, effects tend to be larger in models that incorporate imperfect competition. Even so, the elimination of tariffs alone yields only relatively small benefits in the static models of a NAFTA. The results strongly suggest that the potential benefits of NAFTA are much larger when NTBs are included. With full tariff and NTB liberalization, the estimated increases in real GDP range from 0.27 to 3.38 percent for Mexico and from 0.02 to 2.07 percent for the United States.

Some studies also assess the importance of capital flows. As compared to simulations that liberalize only tariffs and NTBs, increased capital flows into Mexico yield further gains from NAFTA, especially for Mexico. Estimated increases in real Mexican GDP following such capital flows range from 2.6 to 8.1 percent. Overall, the results suggest that such capital flows are a prominent part of the welfare equation for Mexico. At the same time, notwithstanding public concern in the United States, the results of these studies suggest that capital flows from the United States to Mexico under a NAFTA would not appreciably affect U.S. real GDP, due to the size of the U.S. capital market. However, because of the ad hoc manner in which most of these models assess capital flows, while these results can be viewed as highly suggestive, they are in no way conclusive.

In an aggregate sense, labor benefits in all three countries. However, the evidence is mixed with regard to particular labor categories. In general, aggregate employment or wage rates rise in all three countries. Aggregate employment increases range from 0.33 to 6.60 percent for Mexico and from 0.08 to 2.47 percent for the United States. Average real wage increases range from 0.7 to 16.2 percent for Mexico and from 0.02 to 0.20 percent for the United States. A capital inflow into Mexico benefits labor as well, because a larger Mexican capital stock makes Mexican labor more productive.

Urban skilled and professional workers in the United States gain from NAFTA in the Hinojosa and Robinson paper. They also show real wage increases for urban unskilled workers in three of the four scenarios they examine (0.4 to 1.2 percent). In the fourth scenario, urban unskilled workers experience a slight loss in average wages (–0.01 percent). For rural labor, results are rather muddied, ranging from –0.4 to +1.8 percent. High wage manufacturing workers experience slower earnings growth in McCleery's paper as a result of NAFTA. McCleery's results also indicate that U.S. low wage workers may suffer initial earnings losses, though this is coupled with higher earnings in later periods. The net effect is that their discounted income stream is expected to rise.

Overall, the insights from these models regarding the distributional effects on labor income are mixed. The questions raised during the fast-track debate regarding the differential wage effects of NAFTA have yet to be settled, as the existing body of research simply does not provide a basis for definitive conclusions regarding the full direction and magnitude of relative real wage changes for different components of the U.S. labor force, and in particular for unskilled workers. However, it does appear that any negative change in average wages for unskilled U.S. workers would most likely be slight, in the range of 0.5 percent or less.[11]

Conclusions

In general, the different paths taken to model the economywide effects of a NAFTA all seem to lead to similar qualitative conclusions. Dominating practically all of the model results are the relative sizes of the Canadian, Mexican, and U.S. economies. Combined with the fact that the highest tariff and nontariff barriers are in Mexico, NAFTA implies potentially large-scale rationalization and adjustment in Mexico. For the United States, by contrast, effects should prove to be relatively mild. The largest gains for the United States will follow from liberalization of Mexican NTBs. The greatest benefit for the United States may be added stability and prosperity for its southern neighbor at no discernible cost.[12]

One of the primary differences between the actual NAFTA, as it takes shape, and the policy experiments conducted by the CGE modeling projects reviewed here involves timing. The experiments conducted generally contemplated immediate liberalization. Because many, if not most, NTBs will be phased out over a 10- to 15-year time period, the annual effects of the actual implementation of NAFTA will be even less noticeable for all parties than the results reviewed here would suggest. However, the potential does exist for adverse effects and pressure for adjustment assistance, especially on a sectoral level. This is particularly true for agriculture in Mexico and for unskilled labor in the United States. These effects are linked. Pressure for outward migration from the rural areas of Mexico carries the potential for heightened migration to the United States, accompanied by negative pressure on the lower tier of U.S. wage rates. In addition, one should not underestimate the potential role of NAFTA as scapegoat. If the reception of CAFTA implementation in Canada provides any guidance, then NAFTA may be blamed for all negative economic shocks experienced during or following implementation. Governments in all three countries should therefore be prepared to deal with pressure for adjustment assistance and related trade remedies, not only for NAFTA-induced structural adjustment, but for NAFTA-blamed adjustment as well.

This chapter was written while the author was with the U.S. International Trade Commission. All opinions expressed herein are strictly those of the author and should not be attributed to any institution with which he has been affiliated.

Notes

1. The President notified the Congress of his decision to proceed with free trade negotiations with Mexico under "fast-track" negotiating authority on September 25, 1990. Following further discussions with Mexico and Canada, the President notified Congress on February 5, 1991, of the decision of all three governments to broaden the negotiations to include Canada and so to work toward NAFTA. Fast-track provides for Congressional consultation during negotiations, followed by formal notification of an agreement, and a simple yes or no vote on the agreement. It is meant to add credence to the U.S. negotiating position by ensuring against Congressional amendment after an agreement has been negotiated.

2. The Congress had originally requested that the Commission's study be strictly qualitative. This made the later public clarifications of actual magnitudes necessary once the report's findings had begun to be cited in Congressional testimony. The Commission also estimated that the wages of high wage workers would increase by between 0.01 to 0.03 percent. In Mexico, the wages of unskilled and skilled labor would increase by 1.1 to 1.4 percent and 0.4 to 0.7 percent, respectively.

3. See "Response of the Administration to Issues Raised in Connection With the Negotiation of a North American Free Trade Agreement," transmitted to the Congress by the President on May 1, 1991.

4. See Brown (1992) for a discussion of the role of country size and factor endowments in driving the results of trade policy analysis in CGE models. Brown works with a stripped-down version of the Michigan model to illustrate many of the relationships buried inside the most common CGE model specifications.

5. These models thus differ from the older generation of linked-macro models. The linked-macro model approach estimates behavioral relationships from time-series data (*i.e.*, a series of data points in different years) to the fullest extent. However, such models have little microeconomic foundation. As a result, it can be difficult to interpret welfare results. In addition, upstream and downstream linkages are, by necessity, ad hoc. The underlying structure of the model is thus fixed. Yet, by definition, economywide policy changes imply that the underlying reduced-form structure of an economy (as reflected in the structural equations in linked-macro models) may change. This is true, for example, of the Almon model.

6. See Francois and Shiells (1993).

7. See Kehoe (1992).

8. In imperfect substitutes models, the degree of substitutability between domestic products and imports proves to be a critical factor in determining the direction and magnitude of the effects of trade liberalization. See Reinert and Shiells (1992) for an empirical assessment of product similarity between traded NAFTA products.

9. The ITC (1991) model also assumed different labor classes. In that model as well, closure involved labor migration as part of the labor supply conditions.

10. See Goulder and Eichengreen (1992).

11. Robinson, et al. estimate a larger decline in average wage rates for U.S. unskilled workers (–1.7 percent for urban unskilled workers and –1.3 for rural workers). However, these estimates assume immediate liberalization of Mexican agriculture, coupled with the immediate elimination of all Mexican agricultural support programs. The wage declines in the United States that follow are not due to direct trade effects, but rather, in large part, to greater Mexican-U.S. migration flows as Mexican agricultural labor is displaced. In the actual agreement, Mexican liberalization of grain and oilseed markets will be phased in over a 10- to 15-year period, precluding this type of scenario.

12. In the pro-NAFTA camp, much has been made of the potent combination of joint U.S.-Mexican production by U.S. firms as a counter to the competitive advantages of East Asian producers. However, this combination is already made possible under the product-sharing provisions of the U.S. and Mexican tariff codes.

References

Almon, Clopper, 1990, "Industrial Effects of a Free Trade Agreement
between Mexico and the U.S.A." Research report prepared for the U.S.
Department of Labor, Bureau of International Labor Affairs, under
Contract J-9-K-9-0077 (September).

Bachrach, Carlos and Mizrahi, Lorris, 1992, "The Economic Impact of a
Free Trade Agreement Between the United States and Mexico: A CGE
Analysis," in the addendum to *Economy-Wide Modeling of the Economic
Implications of a FTA with Mexico and a NAFTA with Canada and Mexico,*
U.S. International Trade Commission, Publication 2516 (May).

Brown, Drusilla, 1992, "Properties of Computer General Equilibrium
Trade Models With Monopolistic Competition and Foreign Direct
Investment," in the addendum to *Economy-Wide Modeling of the Economic
Implications of a FTA with Mexico and a NAFTA with Canada and Mexico,*
U.S. International Trade Commission, Publication 2516 (May).

Brown, Drusilla; Deardorff, Alan V.; and Stern, Robert M., 1992, "A
North American Free Trade Agreement: Analytical Issues and a Computational Assessment," *World Economy* 15 (January), 11–29.

Francois, Joseph F. and Shiells, Clinton R., 1993, "Dynamic Effects of
Trade Liberalization: A Survey," U.S. International Trade Commission.

Goulder, Lawrence H. and Eichengreen, Barry, 1992, "Trade Liberalization in General Equilibrium: Intertemporal and Inter-Industry Effects,"
Canadian Journal of Economics, No. 2 (May), 253–280.

Harris, Richard G. and Cox, David, 1992, "North American Free Trade
and Its Implications for Canada: Results from a CGE Model of North
American Trade," in the addendum to *Economy-Wide Modeling of the
Economic Implications of a FTA with Mexico and a NAFTA with Canada and
Mexico,* U.S. International Trade Commission, Publication 2516 (May).

Hinojosa-Ojeda, Raul and Robinson, Sherman, 1991, "Alternative Scenarios of U.S.-Mexican Integration: A Computable General Equilibrium
Approach," Department of Agriculture and Resource Economics, Division
of Agriculture and Natural Resources, University of California, Working
Paper No. 609 (April).

Hunter, Linda; Markusen, James R.; and Rutherford, Thomas F., 1992, "Trade Liberalization in a Multinational-Dominated Industry: A Theoretical and Applied General Equilibrium Analysis," in the addendum to *Economy-Wide Modeling of the Economic Implications of a FTA with Mexico and a NAFTA with Canada and Mexico,* U.S. International Trade Commission, Publication 2516 (May).

Kehoe, Timothy J., 1992, "Towards a Dynamic General Equilibrium Model of North American Free Trade," in C. Shiells and J. Francois, eds., *Modeling Trade Policy: Applied General Equilibrium Assessments of North American Free Trade,* Cambridge: Cambridge University Press.

KPMG Peat Marwick, 1991, "Analysis of Economic Effects of a Free Trade Area between the United States and Mexico," KPMG Peat Marwick Policy Economics Group, prepared for the U.S. Council of the Mexico-U.S. Business Committee, Washington, D.C.

Levy, Santiago and van Wijnbergen, Sweder, 1992, "Transition Problems in Economic Reform: Agriculture in the Mexico-U.S. Free Trade Agreement," in the addendum to *Economy-Wide Modeling of the Economic Implications of a FTA with Mexico* and *a NAFTA with Canada and Mexico,* U.S. International Trade Commission, Publication 2516 (May).

McCleery, Robert K., 1992, "An Intertemporal, Linked Macroeconomic CGE Model of the United States and Mexico Focusing on Demographic Change and Factor Flows," in the addendum to *Economy-Wide Modeling of the Economic Implications of a FTA with Mexico and a NAFTA with Canada and Mexico,* U.S. International Trade Commission, Publication 2516 (May).

Reinert, Kenneth A. and Shiells, Clint R., 1992, "Estimating Elasticities of Substitution for Analysis of a North American Free Trade Area," U.S. International Trade Commission Staff Research Study No. 19.

Robinson, Sherman; Burfisher, Mary E.; Hinojosa-Ojeda, Raul; and Thierfelder, Karen E., 1992, "Agricultural Policies and Migration in a U.S.-Mexico Free Trade Area: A Computable General Equilibrium Analysis," in the addendum to *Economy-Wide Modeling of the Economic Implications of a FTA with Mexico and a NAFTA with Canada and Mexico,* U.S. International Trade Commission, Publication 2516 (May).

Roland-Holst, David; Reinert, Kenneth A.; and Shiells, Clint R., 1992, "North American Trade Liberalization and the Role of Non-Tariff Barriers," in the addendum to *Economy-Wide Modeling of the Economic Implications of a FTA with Mexico and a NAFTA with Canada and Mexico,* U.S. International Trade Commission, Publication 2516 (May).

Sobarzo, Horacio E., 1992, "A General Equilibrium Analysis of the Gains from Trade for the Mexican Economy of a North American Free Trade Agreement," in the addendum to *Economy-Wide Modeling of the Economic Implications of a FTA with Mexico and a NAFTA with Canada and Mexico,* U.S. International Trade Commission, Publication 2516 (May).

Trela, Irene and Whalley, John, 1991, "Bilateral Trade Liberalization in Quota Restricted Items: U.S. and Mexico in Textiles and Steel," University of Western Ontario, Department of Economics (May).

U.S. International Trade Commission, 1991, *The Likely Impact on the United States of a Free Trade Agreement with Mexico,* U.S. International Trade Commission, Publication 2353 (February).

————, 1992, *Economy-Wide Modeling of the Economic Implications of a FTA with Mexico and a NAFTA with Canada and Mexico,* U.S. International Trade Commission, Publication 2516 (May).

U.S. Trade Representative, 1991, "Response of the Administration to Issues Raised in Connection with the Negotiations of a North American Free Trade Agreement" (May).

Young, Leslie and Romero, Jose, 1992, "Steady Growth and Transition in Dynamic Dual Model of the North American Free Trade Agreement," in the addendum to *Economy-Wide Modeling of the Economic Implications of a FTA with Mexico and a NAFTA with Canada and Mexico,* U.S. International Trade Commission, Publication 2516 (May).

The Effects of NAFTA on the Mexican Economy

José Romero and Leslie Young

Introduction

The purpose of this chapter is to analyze the economic impact on Mexico of the formation of a free trade area that includes Mexico, the United States, and Canada. By simulating the development of the Mexican economy with and without the North American Free Trade Agreement (NAFTA), the impact of the agreement is measured.

The Model

The authors use a multiperiod, general equilibrium model[1] of the Mexican economy to estimate the effects of NAFTA. The model assumes a small, open economy that takes as given the world interest rate and the price of each traded industry (all except building). The domestic interest rate is equal to the world rate plus a "risk-premium." For each traded good, the domestic price is equal to the world prices plus a tariff percentage. In line with the classification in the Sistema de Cuentas Nacionales de México (Mexican National Accounting System), the model has three capital goods industries (machines, buildings, and vehicles) and nine consumption/intermediate goods activities:

1. **Agriculture** (agriculture, livestock, forestry, hunting, fisheries)
2. **Mining** (coal, iron minerals, nonferrous metals, minerals, stones, other nonmetallic minerals)
3. **Oil** (oil and gas extraction, oil refining, basic petrochemicals)
4. **Food** (processed food, beverages, tobacco)
5. **Textiles** (textiles, apparel, leather goods)
6. **Chemicals** (basic chemicals, fertilizers, resins, medicines, cleaning products, other chemicals)
7. **Metals** (iron and steel, nonferrous metals, metallic

products)
8. **Machines** (electric and nonelectric machinery)
9. **Vehicles** (automobile vehicles and parts, other transportation equipment)
10. **Buildings** (construction)
11. **Services** (electricity, retail, transport, communications, financial services, other services)
12. **Miscellaneous** (wood products, paper, rubber, nonmetallic minerals products, other industries)

The model has several features that make it particularly suitable for an analysis of the impact of NAFTA on the Mexican economy. The exercise involves the econometric estimation of 24 separate models (one cost function for goods and one cost function for capital in each industry). We incorporate those estimations into an intertemporal equilibrium model of the Mexican economy. An important feature of our model is that the dynamics of the response of the Mexican economy to changes in relative prices is based in intertemporal optimization by firms. This is especially important for simulations of trade liberalization because expected future alterations in trade policies always have consequences for decisions made today.

A more common method in applied general equilibrium models has been to "calibrate" the parameters of the model to data for a single year. In view of the wide variations in relative prices that have characterized the Mexican economy since the early 1970s, this approach is highly dependent on the particular year chosen for calibration. Econometric methods make it possible to incorporate behavioral responses to changes in relative prices, based on the historical experience of the last twenty years. The empirical basis for our model sets it apart from other models[2] that have been used in analyzing the economic consequences of NAFTA.

In the model, production takes place in two stages. In stage I, the representative firm in each sector produces two aggregates:

(a) capital, using machines, buildings, and vehicles
(b) materials, using various intermediate goods

In each period the appropriate mix of capital goods used to produce the aggregate capital is that which minimizes the cost of production given the period's prices of the three capital goods. In a similar fashion, the appropriate mix of intermediate goods used to produce the materials is that which minimizes the cost of production given the nine prices of intermediate goods.

In stage II, the firm produces a single "product" using labor, capital, and materials. The product of each industry has different uses: it can be used as an intermediate good for the same or different industry, it can be used to satisfy final demand, and it can be combined with other products in different proportions to produce specific capital goods.

All producers seek to maximize profits. The choice variables in each period are: labor, intermediate goods, and level of investment. Labor and intermediate goods are selected to minimize costs, while the level of investment is selected in a manner that allows producers to reach their optimal capital intensity in the long run (long-run profit maximization). The time required to reach the optimal intensity depends on the adjustment costs that face the economy to produce in each period the nontraded capital goods (construction) needed for investment.

The model assumes full employment and an exogenous annual rate of population growth of 2 percent. Employment in 1989 was 22.4 million workers. At an annual rate of growth of 2 percent, the labor force is expected to reach 27.9 million in 2003.

The experiments assume that each industry's share of the labor force can deviate from its current share by 30 percent either way. This assumption corresponds to the recent history of Mexico (see table 1).

Earlier models assumed perfect labor mobility, yet estimated much smaller gains from NAFTA. In general, we found that the greater the deviations allowed in the structure of employment, the greater the gains from NAFTA. Thus, the benefits from NAFTA to Mexico would be substantially enhanced by government policies that facilitate labor mobility, such as an expansion of educational opportunities.

The model predicts what would be the effects of NAFTA over the twelve sectors in variables, such as: production, employment, capital stock, wages, and rentals. As a point of reference for the simulations that follow, we present in table 2 the observed values of those variables in 1989, the last year for which the information is available.

Table 1
Industry's Share of the Labor Force, 1970–1989
(percentages)

Year	Agr	Min	Oil	Food	Tex	Chem	Met	Mac	Veh	Bldg	Svcs	Misc	Total
1970	34.4	1.2	0.6	3.5	2.7	1.1	1.4	1.1	0.6	6.3	44.2	3.1	100
1971	34.5	1.2	0.5	3.5	2.7	1.1	1.2	1.1	0.6	5.9	44.6	3.0	100
1972	33.0	1.2	0.5	3.4	2.7	1.1	1.2	1.2	0.6	6.5	45.5	3.0	100
1973	32.8	1.2	0.5	3.4	2.7	1.1	1.2	1.4	0.7	7.0	45.3	2.9	100
1974	30.6	1.3	0.5	3.5	2.7	1.1	1.3	1.3	0.7	7.3	46.8	3.0	100
1975	30.3	1.2	0.5	3.4	2.5	1.1	1.3	1.3	0.7	7.5	47.5	2.8	100
1976	28.6	1.2	0.5	3.3	2.4	1.1	1.3	1.3	0.7	7.7	48.9	2.9	100
1977	30.0	1.2	0.5	3.2	2.4	1.1	1.2	1.2	0.6	7.1	48.6	2.8	100
1978	28.9	1.2	0.5	3.2	2.3	1.1	1.3	1.2	0.7	7.9	49.0	2.8	100
1979	26.7	1.2	0.5	3.2	2.4	1.1	1.3	1.3	0.7	8.4	50.3	2.9	100
1980	25.9	1.3	0.6	3.1	2.4	1.1	1.3	1.3	0.7	8.9	50.5	2.9	100
1981	27.0	1.0	0.4	2.9	2.1	1.0	1.1	1.2	0.9	10.4	49.4	2.6	100
1982	26.2	1.1	0.1	3.0	2.1	1.0	1.1	1.1	0.8	10.2	50.8	2.6	100
1983	27.9	1.1	0.4	3.0	2.0	1.1	1.0	0.9	0.7	8.4	51.2	2.4	100
1984	27.5	1.1	0.5	3.0	1.9	1.1	1.0	0.9	0.7	8.8	51.1	2.4	100
1985	27.6	1.2	0.5	3.0	1.9	1.0	1.0	0.9	0.8	8.9	50.8	2.5	100
1986	27.3	1.2	0.5	3.1	1.9	1.1	0.9	0.9	0.7	8.7	51.2	2.5	100
1987	27.6	1.2	0.5	3.0	1.9	1.1	0.9	0.9	0.7	8.7	50.9	2.5	100
1988	27.6	1.3	0.5	3.0	1.8	1.1	0.9	0.9	0.8	8.6	51.0	2.5	100
1989	26.8	1.2	0.5	3.0	1.8	1.1	0.9	0.9	0.8	9.5	50.9	2.6	100

Source: INEGI, "Sistema de Cuentas Nacionales de México."

Table 2
Values, 1989

Industry	GDP (billions of 1980 pesos, world prices)	Employment (thousands of persons)	Capital (hundred billions of 1980 pesos)	Wages (millions of pesos)	Rentals (millions of pesos per each hundred million units of capital)	Average ad valorem tariff (percentages)
Agr	33.229	5,999.24	29.722*	1.16	978.42	13.38
Min	7.271	271.54	12.394	5.63	405.23	9.75
Oil	12.917	111.50	137.191	21.42	45.60	9.36
Food	26.119	673.69	14.157	7.60	1,456.72	14.00
Tex	10.847	408.59	3.617	8.28	1,914.14	16.15
Chem	11.361	244.12	17.148	14.04	620.13	11.22
Met	9.773	201.98	16.751	15.22	560.01	12.99
Mac	7.469	207.46	7.721	13.94	733.15	13.37
Veh	8.236	179.77	9.875	16.03	628.96	16.00
Bldg	25.097	2,133.20	2.137	5.35	2,873.03	0.00
Svcs	316.164	11,398.67	169.459	6.83	1,097.82	0.00
Misc	22.754	580.35	16.105	9.90	1,158.77	11.90
Total	**491.237**	**22,410.11**	**436.277**			

* Estimated

Sources: INEGI, "Sistema de Cuentas Nacionales de México"; Banco de México, Acervos de Formación de Capital, Gerencia de Información Económica; SECOFI, Secretaría de Comercio y Fomento Industrial.

First Scenario

The first scenario assumes that the 1992 level of tariffs will remain in place and that the real rate of interest will continue at its 1992 level of 15 percent. The figures in table 3 show the final values of the simulation for the year 2003.

Table 3 Simulation Results for Year 2003 from Scenario 1 Assumptions: • level of tariffs will remain at the 1992 levels • real interest rate at 15 percent (1992 level)					
Industry	**GDP** (billions of 1980 pesos, world prices)	**Employment** (thousands of persons)	**Capital** (hundred billions of 1989 pesos)	**Wages** (millions of pesos)	**Rentals** (millions of pesos per each hundred million units of capital)
Agr	32.649	5,221.51	29.775	2.05	761.00
Min	5.533	236.34	7.853	9.11	432.27
Oil	27.747	180.23	225.169	36.88	95.34
Food	38.983	1,088.94	30.109	11.57	958.95
Tex	14.945	660.44	5.884	11.50	1,543.72
Chem	15.897	394.59	38.093	16.07	261.92
Met	11.567	326.48	20.183	15.28	364.94
Mac	11.461	335.34	10.273	16.26	664.42
Veh	8.938	290.58	10.070	19.29	538.38
Bldg	47.480	2,475.10	5.808	11.04	2,186.57
Svcs	429.964	15,716.53	210.429	10.20	1,081.27
Misc	29.826	938.07	25.411	13.37	717.83
Total	**674.990**	**27,864.15**	**619.057**		

Second Scenario

The second scenario maintains the 1992 real rate of interest of 15 percent but eliminates all tariffs. The figures in table 4 represent the terminal values of the simulation for the year 2003.

Third Scenario

The third scenario eliminates all tariffs and reduces the current real rate of interest from 15 percent to 12 percent. The figures in table 5 represent the terminal values of the simulation for the year 2003.

Table 4
Simulation Results for Year 2003 from Scenario 2

Assumptions:
• no tariffs
• real interest rate at 15 percent (1992 level)

Industry	GDP (billions of 1980 pesos)	Employment (thousands of persons)	Capital (hundred billions of 1989 pesos)	Wages (millions of pesos)	Rentals (millions of pesos per each hundred million units of capital)
Agr	32.475	5,221.51	29.09	1.74	731.11
Min	5.489	236.34	7.639	6.90	459.62
Oil	25.224	180.23	193.046	32.18	93.64
Food	35.589	1,088.94	26.251	8.24	916.79
Tex	7.720	355.62	2.922	8.28	1,463.11
Chem	15.441	394.59	35.930	13.9	250.32
Met	12.525	326.48	22.471	11.87	351.06
Mac	10.528	335.34	8.766	13.03	635.41
Veh	11.247	290.58	12.919	10.73	570.17
Bldg	37.711	2,059.30	5.434	12.21	2,065.80
Svcs	472.996	16,437.15	235.031	12.46	1,049.87
Misc	28.975	938.07	23.970	11.48	685.00
Total	**695.920**	**27,864.15**	**603.469**		

Table 5
Simulation Results for Year 2003 from Scenario 3

Assumptions:
• no tariffs
• real interest rate at 12 percent

Industry	GDP (billions of 1980 pesos, world prices)	Employment (thousands of persons)	Capital (hundred billions of 1989 pesos)	Wages (millions of pesos)	Rentals (millions of pesos per each hundred million units of capital)
Agr	33.363	5,221.51	30.949	2.27	645.48
Min	5.693	236.34	8.292	10.25	367.47
Oil	33.736	180.23	293.835	45.51	84.08
Food	38.889	1,088.94	30.344	11.32	808.71
Tex	8.240	355.62	3.305	10.67	1,217.96
Chem	18.162	394.59	47.221	17.61	217.96
Met	11.085	326.48	18.939	14.37	314.43
Mac	11.661	335.34	10.683	15.45	559.07
Veh	9.984	290.58	11.075	15.62	454.96
Bldg	49.515	2,200.55	7.726	15.34	1,837.58
Svcs	503.437	16,295.90	273.354	14.77	910.38
Misc	31.456	938.07	27.913	14.16	596.71
Total	**755.221**	**27,864.15**	**763.636**		

Comparison of Scenarios

In table 6 the terminal value of gross domestic product of the different simulations is compared for each industry in the year

2003. At current real interest rates of 15 percent, the long-run effect of NAFTA is a 3.1 percent increase in Mexican gross domestic product at world prices. These benefits are substantially higher if NAFTA reduces real interest rates: if the real rate falls to 12 percent, then gross domestic product, at world prices, increases by 11.9 percent in the long run.

Table 6
Effects of NAFTA on Steady Growth Mexican GDP, World Prices
(billions of 1980 pesos)

Industry	A (tariffs, i=15 percent)	B (free trade, i=15 percent)	C (free trade, i=12 percent	(B-A)/A (percentage)	(C-A)A (percentage)	(C-B)/B (percentage)
Agr	32.649	32.475	33.363	-0.5	2.2	2.7
Min	5.533	5.489	5.693	-0.8	2.9	3.7
Oil	27.747	25.224	33.736	-9.1	21.6	33.7
Food	38.983	35.589	38.889	-8.7	-0.2	9.3
Tex	14.945	7.720	8.240	-48.3	-44.9	6.7
Chem	15.897	15.441	18.162	-2.9	14.2	17.6
Met	11.567	12.525	11.085	8.3	-4.2	-11.5
Mac	11.461	10.528	11.661	-8.1	1.7	10.8
Veh	8.938	11.247	9.984	25.8	11.7	-11.2
Bldg	47.480	37.711	49.515	-20.6	4.3	31.3
Svcs	429.964	472.996	503.437	10.0	17.1	6.4
Misc	29.826	28.975	31.456	-2.9	5.5	8.6
Total	**674.990**	**695.920**	**755.221**	**3.1**	**11.9**	**8.5**

Thus, the long-run effect of NAFTA is a substantial increase in Mexican gross domestic product, even at current real interest rates. The gains are even greater if NAFTA reduces Mexican real interest rates, as we would expect for the reasons given below in the section entitled "A Fall in Real Interest Rates." Our analysis indicates that this could well be one of the most significant benefits of NAFTA to Mexico.

In table 7 we present the values of GDP during the transition of different simulations.

At real interest rates of 15 percent, NAFTA increases the present value of national income over the transition and growth phases by 2.5 percent. The comparison between the present values of national income at different interest rates is dominated by the effects of discounting at these different interest rates, but the last column of table 7 shows that the drop in the interest rate from 15 percent to 12 percent leads to substantial increases in GDP in all periods (except the first).

Table 7
Mexican GDP During the Transition, World Prices
(billions of 1980 pesos)

Industry	A (tariffs, i=15 percent)	B (free trade, i=15 percent)	C (free trade, i=12 percent	(B-A)/A (percentage)	(C-A)A (percentage)	(C-B)/B (percentage)
1993	549.48	558.88	558.11	1.71	1.57	-0.14
1994	561.39	569.53	605.01	1.45	7.77	6.23
1995	583.85	590.33	626.71	1.11	7.34	6.16
1996	585.08	595.26	627.90	1.74	7.32	5.48
1997	597.07	614.80	644.41	2.97	7.93	4.82
1998	610.52	626.03	676.20	2.54	10.76	8.02
1999	623.46	640.86	689.42	2.79	10.58	7.58
2000	635.98	653.66	700.34	2.78	10.12	7.14
2001	648.70	670.30	714.80	3.33	10.19	6.64
2002	661.67	682.78	738.30	3.19	11.58	8.13
2003	674.990	695.920	755.221	3.10	11.89	8.52

The Economic Gains from NAFTA

This section provides an intuitive idea of the economic gains from NAFTA that are captured in our model.

Equalization of Effective Rates of Protection: Static Gains

Consider three sectors A, B, and C, each protected by a nominal 5 percent tariff. If each sector used only Mexican inputs, which are unprotected, their effective rates of protection would be the same and there would be no misallocation of resources across the three sectors, although there would be a misallocation among these sectors and sectors producing nontraded goods. The latter misallocation would be small because of the low level of the nominal tariffs.

By contrast, suppose that the free trade percentage of the final product price representing value added from Mexican sources is 90 percent in A, 50 percent in B, and 50 percent in C. Suppose also that A and B use inputs, which are imported freely, while C uses inputs that are subject to a 20 percent tariff. The standard formula for effective protection[3] measures the percentage by which the domestic value added exceeds the equivalent value at world prices. This formula implies that the tariff structure has increased the value added from Mexican sources by +5.55 percent in A, +10 percent in B, and –10 percent in C, severely distorting the allocation of these resources among these sectors, even though all enjoy the same nominal protection. Moreover, relative to nontradeables, the value added in sector B has increased by 10 percent while that in sector C has fallen by 10 percent, suggesting that NAFTA would move resources from B into nontradeables and from nontradeables into C. Thus, removing modest nominal tariffs can significantly improve the efficiency of resource use.

There can be no presumption that low nominal tariff rates imply low gains. Indeed, as the above examples illustrate, *low* nominal rates of protection of a final good sector tends to imply *high* negative effective protection when combined with moderate tariffs on inputs.

Equalization of Effective Rates of Protection: Dynamic Effects

Machinery and other capital goods are currently subject to substantial nominal tariffs of 16–20 percent. As noted, a sector with highly protected inputs suffers negative effective protection and becomes too small relative to sectors enjoying positive effective protection. This effect is stronger, the greater the share of the final product price absorbed by inputs that are subject to tariffs. For goods that require substantial investment to produce, the relevant "final product price" is the *present value* of the future revenue generated. The very high real rates of interest currently obtaining in Mexico imply that, in highly capital-intensive sectors, the cost of capital goods is particularly high relative to the present value of the revenue stream generated from investment in those goods. Thus, highly capital-intensive sectors suffer particularly high negative levels of effective protection. The tariffs on capital inputs act like a tax on capital accumulation, slowing economic growth by raising the perceived cost of producing for future periods and cutting off investment projects that would enhance labor productivity. The efficiency losses imposed by the tariffs on capital inputs are cumulative, reducing the rate of economic growth.

Efficient Input Use Within a Sector

Tariffs not only misallocate resources across sectors, but also prevent each sector from using the input combination with the lowest foreign exchange cost. For example, within a broad category of "materials," the removal of tariffs on different intermediate goods will lead sectors to choose combinations of intermediate goods that cost the country less foreign exchange. The detailed modeling of intersectoral flows capture the gains from more efficient input use within each sector.

The prevailing high interest real rates imply that these gains will be particularly great because they exacerbate the inefficiencies in input use within a sector that result from tariffs on capital goods. Faced with high rates, an entrepreneur will economize sharply on capital goods, the prices of which have been raised by tariffs, resulting in production techniques that are inefficient for the country as a whole, given their actual opportunity cost.

A Fall in Real Interest Rates

The free trade agreement with the United States represents a very public, internationally binding commitment by Mexico to a certain path of economic development: an open market economy with stable, predictable policies. It also makes clear and stable the terms of Mexican access to the U.S. market. Whatever the complexion of future governments, the access provided to U.S. markets will provide a very substantial reason to adhere to the agreement and to the policies that permit Mexico to benefit from this access.

This removes a great deal of risk from investment in Mexico. With a great deal of the perceived potential risk locked out, there will be a surge of investment, yielding substantial economic growth. Instead of demanding a payback period of just a few years, investors will be willing to accept returns over much longer periods. This will result in projects that make a much greater contribution to the long-term health of the economy. The effective interest rate will be substantially reduced as the risk premium is removed. Access to international capital markets and the terms of international loans will be greatly improved as the international financial community removes the "political risk premium" from the interest rates that they charge for investment in Mexico.

Our analysis indicates that this will be one of its most important benefits, contributing a 8.5 percent increase in gross domestic product. As real interest rates fall, industries will switch to more capital-intensive techniques (see tables 8 and 9), increasing the productivity of the existing labor force and raising GDP.

Increases in GDP and Changes in Welfare

Critics noted that if all additional investment induced by NAFTA were foreign, then a large portion of the gains in GDP would be gains to foreign capital owners. If this were the case then the gains in GDP would be an upwardly biased indicator of changes in

Table 8
Capital Stock in the Steady Growth Path, World Prices
(hundred millions of 1980 pesos)

	A (tariffs, i=15 percent)	B (free trade, i=15 percent)	C (free trade, i=12 percent)	(B-A)/A (percentage)	(C-A)A (percentage)	(C-B)/B (percentage)
Capital stock	657.0	640.4	810.4	-2.5	23.4	26.6

Table 9
Capital-Labor Ratio in the Steady Growth Path
(thousands of 1980 pesos per worker)

Sector	A (tariffs, i=15 percent)	B (free trade, i=15 percent)	C (free trade, i=12 percent)	(B-A)/A (percentage)	(C-A)A (percentage)	(C-B)/B (percentage)
Agr	5.7	5.6	5.9	-2.3	3.9	6.4
Min	33.2	32.3	35.1	-2.7	5.6	8.6
Oil	1,249.4	1,071.1	1,630.3	-14.3	30.5	52.2
Food	27.7	24.1	27.9	-12.8	0.8	15.6
Tex	8.9	8.2	9.3	-7.8	4.3	13.1
Chem	96.5	91.1	119.7	-5.7	24.0	31.4
Met	61.8	68.7	58.0	11.1	-6.2	-15.5
Mac	30.6	26.1	31.9	-14.7	4.0	21.9
Veh	34.7	44.5	38.1	28.3	10.0	-14.3
Bldg	2.4	2.6	3.5	12.4	49.6	33.0
Svcs	13.4	14.3	16.8	6.8	25.3	17.3
Misc	27.1	25.6	29.8	-5.7	9.8	16.5

Mexican welfare. This concern is shared by Mexican citizens who see that investment in Mexico will be dominated by foreigners, resulting in a loss of Mexican sovereignty.

Important evidence to the contrary has accumulated in recent years. The conservative financial policies followed by the Mexican government have led to a major inflow of capital that has stabilized the exchange rate. What is the source of this inflow? Mexican citizens heard the news that their government was following sound policies much earlier than foreigners and have been repatriating their capital from abroad in a reversal of capital flight.[4]

At the moment, increased investment in Mexico by Mexicans has been mainly in the financial economy, but, with the increased certainty about long-term prospects that could result from a free trade agreement, this investment will switch to the real economy where the returns are much higher. However, this information will take longer to penetrate abroad and even longer to be acted upon. In the meantime, it will be acted upon by Mexicans who are already poised to take advantage of the improved investment climate. The enormous funds held by Mexicans abroad will provide a major portion of the requisite financing. The enhanced credibility of Mexico on international financial markets will facilitate further investments with international financial backing, but these investments will be controlled by private Mexican citizens. Much of this will take place before the foreign investors in real projects react to the improved investment climate here, after having commissioned the requisite studies and convinced their board of directors of the new situation. Just as Mexican citizens have been the first to take advantage of the improved financial returns available in Mexico, so they will grab the lion's share of the most attractive real investment projects.

Notes

1. Leslie Young and José Romero, "A dynamic dual model of the North American Free Trade Agreement," Working Paper, El Colegio de México, 1992.
2. These other models include: Bachrach and Mizrahi (1992); Brown, Deardorff and Stern (1992); Levy and van Wijnbergen (1992); McCleery (1992); Robinson, Burfisher, Hinojosa and Thierfelder (1991); Roland-Holst, Reinert and Shiells (1992); Sobarzo (1991); and Trela and Whalley (1991).
3. Effective protection: the tariff applied to imports of a good does not indicate the impact of protection for the domestic industry producing the good if it uses imported inputs that are themselves subject to duty. The domestic industry "adds value" to the imported inputs and the effect of protection on this value added is the key indicator of how protection affects resource allocation. Suppose the world price of clothing is $1.00. To produce a unit of clothing a country imports $0.40 worth of yarn. The domestic industry then adds $0.60 value to the yarn. Suppose a 40 percent "normal" tariff is levied on clothing imports, raising their price to $1.40 and a 10 percent tariff is applied to imports of yarn, raising their cost to $0.44 per unit of clothing behind the tariff wall. The domestic producer receives as value added a $1.40 − $0.44=$0.96. The original value added was $0.60. Hence, the effective protection factor is:

$$\frac{0.96}{0.60} = 1.6$$

and the effective rate of protection is 60 percent. In contrast, the nominal rate of protection was 40 percent.
4. According to Carlos Salinas de Gortari (1993), in the first eight months of 1993, around $1.780 billion dollars deposited abroad by Mexican residents were repatriated.

References

Bachrach, Carlos and Lorris Mizrahi (1992), "The Economic Impact of a Free Trade Agreement between the United States and Mexico: A CGE Analysis," KPMG Peat Marwick, Washington, February.

Brown, Drusilla, Alan V. Deardorff, and Robert M. Stern (1992), "A North American Free Trade Agreement: Analytical Issues and a Computational Assessment," *World Economy*, 15, January.

Levy, Santiago and Sweder van Wijnbergen (1992), "Mexican agriculture in the free trade agreement: transition problems in economic reform," Technical Papers No. 63, OECD Development Center, May.

McCleery, Robert K. (1992), "An Intemporal, Linked, Macroeconomic CGE Model of the United States and Mexico, Focusing on Demographic Change and Factor Flows," *Economic Development and Policy*, East-West Center, Honolulu, February.

Robinson, Sherman, Mary Burfisher, Raúl Hinojosa and Karen E. Thierfelder (1991), "Agricultural policies and migration in a U.S.-Mexico free trade area: a CGE analysis," Working Paper No. 617, Department of Agriculture and Resource Economics, University of California, Berkeley, December.

Roland-Holst, David, Kenneth A. Reinert and Clinton Shiells (1992), "North American Trade Liberalization and the Role of Nontariff Barriers," Mills College, April.

Salinas de Gortari, Carlos (1993), "Anexo al Quinto Informe de Gobierno," Poder Ejecutivo Federal, Presidencia de la República.

Sobarzo, Horacio E. (1991), "A General Equilibrium Analysis of the Gains from Trade for the Mexican Economy of a North American Free Trade Agreement," El Colegio de Mexico, Centro de Estudios Economicos, December.

Trela, Irene and John Whalley (1991), "Bilateral Trade Liberalization in Quota Restricted Items: U.S. and Mexico in Textiles and Steel," University of Western Ontario, Department of Economics, May.

Part II

Industry Effects of NAFTA

4

U.S. Banks, Competition, and the Mexican Banking System: How Much Will NAFTA Matter?

William C. Gruben, John H. Welch, and
Jeffrey W. Gunther

The financial services component of the North American Free
Trade Agreement (NAFTA) represents a new stage in the financial
liberalization that has been occurring to varying degrees in
Canada, Mexico, and the United States. All three countries have
eliminated interest rate controls, reduced reserve requirements,
and lowered barriers to entry for new domestic and international
banks. Mexico's financial opening, however, has been much more
drastic than those of Canada or the United States.

Ten years ago, few would have expected that Mexico would
move to integrate its financial system with those of the United
States and Canada. Following the financial turmoil of the early
1980s, many Mexicans concluded that isolating their financial markets would help avoid financial trauma and that international capital controls and bank nationalization were useful policy tools. However, such policies exacerbated financial instability. Once global
and domestic financial market participants acquired the power to
override such controls, Mexico moved to create one of the more
modern and open financial systems in this hemisphere.

The road to liberalization for Mexico has not been an easy one.
It was interrupted by a reversal of financial opening when the government nationalized the banks in the early 1980s. But the main
lesson of the following history is quite clear: the Mexican government could only temporarily halt financial opening, growth, and
innovation. The recent liberalization effort reflects, to a large extent, the huge growth in the nonbank sectors of the Mexican financial system and the recent reduction of barriers to trade in goods.

Not only do the details of NAFTA represent a major step in
Mexico's recent liberalization efforts, but the general framework of
the agreement also is important. The financial sector portion of the
agreement commences with an explication of general principles
and subsequently focuses on the expression of these principles
through industry-by-industry details. In this regard, NAFTA re-

flects an attempt to apply trade policy concepts to the financial services sector, an innovation stemming from prior efforts to develop the General Agreement on Trade in Services. Sauvé and González-Hermosillo (1993) note that this approach derives from the recognition that the joint pursuit of "business globalization and trade liberalization requires agreement among countries on a guiding set of rules and disciplines relating to matters of establishment, market access, standard of treatment, transparency of regulations and dispute settlement." By establishing both a general framework for greater foreign participation in Mexico's financial markets and particular rules governing that participation, the agreement represents a palpable reduction in the payoff to protectionist lobbying and an increase in the long-term sustainability of financial reform.[1]

This chapter provides an overview of the financial portion of NAFTA and includes analysis of its potential impact on the Mexican banking system. The agreement's general framework, combined with the details of the important financial liberalization that it sets forth, indicates that the agreement will further Mexico's goal of increasing competition and efficiency in the provision of financial services. Differences in the agreement's treatment of various financial services, together with certain characteristics of financial markets in Mexico, suggest that most early entries into the Mexican financial sector under NAFTA likely will occur in nonbank areas, especially brokerage. As competition in the provision of nonbank financial services continues to grow, and as more banks—both foreign and domestic—commence operations in the Mexican market, Mexico's banks will be challenged to make strong gains in efficiency.

The Financing of Import Substituting Industrialization, 1940–74

Until the 1970s, the Mexican financial system was highly regulated, at least by North American standards. The old regime included quantitative restrictions on interest rates, an array of forced lending programs,[2] large barriers to entry, and high required reserve ratios. The financial system reflected import substituting industrialization (ISI), the trade and growth strategy that Mexico and other Latin American countries were pursuing at the time.[3] In the same spirit, the banking sector was effectively protected from direct foreign competition, as Citibank was the only foreign bank since the 1940s to operate in Mexico.[4]

Countries following import substituting industrialization tried to diversify their productive bases by protecting domestic producers of formerly imported goods. Protection involved tariffs, quotas, and direct subsidies. The imports had typically been consumer goods, including durables, such as automobiles, and nondurable luxuries, such as clothing and scotch. ISI motivated local financial systems to specialize in underwriting the purchase of the domestic products that replaced these imports. Because such financing was inherently short term and lenders faced significant inflation and exchange rate risk, the financial system's lending horizons were much shorter than those found in the United States, Canada, and Europe.

The private financial sector did not supply long-term financing of industrial activity, and the trade protection given industry bolstered retained earnings. Accordingly, most fixed investment was internally financed. For industries that required investments too large to base on retained earnings and for exporting industries weakened by protectionism (such as agriculture), the government provided long-term funding through a menu of trust funds and state-controlled credit institutions, the most notable being Nacional Financiera. These institutions not only channeled private and public resources into "priority sectors" but also intermediated (as they still do) resources from foreign lenders and investors.

Banks represented the major private sector institutions in the Mexican financial system, but their behavior was tightly regulated. Most importantly, interest rates on loans and deposits were controlled by Banco de México. Additionally, Banco de México controlled the money supply through the use of flexible marginal reserve requirements. If Banco de México wanted to tighten money, it increased the reserve requirement on new deposits.

Reserve requirement adjustments were a particularly important source of policy flexibility because Banco de México could not undertake open market operations, which require a well-developed market for government debt. Such a market did not exist. But the policy that was flexible for Banco de México was cumbersome and costly for the commercial banks (Brothers and Solis M. 1966). The bank's frequently changing and complex requirements resulted in costly efforts on the part of commercial banks to maintain adequate reserves. Further, to the extent that these reserves did not earn interest, increases in reserve requirements increased the spread between borrowing and lending rates.[5] Cash reserve requirements against demand and savings deposits ranged from 50 percent to 100 percent between the 1940s and the 1960s.

Cash reserves were not the only assets held in required reserves. Banks were forced to maintain a certain percentage of deposits in the form of government securities, creating a captive market for government debt. Banks sometimes had to hold government securities in proportions that ranged from 0 percent to 75 percent from the 1940s through the 1960s. Also, regulations required commercial banks to hold a certain percentage of deposits in the form of credits to the private sector and private sector securities. These directed credits were channeled to what the government deemed priority sectors.

This level of regulation left commercial banks at an increasing disadvantage relative to nonbank intermediaries,[6] especially the *financieras*.[7] *Financieras* became the principle vehicles for financial innovation during this period; they offered high-yielding liquid paper with few of the restrictions that were imposed on commercial banks. Using resources obtained from promissory notes issued to corporations and individuals, *financieras* funded the acquisition of fixed-term obligations, financed working capital and equipment loans, and extended consumer loans.

Financieras were not the only successful financial institutions. Mortgage banks[8] played a significant, but unchanging, role in financial markets during this period. These banks issued special mortgage bonds (*cédulas hipotecarias*) to fund their mortgage lending. Other private financial institutions, such as savings and loan associations and capitalization banks,[9] lost ground because they could not effectively compete for funds (Brothers and Solis M. 1966).

With the growth of nonbank financial intermediation, securities markets became increasingly important, but government regulations impeded the development of markets for long-term debt. Although the Mexican government implicitly maintained the liquidity of all fixed income securities through most of this period, it required them to trade at par. The value was maintained through the loan windows at Banco de México and Nacional Financiera. Because the government proscribed discounting, expected inflation could not be reflected in discount rates, a problem that inhibited the development of a long-term securities market.

While the Mexican financial system—including the nonbank portion—did develop significantly from the 1940s through the 1960s, markets remained very thin by developed country standards. The trading of fixed-interest instruments on the stock and securities exchange was limited because market makers were banks, *financieras*, mortgage banks, capitalization banks, and, ultimately, Banco de México and the Nacional Financiera. Moreover, for the regulatory reasons noted above, the market for long-term obligations was particularly thin. Market thinness and market-inhibiting financial regulations had resulted in costly intermediation during the 1940s, 1950s, and 1960s. These high credit costs and the scarcity of long-term credit, in turn, inhibited the development of Mexican industry.

Financial system problems worsened in the 1970s with the acceleration of inflation during the presidential administration of Luis Echeverria (1970–76). For the banks, the principle problem during this period was disintermediation.[10] Although disintermediation had occurred throughout the postwar period, during the Echeverria administration the acceleration of inflation exacerbated the adverse effects of the interest rate controls and high reserve requirements on the banks. The relatively low level of regulatory constraints placed upon the *financieras* permitted them to adjust to the resurgence of inflation by paying more to attract deposits. Many of the new deposits were diverted from the increasingly uncompetitive banking system. In response, new reforms were instituted in 1974 and 1975. The structure of Mexico's current financial system has its origins in these reforms.

The 1974 and 1975 Reforms

The new Mexican policies of the 1970s supported the consolidation of existing banks and gave them market opportunities formerly restricted to nonbank financial intermediaries. The objective was to allow banks to exploit economies of scale and scope. The means to this objective included a regulatory turn away from a U.S.-style system of strict division between types of financial institutions and toward a Germanic system, in which "supermarket banks," or multiple banks, could offer a wide variety of services.

To this end, financial groups, or conglomerates, were constructed of different types of financial institutions—banks, brokerage houses, insurance companies—connected through a holding company. In 1974, the new Law on Credit Institutions, in part the result of Finance Minister José Lopez Portillo's efforts, went one step further: it created multiple banks through the merger of these different types of institutions (Banco de México 1993). Reflecting their origins, the new multiple banks could not only perform traditional banking functions but could also provide insurance, brokerage services, and custodial and trust services. Banks were also allowed to take stock positions in industrial companies, a privilege that would become controversial (Tello 1984).

The immediate results of the 1974 Law on Credit Institutions included an increasingly concentrated banking system. As figure 1 shows, the number of banks in Mexico decreased from 139 in 1975 to only 60 by 1982, when the bank nationalization occurred. This consolidation would continue even after nationalization. With the inflation of the 1970s, disintermediation made bank adherence to mandated

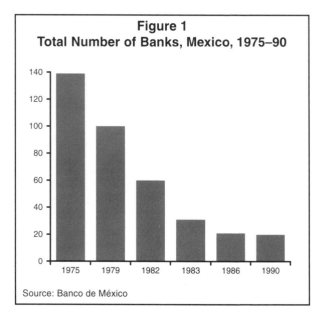

Figure 1
Total Number of Banks, Mexico, 1975–90

Source: Banco de México

interest rate ceilings and directed credit programs impracticable. In the mid-1970s, the government reacted by dramatically increasing legal deposit rates, but it did not free them to reach their market levels. The absence of full liberalization gave added impetus to the nonbank sectors of the financial markets, an impetus that was accelerated by the Securities Market Law of 1975.

This law created brokerage houses and reorganized securities exchanges under the oversight of the newly revamped National Securities Commission (Comisión Nacional de Valores, or CNV), which was originally created in 1946. Not only did these reforms improve oversight and dissemination of information on traded securities, but they also created incentives for individual brokers and financial conglomerates to create brokerage houses. This sector began to grow rapidly, and expansion accelerated when the government created new financial instruments that could be traded in it (Heyman 1989).

Perhaps the most important development in the Mexican securities markets of the 1970s and 1980s was the introduction of government treasury notes, or *cetes*, in 1978. Until then, Petrobonds (created in 1977) had been the major innovation in these markets. Petrobonds represented a share in a trust at Nacional Financiera with rights to certain quantities of government-owned oil, and bond values were accordingly linked to the price of oil (Heyman 1989 and Mansell Carstens 1993). Other innovations of the period included authorization of commercial paper in 1980 and of bankers acceptances in 1981.

Devaluations and the Debt Crisis, 1976–82

Mexican banks had a long tradition of offering dollar-denominated deposits and of extending dollar-denominated loans (Ortiz 1983). Dollarization had decreased during the 1960s and remained low until the mid-1970s, but a burst of inflation during the Echeverria administration provoked fears of an imminent devaluation and a flight back to dollars. The devaluation came in 1976, when the Mexican government elevated the peso price of the U.S. dollar from 12.5 pesos to around 21 pesos. Capital flight and increased dollarization soon followed. The devaluation also precipitated a substantial increase in financial activity, as well as certain financial reforms.

But instead of liberalizing trade to avert future balance of payments problems, the incoming Lopez Portillo administration resolved to uphold the increasingly threadbare import substitution/ industrialization policies of the prior two decades. New oil deposits had been discovered, and this administration projected that it could finance further import substitution schemes with rising oil export revenues. The rush to develop these exports touched off large fiscal deficits and an unsustainable increase in foreign debt. Many of the resources that flowed to Mexico during this period were ultimately wasted (Gavin 1991). A surge in world interest rates in 1979 and a plunge in oil prices in 1980 and 1981 pressed on Mexico's debt-servicing ability from both directions. In August 1982, Mexico confessed that it could not service its foreign debt. Accompanying this collapse were massive capital flight, a severe peso devaluation, the imposition of exchange controls, and the nationalization of the commercial banks.[11]

Bank Nationalization and its Aftermath, 1982–89

In 1982, Mexico went through two major devaluation episodes—one in February and March, the other in August and September. Many inside and outside government contended that more drastic measures were in order (Maxfield 1992 and Tello 1984). Candidates included foreign exchange controls, the effective elimination of Mexdollar accounts, and the nationalization of the banking system.[12]

All were implemented by the Lopez Portillo administration in late August and early September 1982. On August 18, the government had suspended the transfer of Mexdollar accounts abroad and converted these dollar-denominated accounts to pesos at an exchange rate of 70 to the dollar. With market rates around 100 pesos per dollar, this act would—for years to come—create suspicions about what else the government might impose upon the Mexican banking system. On September 1, the government ordained a full array of exchange controls and also nationalized the banking system.[13] To mitigate the damage devaluation had inflicted upon borrowers, a special and highly favorable exchange rate of 40 pesos per dollar was applied to their dollar-denominated loans.

Although most of the Lopez Portillo administration's tactics were conceived to staunch capital flight, they aggravated it. Mexicans forsook Mexdollar deposits for cash dollars and foreign accounts. Banks suffered severe losses in liquidity and contractions in earnings on dollar-denominated loans.

The government's administration of the nationalized banks reflected its concerns about the stability and solvency of the financial system. Mexico implemented bank recapitalization policies and promoted further consolidation. Of the 58 banks originally nationalized, only eighteen remained in 1990 (Banco de México 1993).

Nationalization, however, did not signify wholesale changes in management. Only the bank directors were removed. The de la Madrid administration, which replaced that of Lopez Portillo only a few months after the nationalization, was less sanguine than its predecessor about the virtues of government ownership. Banks were largely left on their own.

Nevertheless, nationalization did reverse some past trends. Chief among these was the reerection of firewalls between the bank and nonbank sectors of the financial system. For example, the de la Madrid administration reprivatized the nonbank assets of multiple banks but retained control of the banks themselves. In many cases, these nonbank assets were purchased by the prior owners through brokerage houses, using "indemnification bonds" as payment.[14]

The growth in the nonbank financial sector in the 1980s, especially in the money market, was enormous and helps to explain why financial innovation was not stymied by the bank nationalization. Between 1982 and 1988, nonbank financial institutions' assets rose from 9.1 percent to 32.1 percent of total financial system assets.

Recall that the government had begun to issue treasury bonds (*cetes*) in 1978. During the de la Madrid administration, the trading of *cetes* in the securities market (Bolsa de Valores) permitted the government an alternative to forced securities sales, expressed as noncash reserve requirements, to the banks. The growth of this alternative outlet for government finance was a particularly important salve for fiscal imbalances at this time. Restrictive rules and regulations were continuing to inhibit the expansion of the banking sector, so that even forced bank financing threatened to be an insufficient source of funds.

Much of the initial growth in the securities market can be explained by the increased issuance of *cetes*, which were followed in 1985 by Bank Development Bonds, in 1986 by Mexican (U.S.) dollar-denominated bonds (*pagafes*) and fixed-interest Urban Development Bonds (BORES), and in 1987 by fixed-interest Development Bonds (*bondes*). The bond market and especially, the money market became increasingly liquid throughout the 1980s (Heyman 1989).

However, with the new surge of the nonbank sector, the banking system again required innovation and deregulation to improve its competitiveness in attracting funds. The government responded in 1989 by removing its restrictions on interest rates and permitting a return to universal banking via the Financial Groups Law of 1990. In 1991, the Salinas de Gortari administration began to sell the banks back to the private sector. At the same time, new financial instruments were also being developed so that the banks could compete effectively for funds. Money market accounts (*cuentas maestras*) appeared in 1986. In 1987, as part of the effort to recapitalize the banks, the government developed Certificates of Claim on Net Worth (CAPS).[15] In what was effectively a first step toward privatization of the banks, the government used these CAPS as a vehicle for trading 34 percent of its bank holdings to the private sector. Banks did not pay dividends on these issues, but the retained earnings represented a capitalized addition to the net worth (capital) of the banks. The CAPs were issued during a general stock market boom and sold at significant premiums.

Between 1982 and 1987, a combination of high inflation, interest rate controls, and high reserve (liquidity) requirements prompted the growth of a black market for credit.[16] Much of the liberalization that followed could not have taken place in the absence of a major fiscal effort by the Mexican authorities. Public sector borrowing requirements dropped from around 17 percent of GDP in 1982 to around -1 percent in 1992, a financial surplus, although it nudged back into a small 0.2 percent deficit in 1993 (figure 2). Having moved toward a balanced budget, the government began to refrain from exacting forced loans from the banks, especially after 1987.

Lowering the liquidity ratio (a broader term for required reserve ratio) and liberalizing interest rates improved the banking system's ability to compete for funds.

The first step toward full liberalization and lower reserve requirements was the 1988 liberalization of the issuance of bankers acceptances. Under the new rules, interest rates on these instruments

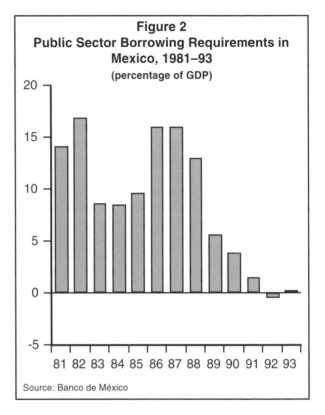

Figure 2
Public Sector Borrowing Requirements in Mexico, 1981–93
(percentage of GDP)

Source: Banco de México

were no longer controlled. Moreover, bankers acceptances were now subject to a relatively low 30 percent liquidity requirement.[17] These conditions gave bankers acceptances an advantage over deposits and CDs in attracting funds. Deposits and CDs were still subject to regulated interest rates and to liquidity coefficients of close to 60 percent.

Additional liberalizations occurred in early 1989. The government removed interest rate ceilings on all deposits and securities and dropped the liquidity coefficient to 30 percent on bank liabilities. Finally, in June 1989, interest payments on checking accounts were allowed (Banco de México 1993).

The Privatization of the Banks, 1990–92

These liberalizations set the stage for a complete privatization of Mexico's eighteen remaining commercial banks, an act initiated by legislation in 1990. In June, the Mexican Congress amended the constitution to allow private sector control of commercial banks. In July, Congress approved the Credit Institutions Law, which restored the multiple bank system (Mansell Carstens 1993).

The return to universal banking did not completely dismantle the segmentation imposed with nationalization. The new legislation allows the formation of three types of financial groups: a) a bank with leasing, factoring,[18] foreign exchange, mutual fund management and origination, and warehousing activities; b) a brokerage firm with leasing, factoring, foreign exchange, mutual fund management and origination, and warehousing activities; and c) a holding company. The holding company must have at least three of the following institutions with no more than one of each type: a bank, an insurance company, a brokerage house, a leasing company, a factoring company, a bonding company, a mutual funds management company, a currency exchange broker, and a warehousing company (Natella, et al. 1991 and Mansell Carstens 1993). Moreover, while banks can now take equity positions in nonbank enterprises, holdings are limited to 5 percent of a firm's paid-in capital.[19] Loans to principle bank shareholders, managers, or directors—or to firms they own—are limited to 20 percent of a bank's loan portfolio.[20] Additionally, the extension of any such loans now legally requires the express approval of the bank's board of directors.

The Credit Institutions Law defined the terms of the subsequent privatization. Ownership structure was (and remains) apportioned according to three types of shares.[21] "A" shares are common stock held by the controlling interest and can represent up to 51 percent of total shares outstanding of any one bank. These may only be held by Mexican individuals, excluding institutional and corporate investors. "B" shares may be held by Mexican individuals, firms, and institutional investors and may represent 19–49 percent of the total shares outstanding. Finally, "C" shares may be held by all Mexicans and foreigners and may represent no more than 30 percent of the shares outstanding (Natella, et al. 1991, Banco de México 1992, and Mansell Carstens 1993). The Mexican government also restricted the share of total bank capital possessed by any individual.

The eighteen banks sold in fourteen months (June 1991–July 1992) at an extraordinarily high average price-to-book ratio of 3.49 (Trigueros 1992 and Carstens 1993). Meanwhile, the government continued to initiate regulatory reforms. Mexico eliminated its remaining liquidity coefficient of 30 percent in September 1991 and abolished exchange controls in December 1991 (Carstens 1993).

The authorities also imposed new capital standards that turned out to be stricter than those contained in the Basle agreement.

What did the recent liberalization accomplish? The most striking benefit of the liberalization and the inflation stabilization was an increase in financial stability, a dramatic fall in interest rates, and robust growth in financial assets. Addi-

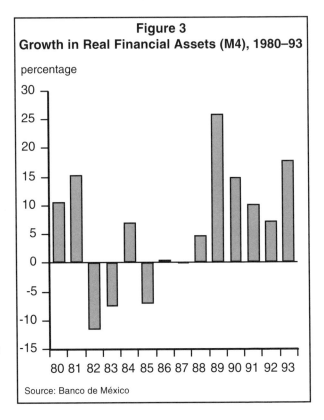

Figure 3
Growth in Real Financial Assets (M4), 1980–93

percentage

Source: Banco de México

tionally, a recovery in lending to the private sector for investment began. Growth in the broad money aggregate M_4 recovered to high and sustainable rates starting in 1988 (figure 3). Over the longer run, continued liberalization within and outside NAFTA should further increase the efficiency of the banking system and lower the cost of financial intermediation in Mexico.

The Financial Services Portion of NAFTA

One way to facilitate the process of business globalization and trade liberalization and accelerate the speed of adjustment to a policy change is to assure that the new policy is easily understood.[22] Accordingly, the two most important doctrines in the financial services portion of NAFTA are relatively simple: each country allows its residents to buy financial services in other NAFTA countries,[23] and foreign subsidiary institutions receive national treatment. The first clause implies a promise that Mexico's capital flight restrictions of late 1982, which inhibited foreign financial services' availability to Mexicans, will not reappear. In the second clause, national treatment means that foreign financial institutions[24] are subject to laws, rules, and regulations comparable[25] to those governing domestic institutions in a given host country.[26] The country for which this doctrine signifies the biggest change is Mexico, where NAFTA allows U.S. and Canadian financial services firms to set up wholly owned subsidiaries for the first time in 50 years.

Although the principal tenets of NAFTA's clauses on financial institutions are relatively simple, several complications arise from the past histories of each country's individual financial service industries, such as banking or securities, and from the connections that different countries permit among such industries. Unlike the United States, Mexico permits the same holding company to own banks, insurance companies, stock brokerage houses, funds management firms, bonding institutions, factoring operations, exchange houses, leasing firms, and warehousing firms. As will be seen, these variations in what NAFTA signatories permit invest the agreement with some peculiar clauses. Moreover, under NAFTA, the structure of Mexican financial services firms owned by U.S. or Canadian firms is important. The Mexican firms must be subsidiaries, rather than branches of their foreign owners. This rule means that a Mexican bank will have its own board of directors, even if it is owned by a U.S. or Canadian firm. More importantly, these subsidiaries can fail, even when the foreign parent bank does not.

The North American Free Trade Agreement phases in liberalization. Mexico will allow U.S. and Canadian commercial banks, insurance companies, brokerage firms, and finance companies their fullest access only after a six-year transition period (beginning in 1994), during which the market will be limited. For example, the capital of foreign insurance affliates could not exceed 6 percent of the aggregate capital of all insurance companies in Mexico during the first year of the transition period, but that share goes to 12 percent on January 1, 1999, and to 100 percent a year later.[27] Similarly, during 1994, bank capital under the control of foreign investors in Mexico could not exceed 8 percent of the value of all bank capital in the country. It increased to 9.4 percent for 1995. In the last year of the six-year transition period, this limit goes to 15 percent.

But even after the phase-in period, NAFTA's characterization of national treatment is limited. Mexico will still be able to treat potential U.S.- and Canadian-owned subsidiaries somewhat differently than it treats domestic firms. As an example, consider Mexico's banking system. Each of Mexico's two largest banking institutions, Banamex and Bancomer, accounts for more than 20 percent of total bank capital in the country. Together, they account for about 45 percent of total bank capital. After NAFTA's phase-in period for banks, neither Canadian nor U.S. groups may acquire an institution that accounts for more than a 4 percent share of the aggregate capital of all commercial banks in Mexico. In addition, once the six-year transition period is over, the Mexican government has the onetime option of freezing *temporarily* the level of capital of Canadian and U.S. banks if that capital reaches 25 percent of total bank capital in Mexico.[28]

The United States, likewise, explicitly restricts what foreign financial institutions of NAFTA signatory countries may do, and some of these restrictions reflect differences between Mexican and U.S. financial institutions. The United States will permit a Mexican financial group that before NAFTA's enactment had acquired both a Mexican bank with U.S. operations and a Mexican securities firm with U.S. operations to operate both for five years after the acquisitions. The U.S. securities affiliate, however, will not be permitted to expand through acquisition. Moreover, the United States requires that the majority of directors of a foreign subsidiary bank be U.S. citizens.

With regard to start-up operations in Mexico, one of NAFTA's attractions for Canadian and U.S. firms is the opportunity to carry out operations denominated in pesos rather than dollars, which will enable firms to accumulate peso liabilities to offset these peso-denominated assets.[29]

The breadth of opportunities offered by NAFTA is important. For example, NAFTA signifies that finance companies may ultimately establish subsidiaries to provide consumer lending, commercial lending, mortgage lending, or credit card services. During the transition period, such operations are subject to the restriction that they may not collectively exceed 3 percent of the sum of the aggregate assets of all banks in Mexico plus the aggregate of all types of limited-scope financial institutions in Mexico, a phrase that refers to companies that provide consumer lending or commercial lending or mortgage lending, or credit card services. After the transition period, such firms receive purely national treatment, which is to say they will not be subject to the caps that banks and securities firms will face after the phase-in.

Even during the transition period, some types of auto-related financing are not subject to the caps that other financial operations will face during the phase-in. Accordingly, it should not be surpris-

ing to note reports that at least one U.S. nonbank firm is already
planning the introduction of auto financing and leasing operations
and that U.S. brokerage firms, meanwhile, are planning cross-border mergers and acquisition activity and the introduction of swaps
and options into the Mexican market.

Attractiveness of Mexico for Entry by U.S. Financial Institutions

Are U.S.-based financial institutions likely to be interested in establishing operations in Mexico under NAFTA? A look at the Mexican
banking system, as an example, offers an indication of what may
make NAFTA attractive to U.S. financial institutions. Mexico's
banking system is highly profitable, highly concentrated, not very
competitive, fairly inefficient, and somewhat less aggressively ori-
ented toward marketing than some developed country systems.

Mexican banks are more profitable than U.S. banks and most
European banks. In 1993, the return on average assets for Mexican
banks was approximately 1.49 percent, versus 1.06 for U.S. banks,
0.09 percent for Japan, and 0.96 percent for Spain (figure 4). When
the Mexican government began to privatize the formerly state-
owned banking system in 1991, some U.S. observers were surprised
to see the selling prices of these banks range from 2.6 times book
value to 5.4 times book (figure 5). Expectations of future profitabil-
ity help explain these prices. Moreover, some observers suspected
that privatization would make Mexican banks compete more intensely with one another, paying higher rates on deposits and
charging lower interest rates. But instead of narrowing, spreads
between interest rates on loans and bank deposits have widened.
During the second half of 1990, interest rate spreads averaged
about 5 percentage points. During 1993, when inflation rates had
declined considerably compared with rates in the 1980s, and a recession was in place during the second half of the year, spreads
fluctuated between 10.30 percent and 11.71 percent (figure 6).[30]

The Mexican banking system is currently highly concentrated,
especially when compared to the U.S. banking system (figure 7). As
of mid-1993, the three largest commercial banks in Mexico held
about one-half of all Mexican commercial bank assets. In contrast,
as of mid-1993, the three largest U.S. banking organizations held less
than one-eighth of total U.S. bank assets.[31] The level of competition
that such concentration implies for Mexico, which lacks a deep nonbank financial market for private debt, may explain why large interest
rate spreads persist.[32]

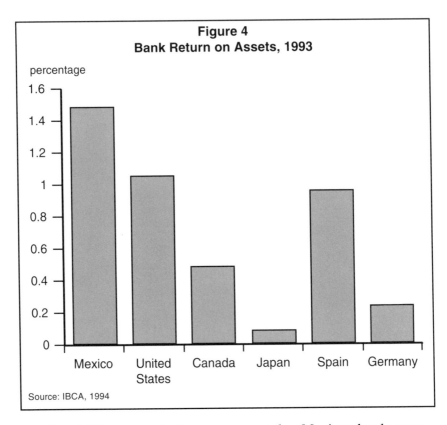

Figure 4
Bank Return on Assets, 1993

percentage

Source: IBCA, 1994

In addition, some indicators suggest that Mexican banks may not have begun to operate very efficiently, at least by commonly applied standards. In 1994.III, the ratio of noninterest expenses to assets in Mexican banks was 5.2 percent, versus 3.6 percent for U.S. banks.[33] It should be noted that Mexico's 5.2 percent in 1994.III represents a decline from 6.3 percent in 1992.IV—after all privatizations had been completed for reasons discussed below, this ratio will probably continue to fall.

Other evidence suggests Mexican banks may devote less attention to marketing than is common in the United States and in Europe. Mexico averages about one bank branch for about every 18,000 people. In the United States, the number is about one branch per 4,000 inhabitants and, in Europe, about one for every 2,000.[34] Nevertheless, as in the case of other bank characteristics, time may not have permitted recent bank behavior to reflect fully the impact of privatization.

Although these factors suggest that under NAFTA Mexico may

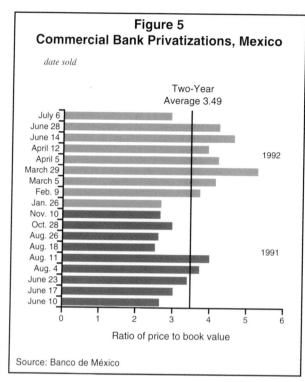

Figure 5
Commercial Bank Privatizations, Mexico

date sold

Two-Year
Average 3.49

1992

1991

Ratio of price to book value

Source: Banco de México

attract U.S. banks, it is important to emphasize that the Mexican financial system is anything but static. The circumstances implied by the financial statistics and ratios will probably not persist.

The first reprivatization of a Mexican bank did not occur until June 1991 and the last, that of Banco del Centro, took place in July 1992. There is much reason to suspect that insufficient time has elapsed for any bank to complete its transition from a public to a private entity. In a study of bank acquisitions by holding companies in the United States, Johnson and Meinster (1973) show that an acquired bank's income and balance sheet ratios do not begin to display statistically significant differences from those of prior management until two years of new ownership. Moreover, the full impact of a change in management appears not to be felt until four years after the acquisition (Johnson and Meinster 1975). As of this writing, less than four years have passed since any Mexican banks were privatized.

Tenure of ownership is not the only factor contributing to the state of flux in Mexican banking. In 1993, Mexico opened its banking system to new domestic charter applicants and, in 1994, the banking system opened to new foreign charter applicants. Considering the increase in domestic banks as a result of the extension of new charters, the period 1994–2000 would likely see profound changes in the Mexican financial system even in the absence of NAFTA.

In addition to the rapidly changing nature of financial institu-

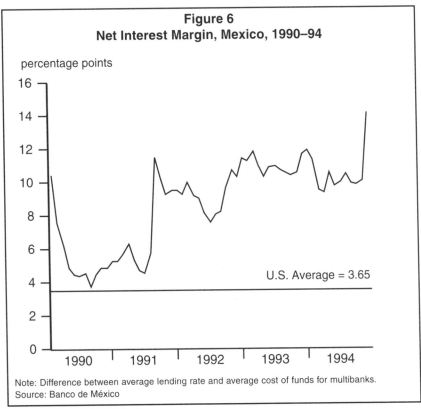

Figure 6
Net Interest Margin, Mexico, 1990–94

percentage points

U.S. Average = 3.65

Note: Difference between average lending rate and average cost of funds for multibanks.
Source: Banco de México

tions and markets, other factors in Mexico raise questions about the intensity and rapidity with which Canadian and U.S. banks may choose to enter the Mexican market. While Mexico may be under-branched and while "rising incomes are expected to increase the demand for banking services by Mexicans, most of whom live outside the major cities and currently have no banking relationship at all" (Laderman and Moreno 1992), Mexican banks have well-established positions in the retail market, which U.S.- owned institutions may have difficulty achieving.[35]

With regard to wholesale banking, Mansell Carstens (1993) notes that Mexican banks have faced competition from foreign firms in this sector for years. While foreign banks have not been permitted to establish themselves as banks *per se* in Mexico, they have had representative offices. Moreover, Mexican banks, private and public corporations, and the government have relied for decades on these institutions. Mansell Carstens (1993) remarks that, "for the wholesale banking sector, NAFTA may be a nonevent."

A related detail may offer a useful perspective on the extent of competition that Canadian and U.S. financial institutions could face from Mexican entities. Although the Mexican bank nationalization that occurred in 1982 formally removed only bank directors and left other employees at their desks, many of these employees departed for securities firms, which took on a

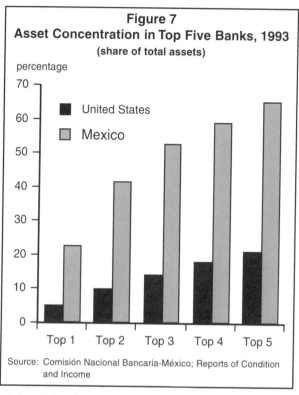

Figure 7
Asset Concentration in Top Five Banks, 1993
(share of total assets)

Source: Comisión Nacional Bancaria-México; Reports of Condition and Income

rising share of financial activity. Later, Mexican securities firms turned out to be the major purchasers of privatized Mexican banks. Since many securities industry executives were bankers before the nationalization, the recent financial deregulation has meant a reunification of financial products and personnel. Does this mean that Mexican banks have an information advantage that would make a U.S. bank's entry into the Mexican market a highly competitive event? It seems to suggest that, because of personnel movement out of banking and into the securities business and then back, human capital appropriate to the joint provision of securities services and traditional banking products may be particularly abundant in the Mexican financial system.[36]

Perhaps the main barriers to entry by U.S. banks are the capital requirements and the maximum market share restrictions on U.S. bank holdings. The initial minimum capital requirement for a new entrant into the banking system is currently 0.12 percent of the sum of the net capital of all commercial banks in the banking system, while the maximum allowed is 1.5 percent. As of December 1994, the minimum requirements converted to about $11 million, compared with $2 million in the United States, while the maximum is about $137 million.

NAFTA's Implications for U.S. Border Banks

Border banks' specific knowledge and skills favor their penetration into Mexican retail markets. These banks generally are familiar with retail banking opportunities in Mexico. Their proximity to Mexico enables them to provide deposit services to Mexican citizens and extend credit to Mexican businesses. Moreover, the local banking markets on the U.S. side of the border are, in many respects, similar to the banking environment in Mexico. The familiarity of border banks with Mexican markets should help these banks assess the credit quality of small and midsize businesses in Mexico, reducing any information advantage that established business relationships impart to Mexican banks.

Although the proximity of border banks to Mexico enhances their position as potential entrants, other factors suggest that their entry into Mexico under NAFTA will be limited. Mexican financial companies provide commercial banking, brokerage, and insurance services jointly through an extensive network of branch offices. The established retail market position of Mexican banks increases the difficulty entering U.S. banks—particularly border banks, most of which are relatively small—will face in attracting a broad base of retail customers.

Perhaps the greatest obstacle for border banks is the minimum capital requirement established by the Mexican authorities for new banks. The required minimum level of capital that would apply to new banks established by U.S. financial services providers under NAFTA is, as of this writing, approximately $20 million. Moreover, each of the new Mexican banks recently approved by the Mexican authorities has been established with more than $40 million in capital, suggesting that investments well above the published minimum are encouraged. This level of capital could pose a serious barrier to entry by smaller institutions along the border. As of year-end 1992, 48 banking organizations operated at least one bank in Texas border counties. As shown in the pie chart, the minimum capital requirement of $20 million was more than five times greater than existing bank capital at 32 percent of these banking firms.[1] And the minimum capital requirement exceeded 100 percent of bank capital at 86 percent of the firms. To meet the minimum capital requirement for establishing a bank in Mexico, while maintaining an adequate level of capitalization among their domestic banks, these banking organizations would need to raise large amounts of external capital. And it generally is difficult for small banks to raise equity externally. Similar adjustments would be required of all but the largest U.S. banking organizations that currently operate a bank along the Mexican border.

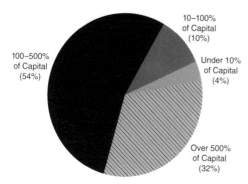

100–500% of Capital (54%)

10–100% of Capital (10%)

Under 10% of Capital (4%)

Over 500% of Capital (32%)

The regulatory constraint posed by Mexico's minimum capital requirement, coupled with the extensive market resources of Mexican banks, suggests that most U.S. border banks will be unlikely to exploit their familiarity with Mexican markets by establishing banks in Mexico. Rather, the factors considered here indicate that NAFTA represents the greatest opportunity for relatively large U.S. banking organizations. The primary benefit of NAFTA for most of the border banks will be an indirect one resulting from an increase in trade and economic activity in the border region.

1. Total bank capital is approximated by the sum of the year-end 1992 capital levels of an organization's individual banks.

More recently, however, changes in Mexican banking law allowed new special treatment for the purchase of Mexican banks. Under new laws, foreign institutions may purchase as much as 51 percent of a Mexican bank entity provided that the capitalization involved not exceed 6 percent of total bank capital. This permits acquisition of all but Mexico's three largest banks. These banks command more than half of Mexico's banking system, however.

In sum, NAFTA allows U.S. banks to enter in the phase-in period in a somewhat limited portion of the market. U.S. banks in many cases will be motivated to grow their own Mexican subsidiaries.

A broader issue involving the development of the Mexican financial system is the connection of this process to other components of Mexico's liberalization programs, which attracted large influxes of foreign capital into the country. These inflows of foreign capital, and their translation into pesos, bolstered both the demand for the peso and its rate of exchange against other currencies. Partly as a result of the strong peso (or weak U.S. dollar) and partly because Mexico had dramatically lowered its barriers to foreign trade, the United States increasingly became a low-cost supplier for Mexican buyers. Indeed, U.S. producers began to out-compete Mexican producers in so many Mexican markets that Mexico's imports from the United States more than quadrupled between 1987 and 1994. Partly as a result of rising U.S. and other foreign competition, Mexican tradeable goods producers began during the 1990s to default on their debt to Mexican banks at relatively rapid rates. Loans with a moderate or high risk of default rose from 4.8 percent of total loan volume in December 1991 to 7.8 percent in September 1994. Likewise, as figure 8 shows, the overall ratio of nonperforming loans to total loans has risen significantly.

The increase in problem loans, in part, reflects greater risk-taking at Mexican banks. In counterpoint, Garber and Weisbrod (1991) have argued that the important role of banks in Mexico's financial system imparts a substantial franchise value to Mexican banks, particularly those with high market shares and strong reputations. Accordingly, the incentive to protect this franchise value from the loss due to failure may partially offset banks' propensities to extend large volumes of high risk loans. Even

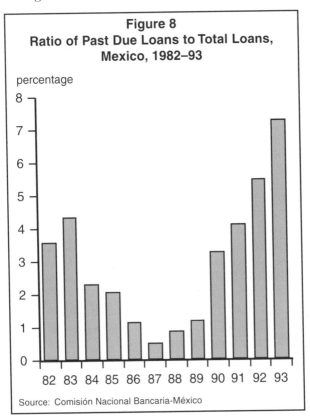

Figure 8
Ratio of Past Due Loans to Total Loans, Mexico, 1982–93

percentage

Source: Comisión Nacional Bancaria-México

so, there is much to suggest that the incentive has not fully offset the tendency to take risks. Problems with credit card debt defaults—which seem to have been aggravated by a combination of scarcity of organized consumer credit information together with significant increases during the present decade in the extension of credit cards—have been particularly acute.

In the wake of the capital flight and inflation attendant to Mexico's devaluation of December 1994, rapidly rising interest rates on variable rate short-term loans began to trigger even more loan defaults and to raise questions about the solvency of Mexico's banking system. As of this writing, five banks are effectively insolvent and under the administration of Mexico's bank regulators. It is in response to this crisis that maximum capital limits for Mexican banks that could be purchased by foreigners—limits that formerly were identical to the 1.5 percent-of-total-banking-system-net-capital limit still in effect for new banks established as subsidiaries of foreign institutions—have been raised to 6 percent. Similarly, as originally agreed under NAFTA, bank net capital under control of foreign institutions was not to exceed 9.4 percent of total commercial banking system net capital; in response to bank solvency problems that could be ameliorated by foreign institutions' acquistion of existing banks, legal changes have raised the percentage of system-wide net bank capital that may be controlled by foreign institutions to 25 percent effective July 1995.

Even in the wake of financial crisis, however, the relatively illiquid nature of Mexico's financial markets should continue to offer banks there a central role in supplying liquidity and monitoring the financial condition of borrowers. An interesting detail in the wake of what seem to be severe information-generated problems in the bank credit card markets is that several Mexican "grupos" have allied with U.S.-based consumer credit reporting agencies to provide such services in Mexico.

As Mexico's financial markets continue to broaden and deepen, Mexico's relatively unrestrictive regulations pertaining to financial structure offer broader avenues for avoiding the erosion of market share than those afforded U.S. banks in the 1980s.[37]

Other Mexican Financial Markets

Bank concentration need not inhibit competitive provision of banking services but, up to now, it seems to have done so in Mexico. One reason Mexico's banking system seems to lack competition appears to involve a shortage of contestable markets. That is, the viability of entry by new banking firms or the existence of deep and broad markets for nonbank funding of private enterprise seem not to have been sufficient to discipline banks toward competitive behavior. While stock and securities markets exist in Mexico and while factoring and leasing operations and other nonbank sources of de facto finance for private borrowers have also existed for years, many of these institutions have had problems of their own that have impaired their competitive strength.

Consider the stock market in Mexico. In general, stock markets transfer capital from savers to investors (the primary market), provide liquidity to owners of fixed capital (the secondary market), and improve the efficiency and performance of firms through the market for corporate control (the secondary market). However, the performance of the stock market depends not only on market access but also on the market's ability to discipline its corporate participants.

The Mexican stock market is small compared with those of developed countries. An important reason involves contestable markets, but of a somewhat different sort than those stressed in previous discussions. Here, the contest involves the threat of takeover when a company's managers behave in their own interests rather than in the interests of the stockholders. McConnell and Servaes (1990) provide evidence that self-serving managerial behavior increases with the percentage of insider ownership and that increases in insider ownership accordingly lower the value of stock.

High insider ownership rates are common in Mexico, and the result has been an illiquid market. Under the current Mexican regime of comparatively loose regulation of company performance reportage, in a milieu of heavy insider stock holdings, participants in the Mexican market are suspicious of managers and discount stock values accordingly.

Moreover, the market suspicions that have been inspired by Mexico's longtime corporate issuers naturally contaminate efforts of new firm entrants to fund themselves efficiently in the equity market. Accordingly, Mexico's stock market is less liquid than that of developed countries and offers even less competition with the banking system than do stock markets in developed countries.[38]

Other forms of private firm securities likewise play a smaller role in Mexico than in developed countries. As an example, consider commercial paper, an open market substitute for bank loans. The ratio of commercial paper holdings to bank lending is less than one-fourth as high as in the United States. And the banks themselves behave as if they are money market mutual funds. They place their own funds and those of the trusts they operate into commercial paper that they themselves market (Garber and Weisbrod 1991).

More generally, until now the overwhelming share of securities traded in the Mexican Bolsa de Valores has been of government issue. Because of the thinness of nonbank financial markets for nongovernmental borrowers, firms that could go abroad for funding have. It has been common for Mexico's great conglomerates to issue fixed-income securities in U.S. or European markets, and it is not unusual for the government to do the same.

Over time, however, the role of government issues in the Mexican securities market has diminished and will probably continue to decline. Recent innovations, expected developments (such as a Mexican options market), as well as broadening and deepening of existing markets, suggest a diminishing role for traditional lending services in Mexican financial markets, much as has been the case in the developed world. The worldwide revolution in information processing that has increased the abilities of nonbank financial institutions to tailor securitized debt to the special needs of particular borrowers will likely continue to affect Mexican domestic financial markets (Walter 1992). That is, Mexican firms may be increasingly able to offer services at a level of particularity that up to now has been restricted to bank lending.

However, the same is true for Canadian and U.S. brokerage firms that could enter Mexican markets under NAFTA. Moreover, Canadian and U.S. firms already have experience and technology of the types that Mexican institutions are just now gaining. Accordingly, this is the area of the Mexican financial market that may see the greatest foreign penetration. Growth in such securities and trading by both Mexican and foreign institutions may prevent the fall in the liquidity of the Mexican financial system that Garber and Weisbrod (1991) expected to result from reductions in the number of Mexican treasury instruments outstanding. Private issues may offset those of the government.

Another motivating factor for the entry of foreign securities brokerage firms under NAFTA is the agreement's relatively favorable treatment of this industry. While the maximum level of start-up capital for a new entrant into Mexico's banking system is 1.5 percent of the sum of net capital of all commercial banks, the comparable restricted maximum for new foreign entrants in the securities brokerage industry is a more liberal 4 percent during the transition period—before being removed entirely in the year 2000. Of course, the 4 percent rule is more restrictive than the 6 percent of systemwide bank capital maximum that is allowable when considering foreign institutions' applications to acquire existing Mexican banks, even though it is more liberal than the 1.5 percent maximum for establishing foreign institution-owned new or de novo banks in Mexico.

A possible role in the Mexican financial system for foreign financial firms is that of an offshore banking center. In July of 1990, for example, the Law on Credit Institutions changed to allow Mexican banks to create dollar-denominated deposits for nonresident depositors. Currently, however, several factors remain to discourage foreign institutions from establishing offshore operations in Mexico. First, the Mexican income tax for such institutions is 35 percent, a relatively high level compared with those obtaining in traditional offshore banking centers. In addition, Mexican labor laws require any company in Mexico to share 10 percent of its profits with its workers. Inasmuch as financial institutions in general, and offshore banks in particular, realize relatively high profits per employee, these laws may also dissuade potential offshore bankers from establishing operations in Mexico (Mansell Carstens 1992).

Conclusion

Although the possibility of U.S. and Canadian bank entry into the Mexican market has received a fair amount of attention, there is reason to suspect that de novo entry into the Mexican banking market may be less inviting than other NAFTA-related financial apertures. Because of the capital ceilings for such de novos, U.S. banks that enter must be relatively small. Typically such smaller institutions deal in retail banking and consumer financing. Most U.S. banks, however, are not familiar enough with the Mexican market to compete effectively in retailing. On the other hand, the more liberal treatment given brokerage, bonding, leasing, factoring, insurance, and warehousing suggests that equity and bond markets may prove somewhat more attractive than de novo banking. In light of recent legal changes attendant to growing solvency problems for existing Mexican banking institutions, bank acquisition where possible may prove at least as attractive early on as de novo activity.

Much of nonbank entry will likely involve securities brokerage firms. Mexico already imports a large amount of brokerage services from the New York Stock Exchange (NYSE) through the flotation of American Depository Receipts (ADRs) and from world bond markets through the large flotations from PEMEX, some large banks, and also some smaller firms. Hence, brokerage operations with strong links to U.S. investment banks will enjoy a strong position not only for arbitrage between the Mexican and New York markets but also to tailor asset and liability products to the needs of firms that conduct business internationally.

Certainly, increasing competition in the nonbank sectors from foreign participation in combination with a number of new Mexican banks will put pressure on banks to improve their efficiency. As we have described, this process is already well under way. The Mexican financial system, although not competitive at present, shows signs that very soon the institutions and markets will offer better financial services at significantly lower cost.

But a number of questions remain. One concerns the role that banks will play relative to securities markets. The remaining statutory barriers to entry in Mexican banking and the problems with the Mexican market for corporate control indicate that banks will maintain a privileged position in the Mexican financial system for many years to come. But the decline of banking in the United States and Europe cannot be explained solely by overregulation, implying that perhaps the importance of Mexican banks may also erode over time. Technological advances in information processing and financial instruments has given securities markets an edge, as witnessed by the major increase in securitization (Kaufman 1991). If U.S. and Mexican specialist institutions can offer nonbank services more efficiently than banks, then one would expect the importance of banks to wane. The favorable treatment of securities brokerage by NAFTA would be expected to promote such a competitive process. These considerations make projections of the future structure of the Mexican banking system extremely difficult. But no matter what the ultimate outcome, the evolution of the Mexican banking system should prove a fertile experiment in financial market liberalization.

We would like to thank Agustín Carstens and Moises Schwartz of the Banco de México and Yves Maroni of the Board of Governors of the Federal Reserve System for their comments. Of course, all remaining errors are our own and the usual caveats apply. This chapter is adapted from work appearing in *Financial Industry Studies,* October 1993, Federal Reserve Bank of Dallas.

Notes

1. Also, by increasing the credibility of policy permanence, NAFTA can reduce response time to a policy change. An important reason for having free trade agreements like NAFTA, as Gould clarifies, is that "unlike most legal contracts, enforcement of these agreements is entirely voluntary, and their credibility does not depend on the objectives and interests of only two parties, but on the relative power of competing interests within two or more subscribing countries." Incredible policy changes may have neutral or even perverse effects. In the early 1980s, Peru's attempt at trade liberalization lacked credibility. Suspecting that tariffs would rise again, investors imported large quantities of foreign goods and reduced domestic investment (Gould 1992).

2. Banks were required to lend a certain portion of their deposits to firms in priority sectors.

3. A succinct analysis of import substituting industrialization can be found in Baer (1992). For a detailed analysis of the Mexican banking system during this period, see Brothers and Solis M. (1966). For a similar analysis of another country, Brazil, which pursued import substitution, see Welch (1993a).

4. An important point is that Citibank's office was a branch, not a subsidiary.

5. In a perfectly competitive banking system in which profits are zero, the relationship between lending rates, i_L, and deposit rates, i_D, is

$$i_L = \frac{1}{1-k} i_D,$$

where k is equal to the required reserve ratio.

The spread or the difference between i_L and i_D is therefore

$$i_L - i_D = \frac{k}{1-k} i_D$$

If k increases, the spread increases. Notice also that if interest rates rise, so does the spread. For further details of this relationship, see McKinnon and Mathieson (1981).

6. The term "nonbank intermediary" simply refers to a financial entity

that is not a bank but still accumulates funds (by taking issuing bonds, notes, bills, or acceptances) from some sources and then lends or otherwise distributes them to another party.

7. *Financieras* were financial institutions that resembled banks but with a narrower scope of operation. A *financiera* could be seen as a sort of development bank, i.e., it focused on making long-term loans to industry. To secure funds, *financieras* accepted time deposits with a minimum duration of one year. *Financieras* also issued their own ten-year (or longer) certificates of obligation called financial bonds (*bonos financieros*). It was not unusual for a private *financiera* to be part of a collection of financial institutions held by a holding company. As such, they were often recipients of large amounts of funds that were able to be employed in the purchase of claims on industrial and consumer borrowers not suitable for direct holding by the financial intermediaries—other types of institutions within the holding company, for example —that made the funds available.

8. Mortgage banks specialized in home mortage-based lending and collected funds through the issuance of special mortgage bonds, as noted.

9. Capitalization banks focused on long-term lending for capital goods.

10. Disintermediation occurs when funds shift out of one type of financial intermediary (in the case under discussion, banks) and either into another type (here, *financieras*) or out of the financial system altogether. In the United States before the financial deregulations of the late 1970s and early 1980s, restrictions on bank and savings and loan deposit rates would cause deposits to flow out of these institutions and into less regulated assets when rates went up.

11. Two commercial banks escaped nationalization: Banco Obrero, which was owned by the unions, and Citibank Mexico.

12. See Moore (1993) for additional analysis of the pervasive effects of Mexico's high government deficit on the Mexican financial system.

13. Fifty-eight of the existing 60 banks were nationalized. As noted above, only Banco Obrero and Citibank Mexico were spared. When nationalization was implemented, articles 28 and 123 were amended to exclude the private sector from holding a controlling interest in a bank (Bazdresch Parada 1985 and Tello 1984).

14. The prior bank owners were indemnified with these bonds, which had a maturity of ten years and an interest rate tied to the CD rate (Heyman 1989).

15. These were issued in the form of "B" shares that can only be held by Mexicans; consortia cannot form a controlling interest.

16. The term "liquidity coefficient" refers to required reserves that can be held in liquid interest-bearing assets such as *cetes*. This is different from "required reserve coefficient," which typically refers to the percentage of liabilities that must be held in cash reserves or non-interest-bearing (or low interest-bearing) deposits at the central bank.

17. Bankers acceptances in Mexico are short-term (maturity not exceeding 180 days) promissory notes issued on a discount basis by banks. Unlike their counterpart in the United States, bankers acceptances in Mexico are not linked to goods traded internationally (Heyman 1989).
18. A factoring company buys a firm's accounts receivable for less than their face value, does its best to collect the payments on the accounts at face value, and profits on the difference.
19. There is one relaxation of this provision. A bank can hold up to a maximum of 15 percent of a firm's paid-in capital as long as possession does not continue for more than three years. Moreover, even three years' possession is permissible only after approval by two-thirds of the bank's board members and authorization by Mexico's Ministry of Finance (Banco de México, 1993).
20. These loans must be approved by two-thirds of the directors (Natella, et al. 1991).
21. CAPS issued in 1987 were subsequently turned into shares.
22. NAFTA also represents much effort to ensure procedural transparency; in fact, transparency is one of the general principles on which this principles-based agreement is founded. In processing applications for entry into its financial services markets, each NAFTA country has committed itself to clarifying its requirements for completing applications, to providing information on the status of an application on request, to making an administrative determination on a completed application within 120 days, to publishing measures of general application no later than their effective date, to allowing interested persons the opportunity to comment on proposed measures, and to establishing inquiry points to answer questions about its financial services measures.
23. NAFTA countries have generally agreed not to increase current impediments to cross-border trade. However, the United States has declined to make such a commitment with regard to cross-border trade in securities with Canada, even though such an agreement does exist between the United States and Mexico. Likewise, Canada has not committed to such a "standstill" agreement with the United States. While NAFTA countries generally have agreed to permit their residents to purchase financial services provided from the territory of another party to the agreement, the transaction must originate at the request of the purchaser. Active solicitation of business from a seller in one NAFTA country to a purchaser in another is not part of the agreement.
24. The financial services chapter of NAFTA focuses more on institutions than on products. NAFTA's focus is a departure from that of other agreements, such as the General Agreement on Trade in Services, in that NAFTA treats financial services as institution-specific, so that the rules for one type of lending or deposit-accepting

institution are different from those of another. Under NAFTA, the same category of service may face different regulations or restrictions in accordance with the category of institution providing the services.
25. The term "comparable" is important. Sauvé and González-Hermosillo note that NAFTA borrows from the General Agreement on Trade in Services in defining national treatment in a de facto rather than *de jure* sense. A *de jure* national treatment means that the very same laws apply to foreign firms as domestic. A *de facto* standard takes account of the potential inequality of effects that regulatory requirements might have if they were applied identically to domestic and foreign institutions. Accordingly, *de facto* treatment may allow somewhat different laws and regulations to apply to foreigners than apply to locals, "so long as their effect is equivalent and does not place the former at a competitive disadvantage in the host country market." (Sauvé and González-Hermosillo 1993). Of course, not all parties will agree in every future case on what equal effects are. There is a dispute settlement mechanism to address these potential differences.
26. The host country provision contrasts with that of the European Economic Community, which allows Country A's subsidiary financial institutions operating in Country B to behave in accordance with Country A's regulations instead of Country B's.
27. NAFTA also allows foreign insurance providers to enter Mexico through a partial equity interest in a new or existing Mexican insurance company. Under this alternative entry mechanism, the share of a Mexican insurance company's voting common stock owned by foreign insurance providers is subject to limits that are relaxed during the transition period.
28. The freeze is permitted to last only three years and can only be implemented during the period 2000–2004. NAFTA provides a similar option for Mexico with regard to securities firms, but there the aggregate capital percentage that triggers the option is 30 percent, although the same three-year maximum freeze period holds. Note that Canada exempts Mexican firms and individuals from its prohibition against nonresidents' collective acquisition of more than 25 percent of the shares of a federally regulated Canadian financial institution. Canada had already extended this exemption to the United States as part of the Canada-U.S. Free Trade Agreement (FTA). Mexican banks are also exempted from the combined 12 percent asset ceiling that applies to non-NAFTA banks and also need not seek the approval of the minister of finance as a condition of opening multiple branches in Canada. Financial services commitments of Canada and the United States under the Canada-U.S. FTA will be incorporated into NAFTA.
29. In general, to gain peso exposure, U.S. and Canadian financial institutions must locate operations in Mexico, as offshore peso

trading is strictly prohibited. However, certain operations between U.S. and Mexican markets also provide vehicles for peso exposure.

30. In a discussion of this point, Mansell Carstens notes that spreads have remained high and are likely to continue to remain high over the next two years, not only because of the oligopoly power in the provision of commercial bank services, but because "commercial banks have been moving into high yield consumer lending" (Mansell Carstens 1993). She notes that consumers had not had access to credit since the early 1980s; that banks have enjoyed a seller's market in satisfying the backlog of credit demand; that banks will probably expand their credit card, consumer durable, and mortgage lending programs to middle and lower income groups; and that such operations typically involve large spreads.

31. The bank assets of individual U.S. banking organizations are approximated by the sum of the assets of their bank affliates. U.S. concentration measures based on deposits are similar to the asset concentration figures reported here. Note that the national concentration measures used here do not necessarily reflect the degree of concentration within local market areas in either Mexico or the United States.

32. Concentration, in and of itself, need not preclude competitive provision of banking services. Shaffer (1993) finds that the Canadian banking system, which is comparable to Mexico's in terms of market concentration, still behaves competitively. The historical difference has been the contestability of Canadian markets for the types of financial services that Canadian banks offer. That is, market entry has traditionally been more viable in Canada, and securities markets for private debt are broader and deeper than those in Mexico. Later in this chapter, we more fully address problems of Mexico's nonbank private debt markets in providing competition for the banks.

33. International comparisons of financial ratios probably offer a general picture of differences between the Mexican banking system and its counterparts in other countries, but care must be exercised and tenths of a percentage point ought not to be taken seriously. For a more extensive clarification of international comparisons of financial ratios in the context of NAFTA countries, see Gavito Mohar, Sánchez Garcia, and Trigueros Legarreta (1992). Despite their cautions, those authors still draw conclusions about the essential differences between Mexican and U.S. financial performance, and the conclusions are very similar to those we draw.

34. See Mansell Carstens (1993) for further discussion of this issue.

35. In a discussion of this point, Mansell Carstens (1993) notes that the smallest of Mexico's three largest banking institutions (Banca Serfin) has 596 branches and that both Banamex and Bancomer have more.

36. The stock of financial experience in Mexico's banks contrasts sharply with that of many U.S. financial institutions in the 1980s. The partial

erosion of barriers to competition at that time in the United States led many U.S. thrifts to enter into areas in which they had little or no previous experience. Similarly, the financial deregulation of the 1980s broadened the types of financial controls that U.S. banks and thrifts were required to maintain on their own, leading to substantial financial difficulties at some institutions.

37. See Gunther and Moore (1992) for a discussion of the relatively unrestrictive product and geographic expansion laws that distinguish Mexico's banking system from that of the United States.

38. For further development of these issues, see Welch (1993b).

References

Baer, Werner (1992), "U.S.-Latin American Trade Relations: Past, Present, and Future," in Gerald P. O'Driscoll, Jr., ed., *Free Trade within North America: Expanding Trade for Prosperity* (Norwell: Kluwer Academic Publishers).

Banco de México (1993), *The Mexican Economy 1993* (México: Banco de México).

Bazdresch Parada, Carlos (1985), "La Nacionalización Bancaria," *Nexos,* January.

Brothers, Dwight S. and Leopoldo Solis M. (1966), *Mexican Financial Development* (Austin: University of Texas Press).

Carstens, Agustín G. C. (1993), "The Mexican Financial System," lectures presented at the Federal Reserve Bank of Dallas, January.

Garber, Peter M. and Steven R. Weisbrod (1991), "Opening the Financial Services Market in Mexico," paper presented at the Conference on the Mexico-U.S. Free Trade Agreement, Brown University, October 18–19.

Gavin, Michael (1991), "The Mexican Oil Boom," Discussion Paper No. 548, Department of Economics, Columbia University, May.

Gavito Mohar, Javier, Sergio Sánchez Garcia, and Ignacio Trigueros Legarreta (1992), "Los Servicios Financieros y el Acuerdo de Libre Comercio: Bancos y Casas de Bolsa," in Eduardo Andere and Georgina Kessel, eds., *México y el Tratado Trilateral de Libre Comercio: Impacto Sectorial* (México City: ITAM and McGraw-Hill).

Gould, David M. (1992), "Free Trade Agreements and the Credibility of Trade Reforms," Federal Reserve Bank of Dallas, *Economic Review,* first quarter.

Gunther, Jeffrey W. and Robert R. Moore (1992), "Mexico Offers Banking Opportunities," Federal Reserve Bank of Dallas, *Financial Industry Issues,* fourth quarter.

Heyman, Timothy (1989), *Investing in Mexico* (Mexico: Editorial Milenio).

Johnson, R.D. and D.C. Meinster (1975), "The Performance of Bank Holding Company Acquisitions: A Multivariate Analysis," *The Journal of Business*, 48.

———— (1973), "The Analysis of Bank Holding Companies' Acquisitions: Some Methodological Issues," *Journal of Bank Research*, 4.

Kaufman, George G. (1991), "The Diminishing Role of Commercial Banking in the U.S. Economy," Federal Reserve Bank of Chicago Working Paper No. WP-1991-11, May.

Keeley, Michael C. (1990), "Deposit Insurance, Risk, and Market Power in Banking," *American Economic Review*, 80, December.

Laderman, Elizabeth and Ramon Moreno (1992), "NAFTA and U.S. Banking," *FRBSF Weekly Letter*, no. 9240.

Mansell Carstens, Catherine (1993), "The Social and Economic Impact of the Mexican Bank Reprivatization," paper presented at Institute of the Americas, La Jolla, January.

———— (1992), *Las Nuevas Finanzas en Mexico* (Mexico City: Editorial Milenio).

Maxfield, Sylvia (1992), "The International Political Economy of Bank Nationalization: Mexico in Comparative Perspective," *Latin American Research Review*, 27, no. 1.

McConnell, John J. and Henri Servaes (1990), "Additional Evidence on Equity Ownership and Corporate Value," *Journal of Financial Economics*, 27, October.

McKinnon, Ronald I. and Donald J. Mathieson (1981), "How to Manage a Repressed Economy," *Princeton Essays in International Finance*, no. 145, December.

Moore, Robert R. (1993), "The Government Budget Deficit and the Banking System: The Case of Mexico," Federal Reserve Bank of Dallas, *Financial Industry Studies*, October.

Natella, Stefano, Thomas H. Hanley, Justin Manson, Suhas L. Ketkar, and Veronica Dias (1992), *The Mexican Banking System II* (New York: CS First Boston).

———— (1991), *The Mexican Banking System* (New York: CS First Boston).

Ortiz, Guillermo (1983), "Dollarization in Mexico: Causes and Consequences," in Pedro Aspe Armella, Rudiger Dornbusch, and Maurice Obstfeld, eds., *Financial Policies and the World Capital Market: The Problem of Latin American Countries* (Chicago: University of Chicago Press).

Sauvé, Pierre and Brenda González-Hermosillo (1993), "Financial Services and the North American Free Trade Agreement: Implications for Canadian Financial Institutions," unpublished paper, External Affairs and International Trade Canada and Bank of Canada, Ottawa.

Shaffer, Sherrill (1993), "A Test of Competition in Canadian Banking," *Journal of Money, Credit, Banking*, 25, no. 1.

Tello, Carlos (1984), *La Nacionalización de la Banca en México* (Mexico City: Siglo XXI Editores).

Trigueros, Ignacio (1992), "El Sistema Financiero Mexicano," mimeo, ITAM, December.

Walter, Ingo (1992) "A Framework for the Optimum Structure of Financial Systems," New York University Salomon Center Working Paper Series No. S-92-47.

Welch, John H. (1993a), *Capital Markets in the Development Process: The Case of Brazil* (Pittsburgh: University of Pittsburgh Press).

——— (1993b), "The New Face of Latin America: Financial Flows, Markets, and Institutions," *Journal of Latin American Studies*, 25, February.

5

The North American Free Trade Agreement, Domestic Price Reforms, and the Agricultural Sector of Mexico

Antonio Yúnez-Naude

Introduction

The liberalization of the Mexican economy since the debt crisis of 1982 constitutes one of the major events of Mexico's contemporary political economy. The North American Free Trade Agreement (NAFTA) must be taken as part of this process of change. NAFTA will be an important element in guaranteeing that both internal price reforms and trade liberalization will continue in the future. The objective of this chapter is to estimate the impacts of agricultural price reforms and the trilateral trade negotiations on Mexican agricultural output, labor income, and trade.

The Agricultural Sector of Mexico

The Mexican agricultural[1] sector has been suffering from stagnation. Since 1965, the average rate of growth of per capita agricultural production has been negative,[2] indicating stagnation in both productivity and agricultural production. The average rate of growth of harvested land increased by just 0.3 percent between 1965 and 1985.[3] This has been particularly so for corn, the most important crop in Mexico and the most important food for the country's poor population. Corn production accounted for 47.2 percent of total harvested area in the 1980–82 period and for 28.7 percent of the value of total agricultural production in 1980 (table 1). The harvested area used in the production of corn decreased 0.4 percent between 1965 and 1985. More than 75 percent of the corn produced in Mexico is produced on rainfed (nonirrigated) lands (table 2). It is important therefore to recognize that any changes in the structure of the rainfed corn supply will have a significant effect on total agricultural output in Mexico. The production of beans (another basic food for Mexican consumption) has also been sluggish. The harvested area of this crop—most of which is also produced on rainfed lands—decreased 0.7 percent between 1965 and 1985.

Table 1
Basic Features of Agricultural Production in Mexico, 1965-85

Crops	Shares of (percentages)		Annual average rates of growth (percentages)		
	Harvested area	Total agricultural production	Harvested area	Production volume	Per capita production
	1980-82	1980	1965-85	1965-67/1983-85	
Basic crops					
Rice	1.1	1.2	0.2	1.9	-0.8
Beans	12.1	6.5	-0.7	0.4	-2.2
Corn	47.2	28.7	-0.4	2.0	-0.6
Wheat	6.1	4.7	1.7	4.7	1.9
Sesame	1.2	0.8	-2.9	2.1	-0.6
Cotton	3.0	1.3	-5.2	2.9	0.2
Safflower	2.4	1.6	4.7	1.6	-1.0
Soybeans	2.1	1.1	11.2	11.0	8.2
Barley	1.9	0.9	1.0	5.2	2.5
Sorghum	10.6	7.5	6.0	7.6	4.8
Industrial crops (& traditional exports)					
Cocoa	0.5	0.9	-0.2	2.8	0.1
Coffee	3.2	4.7	2.0	4.8	2.1
Sugarcane	3.5	6.0	0.2	41.7	38.0
Henequen	1.0	0.6	-2.9	-4.4	-6.9
Tobacco	0.3		-2.3	-2.2	-4.8
Oleaginous					
Sunflower	0.1	0.0	-7.0	-3.4	-5.9
Coconut	0.6	0.8	6.4	-0.7	-3.3
Animal feeds					
Alfalfa	1.5	3.7	3.7	4.1	1.4
Vegetables					
Chilies		1.8			
Tomatoes	0.5	3.3	2.0	5.2	2.5
Fruits					
Avocados		2.5			
Strawberries	0.0	0.3	-2.1		
Oranges	1.2	2.3	2.5	1.2	-1.5
Bananas		1.7			

Note: Different intervals are used in the tables describing the evolution of Mexico's agricultural production and trade because complete information is unavailable. Sources: Yúnez-Naude and Blanno Jasso (1990), tables 14 and 16 (columns 1 and 3-5); tables 2, infra (column 2).

The agrarian structure of the country is characterized by the coexistence of small, rainfed, family-based plots with dynamic, irrigated, capitalistic farms. The stagnation in the production of corn and beans is mainly concentrated in poor, small, privately owned

Table 2
Production of Basic Crops in Mexico, 1977-90

Crop	Value* 1980 (millions of pesos)	Share of (percentages)		Volume of production, annual average rates of growth (percentages)**			
		Value per crop 1980	Total crop harvested area 1977/85	1980-81/ 1982-84	1982-84/ 1985-87	1985-87/ 1988-90	1980-81/ 1988-90
Rice	2,618			-14.0	36.4	-29	-5.9
Irrigated	1,909	72.9	59.8	-22.5	38.7		
Rainfed	709	27.1	40.2	10.2	31.7		
Beans	14,137			-6.0	-5.2	-9.3	-6.9
Irrigated	4,081	28.9	13.3	-9.9	-9.2		
Rainfed	10,056	71.1	86.7	-4.4	-3.7		
Corn	62,107			-10.6	4.0	-3.2	-3.5
Irrigated	15,267	24.6	13.9	-4.5	5.4		
Rainfed	46,841	75.4	86.0	-12.4	3.6		
Wheat	10,173			37.8	16.5	-17	10.1
Irrigated	9,644	94.8	86.5	40.1	16.4		
Rainfed	529	5.2	13.5	3.5	20.4		
Sesame	1,625			-39.1	-1.2	-29.9	-25
Irrigated	622	38.3	26.2	-4.8	19.3		
Rainfed	1,003	61.7	73.9	-54.7	-20.9		
Cottonseed	2,906			-31.3	-20.2		
Irrigated	2,693	92.7	88.4	-31.5	-18.1		
Rainfed	213	7.3	11.6	-28.7	-54.5		
Safflower	3,446			-40.9	-24.9	1.2	-23.4
Irrigated	2,585	75.0	54.3	-48.6	11.3		
Rainfed	860	25.0	45.6	-19.5	9.6		
Soybeans	2,478			31.0	22.1	-26.6	5.5
Irrigated	2,299	92.8	82.8	28.7	22.4		
Rainfed	179	7.2	17.2	52.1	19.5		
Barley	2,006			-1.3	4.8	-22.2	-7
Irrigated	596	29.7	19.0	13.5	13.4		
Rainfed	1,409	70.3	81.0	-8.1	-0.1		
Sorghum	16,343			-9.5	22.3	-5.2	1.6
Irrigated	7,322	44.8	35.6	1.7	12.1		
Rainfed	9,021	55.2	64.4	-18.2	32.2		
Total basic crops	117,839	54.4***		4.6	9.8	-7.9	-1.2
Total ag. GDP	216,592						

* Refers to the agricultural year, i.e., includes the spring-summer cycle of 1980 and the autumn-winter cycle that began in 1979.
** Based on two- or three-year averages.
*** Share in value of total agricultural production.
Sources: National Water Commission database (CNA), tables 11f, 33f, 37f, and 61f (columns 1, 2, and 4-7); Yúnez-Naude and Blanno Jasso (1990), table 19 (column 3).

nonirrigated farms and in the *ejidos,* units of production and consumption in poor rainfed lands.[4] Most of the *ejidos* can be classified as peasant plots.[5]

The production of corn and beans has been affected not only by small or sluggish increases in productivity and by reductions of the harvested area dedicated to these crops, but also by a process of substituting sorghum and soybeans in irrigated lands for rainfed corn and beans production.[6] In fact, among agricultural products, soybeans and sorghum showed the highest rates of growth in harvested area between 1965–85. The harvested area also increased for other agricultural products such as wheat, coffee, and tomatoes during the same period. From 1965–67 to 1983–85, the volume of production of these crops increased as well (tables 1 to 3). With the exception of coffee, all these products are mainly produced in irrigated lands (table 3). Coffee, tomatoes, and other vegetables are mainly export crops and have displaced cotton as the major agricultural traded good of Mexico (table 4). Sorghum and soybeans, on the other hand, are used primarily as inputs to produce processed animal feeds.

In summary, since 1965, Mexico's agricultural supply has been characterized by slowdowns in the production of corn and beans on rainfed plots and the substitution of these crops for sorghum and soybeans by capitalist and some rainfed producers. The stagnation of agriculture can be explained by the negative growth in the production of corn and, to a lesser extent, beans. Change in the agricultural sector, however, is related not only to the stagnation in the production of corn and beans, but also to the orientation of agricultural supply toward the production of crops for animal feeding (sorghum and soybeans) and for the foreign market (tomatoes, other vegetables, and coffee).

Increases in the domestic production of soybeans and sorghum, however, have been insufficient to compensate for increases in the domestic demand for these products; therefore, Mexico's imports of both crops have been steadily increasing since the 1960s (table 4). The gap between the domestic supplies of and the demands for corn and beans has also been growing.[7] Increasing imports of corn, beans, sorghum, and soybeans and an insufficient growth in Mexico's exports of agricultural products to compensate the increasing purchases in the exterior have produced both a continuous reduction of the trade surplus that the agricultural sector enjoyed up to the mid-1970s and the emergence of deficits during several years of the 1980s. While the sector had a positive balance

Table 3
Production of Nonbasic Crops in Mexico, 1977-90

Crop	Volume* 1980 (millions of pesos)	Share of harvested area 1977-85 (percentages)	Volume of production, annual average rates of growth (percentages)**			
			1980-81/ 1982-84	1982-84/ 1985-87	1985-87/ 1988-90	1980-81/ 1988-90
Industrial crops / traditional exports						
Cocoa	1,867		10.5	25.7	10.4	15.3
Irrigated		1.4				
Rainfed		98.6				
Coffee	10,184		40.5	19.3	44.8	34.4
Irrigated		26.9				
Rainfed		79.8				
Sugarcane	13,050		3.6	2.6	-11	-1.8
Irrigated		40.4				
Rainfed		59.6				
Henequen	1,338		-26.7	-25.1	-11.2	-21.3
Irrigated		0.0				
Rainfed		100.0				
Oleaginous						
Sunflower	23		52	47.9	-59.1	-2.8
Irrigated		18.8				
Rainfed		80.9				
Copra	1,810		8	-2.5	8.4	4.5
Irrigated		21.3				
Rainfed		78.9				
Animal feeds						
Alfalfa	7,948		-6.9	-12.8	17.6	-1.5
Irrigated		97.8				
Rainfed		2.2				
Vegetables & fruits						
Fresh chiles	3,933		5.1	24.6	11.1	13.3
Tomatoes	7,224		17.3	-33.6	79.5	11.8
Irrigated		84.7				
Rainfed		15.5				
Avocadoes	5,475					
Strawberries	615		1.2	-13.8	29.1	4
Irrigated		99.0				
Rainfed		1.4				
Lemons	2,154		26	1.7	-28.4	-2.9
Apples	2,236		18.3	20.5	1.8	13.2
Oranges	5,041		9.5	-4.1	-22.9	-6.8
Irrigated		27.7				
Rainfed		73.3				
Bananas	3,714		18.1	-2.8	-17.1	-1.6
Total "nonbasic"	66,611	30.8*	1.9	-2.4	-2.8	-1.1
Total agricultural GDP	216,592					

* Share in value of total agricultural production.
** Based on two or three-year averages.
Sources: see table 2.

Table 4
Volume of Trade of Major Agricultural Products in Mexico, 1965-1990

	Thousands of metric tons				Annual average rates of growth (percentages)	
	1965-70	1977-82	1980-81	1988-90	1977-82/ 1965-70	1988-90/ 1980-81
Imports						
Rice	9	43			123.7	
Beans	2	231	467	160	1078.0	-30.10
Corn	133	1,764	3,421	3,685	264.7	2.5
Wheat	0	656	975	653		-12.5
Soybeans	24	628	816	1,035	414.2	8.3
Sorghum	26	1,417	2,522	2,224	631.2	-4.1
Barley	22	77	133	81	88.7	-15.2
Exports						
Coffee	86	130	122	197	22.9	17.5
Henequen	31					
Chickpeas	4	71	74	55	311.3	-9.5
Tomatoes	246	383	333	433	24.8	9.1
Garlic	5	1			73.8	
Onions	17	52			72.5	
Pumpkins & zucchini	6	43			160.0	
Cucumber	36	192			129.9	
Other vegetables*			427	844		25.5
Strawberries	14	10	5	16	-16.2	51.9
Melon & watermelon	96	199	170	341	43.6	26.1
Oranges	43	19			-33.4	
Pineapple	12	34			66.0	
Grapes	1	11			279.9	
Cotton	335	168	177	79	-29.2	-23.7
Tobacco	8	22	23	10	67.9	-22.9

* Excludes tomatoes.
   Sources: Yúnez-Naude and Blanno Jasso (1990), table 10 (columns 1 and 2); CNA, tables 83f and 84f (columns 3 and 4).

of $490.8 million in the 1965–70 period, it had an estimated deficit of $288.4 and $91.4 million in 1989 and 1990, respectively (table 5).

What place do exports and imports of agricultural products have in total Mexican trade? When comparing periods 1980–90 and 1988–90, no significant changes in import shares among economic sectors (table 6) can be found. However, there were significant changes in export shares (table 7). Although the share of agriculture in total exports stayed constant—at about 6.5 percent for crops and 1.4 percent for livestock—between these periods, manufacturing (other than agroindustry) increased its participation from 33 percent in 1980–90 to 52 percent in 1988–90, and mining (oil, in particular) decreased its share from 54.2 percent to 34.2 percent during the same periods.

Table 5				
International Trade, Mexico, 1965-90				
(thousands of U.S. dollars)				
	Agriculture and silviculture	**Livestock and apiculture**	**Subtotal**	**Total trade**
Imports (FOB)				
1965-70	32,333	48,667	81,000	1,908,617
1971-76	363,500	113,333	476,833	4,984,433
1977-82	1,120,437	271,330	1,391,767	13,936,788
1983-85	1,515,442	389,535	1,904,977	11,005,787
1986	900,195	437,123	1,337,318	11,432,364
1987	908,626	480,688	1,389,314	12,222,852
1988	1,396,514	376,509	1,773,023	18,903,359
1989	1,746,923	248,485	1,995,408	23,409,700
1990 p			2,071,014	29,798,516
Exports (FOB)				
1965-70	477,500	94,333	571,833	1,205,967
1971-76	832,333	122,167	954,500	2,445,800
1977-82	1,416,991	142,130	1,559,121	12,738,033
1983-85	1,434,058	196,369	1,630,427	22,723,957
1986	1,848,669	361,822	2,210,491	16,030,999
1987	1,752,601	288,435	2,041,036	20,656,187
1988	1,400,922	270,920	1,671,842	20,657,633
1989	1,461,457	245,502	1,706,959	22,764,900
1990 p			2,162,442	26,773,099
Balances				
1965-70	445,167	45,667	490,833	(702,650)
1971-76	468,833	8,833	477,667	(2,538,633)
1977-82	296,553	(129,200)	167,353	(1,198,755)
1983-85	(81,383)	(193,166)	(274,550)	11,718,171
1986	948,474	(75,301)	873,174	4,598,635
1987	843,975	(192,253)	651,722	8,433,335
1988	4,408	(105,589)	(101,181)	1,754,274
1989	(285,466)	(2,983)	(288,449)	(644,800)
1990 p			(91,428)	(3,025,417)

P=preliminary
FOB=free on board
Source: Banco de México, Indicadores Económicos, various issues.

Agricultural Trade Between Mexico and the United States

The difference between the dimensions of the Mexican and the U.S. economies[8] is reflected in their respective agricultural and livestock sectors. During the 1980s, U.S. per capita gross national product (GNP) was 6.5 times that of Mexico; U.S. average agricultural and livestock gross domestic products, about 8.5 times; and the amount of U.S. arable and permanent cropland, 8.8 times larger (table 8).

The agricultural sector is relatively more important to the Mexican economy. With the exception of corn (U.S. corn farmers are three times more productive), the land productivity (kg/ha) per

Table 6
Mexican Imports (FOB): 1980-90
(thousands of U.S. dollars)

	Averages	Shares in total value of imports (percentages)			Shares in subtotals (percentages)		
	1980-90	1980-90	1980-81	1988-90	1980-90	1980-81	1988-90
Agriculture	1,485,767	8.8	9.6	6.9	100.0	100.0	100.0
Natural rubber	58,913				4.0	3.5	4.0
Barley	11,446				0.8	1.2	1.0
Beans	111,069				7.5	14.2	7.1
Fruits (fresh & dried)	14,594				1.0	0.9	1.9
Vegetables	24,493				1.6	1.6	1.0
Corn	369,4262				4.9	25.6	25.5
Other oleaginous seeds	160,797				10.8	6.7	8.8
Cotton (seeds)	18,365				1.2	0.7	2.6
Soybeans	255,175				17.2	12.0	17.7
Sorghum	266,145				17.9	18.2	15.9
Wheat	82,498				5.6	9.3	5.1
Other fresh products	112,847				7.6	6.2	9.3
Livestock, etc.	206,102	1.2	0.8	1.2	100.1	100.0	100.2
Live cattle	64,864				31.5	18.0	39.1
Wool (rough)	22,056				10.7	18.0	8.3
Furs and skins	83,140				40.3	40.2	34.5
Fishing & hunting	4,966				2.4	5.0	2.6
Other	31,258				15.2	18.8	15.8
Mining	259,195	1.5	1.3	1.5			
Agroindustry	1,032,502	6.1	5.3	8.2	100.0	100.0	100.0
Soy oil	29,098				2.8	1.2	1.7
Processed animal feeds	57,614				5.6	5.6	6.1
Sugar	187,249				18.1	40.9	12.4
Meats (fresh or frozen)	115,478				11.2	4.2	14.7
Fruits (preserved)	7,049				0.7	1.4	0.4
Milk (powdered)	194,313				18.8	10.9	21.3
Milk (other)	23,238				2.3	7.4	0.1
Spirits	22,219				2.2	4.6	1.8
Butter	34,133				3.3	4.3	2.3
Other animal fats & vegetable oils	90,402				8.8	2.1	10.6
Pig skin	31,248				3.0	1.6	3.2
Fish & seafoods	8,299				0.8	1.1	0.8
Processed feeds	22,745				2.2	1.2	3.5
Tallows	50,656				4.9	3.7	3.5
Other	158,945				15.4	9.6	17.6
Manufacturing*	13,748,355	81.4	81.8	81.4			
Services	49,549	0.3	0.1	0.6			
Nonclassified	94,698	0.6	0.9	0.2			
Total imports	16,883,435	100.0	99.8	100.0			

FOB=free on board
*Other than agroindustry
Source: National Agricultural Council (CNA), table 82f.

Table 7 Mexican Exports (FOB): 1980-90 (thousands of U.S. dollars)						
	Averages	Shares in total value of imports (percentages)			Shares in subtotals (percentages)	
	1980-90	1980-90	1980-81	1988-90	1980-90	1980-81	1988-90
Agriculture	1,364,631	6.5	8.1	6.5	100.0	100.0	100.0
Cotton	153,636				11.3	22.5	6.90
Cocoa	4,738				0.30	0.20	0.10
Coffee grains (raw)	453,993				33.3	26.7	28.0
Strawberries (fresh)	8,451				0.6	0.3	1.2
Chickpeas	36,360				2.7	4.2	2.0
Tomatoes	237,677				17.4	15.5	19.0
Vegetables (fresh)	215,588				15.8	13.2	19.6
Melons	68,056				5.0	5.2	6.3
Other fresh fruits	49,209				3.6	1.4	6.2
Tobacco	30,528				2.2	3.4	1.6
Other	106,303				7.8	7.3	9.1
Livestock, etc.	230,340	1.1	0.6	1.4	100.0	100.0	100.0
Cattle	176,108				76.5	63.0	76.0
Honey (bees)	33,922				14.7	29.3	10.2
Other	1,587				0.7	0.6	0.8
Fishing & hunting	18,723				8.1	7.2	13.0
Mining	11,384,815	54.2	71.70	34.2			
Agroindustry	948,271	4.5	4.20	5.3	100.7	100.0	100.0
Abulon (preserved)	12,549				1.3	1.6	1.8
Tunafish (frozen)	21,420				2.3	0.7	3.7
Sugar	33,623				3.5	0.0	6.5
Shrimp (frozen)	354,895				37.4	50.4	24.5
Beer	101,814				10.7	3.6	13.6
Coffee (toasted)	40,975				4.3	2.3	4.3
Cattle meats	11,184				1.2	0.4	1.8
Strawberries (frozen)	24,112				2.5	4.3	2.0
Orange juice	32,344				3.4	0.9	5.7
Lobster (frozen)	13,717				1.4	1.8	1.4
Vegetables (preserved)	92,836				9.8	8.5	11.5
Cocoa oil	17,739				1.9	2.3	1.5
Honey	15,643				1.6	3.1	0.9
Tequila & other spirits	51,551				5.4	5.6	6.0
Other	130,256				13.7	14.7	14.9
Manufacturing*	7,007,593	33.4	15.40	51.9			
Services	52,863	0.3	0.0	0.6			
Nonclassified	3,778	0.0	0.0	0.0			
Total	20,992,629	100.0	100.0	100.0			100.0

FOB=free on board
*Other than agroindustry
Source: National Agricultural Council (CNA), table 81f.

Table 8
Macroeconomic and Agricultural* Indicators,
Mexico and the United States
(averages, 1980-1987)

	Mexico	United States	U.S./Mexico
Population (millions)	76.06	235.86	3.10
Rate of growth (percentage/year)	2.28	1.00	0.44
Agricultural population (percentage)	25.36	1.45	0.06
Total labor force (percentage)	21.58	34.25	1.59
Agricultural labor force (percentage)	7.31	0.66	0.09
GNP total (millions of U.S. dollars)	149,538.38	3,054,882.75	20.43
GNP per capita (dollars per person)	1,997.50	12,983.75	6.5
Agriculture share in GDP (percentage)	7.50	1.38	0.18
Factors of production			
Arable & permanent cropland (1,000 ha)	21,599.88	190,092.25	8.80
Permanent pastures (1,000 ha)	74,499.13	240,485.00	3.23
Irrigated area (1,000 ha)	4,933.75	19,154.25	3.88
Agricultural labor force/1,000 ha (no.)	220.25	8.13	0.04
Tractors/1,000 ha (no.)	5.25	21.88	4.17
Tractors/1,000 agricultural workers (no.)	15.00	1,715.75	114.38
Fertilizer use (kg/ha)	57.25	86.88	1.52
Production values (millions of U.S. dollars)			
Total agriculture	15,685.88	135,716.13	8.65
Total crop	8,522.88	74,752.13	8.77
Total livestock	7,163.00	60,964.13	8.51
Crop production (kg/ha)	302.13	393.13	1.30
Agricultural production/agricultural worker	1,610.50	49,547.75	30.77
Yields, selected crops (kg/ha)			
Wheat	4,135.50	2,448.38	0.59
Rice, paddy	3,570.26	5,621.00	1.57
Corn	1,796.75	6,729.63	3.75
Barley	1,927.13	2,821.25	1.46
Oats	1,273.25	2,015.75	1.58
Sorghum	3,331.50	3,756.25	1.13
Soybean	1,850.63	2,047.25	1.11
Sunflower	980.25	1,307.13	1.33
Seed cotton	2,789.88	1,683.63	0.60
Yields, livestock products (kg/animal)			
Cattle	191.88	271.63	1.42
Pigs	73.38	78.75	1.07
Sheep	15.88	25.63	1.61
Milk	1,291.00	5,755.63	4.46
Eggs	13.13	14.63	1.11

* Includes livestock
ha=hectares; no.=number; kg=kilograms
Sources: United States Department of Agriculture (USDA); Economic Research Service (ERS), 1989, provided by John Link.

major crops is very similar in both countries. However, labor is 30 times more productive in the United States. Other contrasts mark the population and production bases of the two countries. While 25.4 percent of the total population in Mexico was living in rural

Table 9
Importance of Agriculture* in Mexican and U.S. Trade, 1961-1987
(averages)

	1961-1969 (percentage)	1970-1979 (percentage)	1980-1987 (percentage)
Mexico			
Agricultural exports on domestic agricultural production	7.34	10.11	11.50
Agricultural imports on domestic agricultural production	1.40	6.04	15.27
Agricultural exports on total exports	56.10	33.06	8.92
Agricultural imports on total exports	7.58	12.70	16.35
United States			
Agricultural exports on domestic agricultural production	6.39	17.28	27.00
Agricultural imports on domestic agricultural production	4.91	9.28	14.53
Agricultural exports on total exports	21.79	20.84	16.36
Agricultural imports on total exports	18.88	9.57	6.16
Mexico-United States trade			
U.S. in Mexico's total exports	58.14	101.99	83.47
U.S. in Mexico's total imports	62.00	78.55	87.05
Mexico in U.S. total exports	3.39	4.45	5.69
Mexico in U.S. total imports	2.54	3.18	5.28
U.S. in Mexico's agricultural exports	47.52	67.66	81.90
U.S. in Mexico's agricultural imports	60.02	75.05	71.53
Mexico in U.S. agricultural exports	1.14	2.59	4.68
Mexico in U.S. agricultural imports	6.17	7.29	7.49

* Includes livestock and agricultural inputs (tractors, total fertilizers, and pesticides)
Sources: United States Department of Agriculture (USDA); Economic Research Service (ERS), 1989, provided by John Link.

areas in 1980–87, rural residents represented only 1.45 percent of the total population in the United States during the same period. The labor force working in the agricultural and livestock sectors accounted for 7.31 percent of total Mexican population in 1980–87, but it only accounted for 0.66 percent in the United States during the same period. The agricultural sector of Mexico represented 7.5 percent of Mexican GDP from 1980–87, but only 1.38 percent of U.S. GDP for the same period.

There is also dissimilarity between the significance of Mexican and U.S. markets for agricultural and livestock trade. While 81.9 percent of Mexican exports of agricultural and livestock products went to the United States between 1980–87, only 4.68 percent of U.S. agricultural and livestock exports went to Mexico during the same period (table 9). Furthermore, 71.53 percent of Mexican imports of agricultural and livestock products came from the United States, but only 7.49 percent of U.S. imports of these products came from Mexico. However, the participation of Mexico in U.S. trade has increased steadily since 1961.

Corn, soybeans, and sorghum accounted for 59.7 percent of total Mexican agricultural imports from the United States in 1980–88 (table 10). Mexico exported mainly coffee, fresh vegetables, and fruits to the United States in the same period. Livestock exports to the United States were more specialized: young calves accounted for 92 percent of Mexican livestock exports to the United States between 1980–88. Most Mexican livestock imports from the United States were processed products, such as hides and skins, dairy products, and animal fats. Mexico had an average deficit of about $300 million in agricultural and livestock products between 1980–88 (of which $221 million was in livestock products, as shown in table 10).

Effects of Trade Liberalization and Price Reforms on Mexican Agriculture

De la Madrid's administration (1982–88) started the liberalization of the Mexican economy, a process strengthened by the Salinas government (1988–94). In 1990, tariffs and/or licensing were eliminated for copra (dried coconut meat yielding coconut oil), cottonseed, safflower, sesame, and soybeans, as well as for rice, sorghum, and cattle. Despite these reforms, price controls and nontariff barriers (i.e., import permit requirements) remain in place for several agricultural products. In reality, the process of agricultural liberalization has been limited by sharp annual fluctuations in domestic supplies, imports of major agricultural goods, and lobbying by producers' associations that forced the government to establish price controls for certain products. Three kinds of price controls were established in 1990: (1) "guarantee" prices, or prices fixed by the government, were reduced from ten "basic" crops (as listed in table 1) to two "basic" products: corn and beans; (2) "negotiated" prices, or prices randomly bargained with interest groups, such as wheat prices; and (3) price controls that vary with the volume of imports, such as prices for sorghum and soybeans. Imports of beans, corn, wheat, and milk still require permits and/or are carried out by CONASUPO (Compañía Nacional de Subsistencias Populares, or National Company for Popular Subsistence). Products such as barley and rice are also subject to some regulatory scheme.

Today, nontariff barriers are the fundamental type of regulation for the three major imported crops, corn, sorghum, and soybeans. In fact, the tariffs on these crops are very low. In 1989, the average tax for corn imports was only 0.7 percent and zero for sor-

Table 10
Mexican Agricultural Trade with the United States:
Participation of Major Products, 1980-1988
(averages in millions of U.S. dollars)

Commodity	Value	Share (percentage)	Value	Commodity	Value	Share (percentage)
			Agriculture			
Imports				**Exports**		
Corn	354.28	25.67		Coffee[3]	343.26	26.76
Soybeans[1]	248.59	18.01		Tomatoes	194.27	15.14
Sorghum	221.45	16.05		Peppers	59.93	4.67
Dried beans[1]	81.6	5.91		Cucumbers	54.52	4.25
Wheat	57.3	4.15		Grapes	24.3	1.89
				Melons	19.52	1.52
				Cocoa, butter	18.47	1.44
				Other fruits[4]	29.44	2.30
Subtotal	963.22	69.79		Subtotal	743.72	57.98
Total crops[2]	1,380.12	100.00		Total crops[2]	1,282.81	100.00
Agricultural balance			-97.31			
			Livestock			
Imports				**Exports**		
Hides & skins	81.93	20.93				
Dairy products	74.53	19.04				
Animal fats	68.36	17.47				
Live beef & cattle	42.20	10.78		Calves[5]	157.48	92.44
Poultry	31.37	8.01		Other livestock	12.88	7.56
Subtotal	298.40	76.24				
Total livestock	391.40	100.00		Total livestock	170.36	100.00
Total balance			-221.03			

1: Excludes seeds.
2: Includes fresh, frozen, and processed products.
3: 93.3 percent of this coffee is crude.
4: Mangoes = 1.48 percent of crop exports; strawberries, 0.4 percent; oranges, 0.3 percent; and pineapple, 0.12 percent.
5: Calves between 200 and 700 pounds.
Source: Database from Foreign Agricultural Service (FAS), USDA.

ghum and soybeans. However, in that same year, their domestic producers' prices were much higher than those prevailing in the international market. This difference was: 41 percent for corn, 22 percent for sorghum, and 22 percent for soybeans. Although the average tariffs applied to the imports of crops other than corn, sorghum, and soybeans are low, they are higher than those charged for the imports of these three goods. For example, in 1989 they were: 6 percent for fruits, 18 percent for wheat, and 5.2 percent for most other agricultural products still subject to tariffs.[9]

The Impacts of Trade and Price Liberalization on Mexico's Agriculture

A computable general equilibrium (CGE) model was constructed[10] to estimate the impact that freer trade in North America and price reforms of Mexico's agriculture products will have on Mexico's agricultural sector.

The Model

The emphasis of the CGE model is on production and trade. Its classification of sectors takes into account the peculiarities of Mexico's agricultural supply. The model is static and Walrasian, representing a small economy with government. Notwithstanding that the model is static, investment is included as a component of production, which can then be used in the subsequent period as a primary factor of production. The value of investment by sector of origin is taken as exogenous, whereas investment by sector of destination is ignored.

Supply and demand are derived from optimizing the behavior of the economic agents. Production is determined by value added and intermediate demand, and its functional forms are assumed to exhibit constant returns to scale. An aggregate sectoral CES (constant elasticity of substitution) production function is used for modeling value added. The function components are labor and capital, both for nonagricultural sectors and, together with land, for agricultural activities. Although intermediate inputs are assumed to be demanded in fixed proportions, substitution between domestic and foreign inputs is allowed.

Labor and capital are assumed to be homogeneous and freely mobile between sectors. These factors, together with land, are taken to be fixed[11] and owned by households. Labor, capital, and land constitute households' initial endowments, which are sold at market prices. There is only one consumer, whose total income comes from the selling of initial endowments and is split among consumption, taxes, and savings in fixed proportions.

Direct taxes to households and indirect taxes to production and trade activities provide government income. The consumption by consumers of sectoral commodities is assumed to be fixed. Demand for imports is modeled in two stages, using the Armington (1969) assumption. Domestic output is sold to the national market and to the rest of the world. Trade with Canada and the United States is referred to as NA (North America) and with the remaining trading partners of Mexico as ROW (rest of the world). The flows of foreign capital are assumed to be fixed and the "real exchange rate" is endogenous or flexible. This means that the balance of trade is exogenous and that the exchange rates vary to equalize the supply and demand of "foreign currencies."

The consumer price index is taken as the numeraire. The model takes into account that the major crops traded between Mexico and the United States are also the most important agricultural goods produced in Mexico (tables 1 and 10). The Mexican agricultural sector is divided into twelve components.[12] To capture the heterogeneity prevailing in Mexico's rural areas, the model distinguishes agricultural activities according to the type of land used,[13] assuming, for example, that soybeans, vegetables, and wheat are produced under irrigated conditions and that coffee is basically a rainfed crop. The remaining components of agricultural supply are obtained from both types of lands, and they are modeled accordingly (tables 2, 3, and 11). Substitution possibilities in goods produced on rainfed lands are assumed to be zero (table 11), whereas any irrigated crop can be replaced for any other one using this type of land. Finally, irrigated crops are taken as the ones that are exported, and the substitution elasticities between factors used in their production are assumed to be higher than the corresponding ones for rainfed lands.[14]

The Simulation of Policy Changes
The simulation exercise includes the elimination of both tariff and

Table 11
Specifications for Modeling the Agricultural Sector of Mexico

Crop	Production	Exported	Substitution possibility for other crops
Corn	rainfed	no	no
	irrigated	yes	yes
Beans	rainfed	no	no
	irrigated	yes	yes (for any irrigated crop)
Sorghum	rainfed	no	no
	irrigated	yes	yes (for any irrigated crop)
Wheat	irrigated	yes	yes (for any irrigated crop)
Soybeans	irrigated	yes	yes (for any irrigated crop)
Coffee	rainfed	yes	yes (only for "other" rainfed crops)
Vegetables and fruits	irrigated	yes	yes (only for coffee)
Other	rainfed	no	yes (only for coffee)
	irrigated	yes	yes (for any irrigated crop)

nominal implicit protection (NIP, see note 9).[15] To measure the impact of deregulation, it is assumed that tariffs for all commodities traded among the three North American countries are eliminated and that NIP for Mexico's three major imported crops (corn, soybeans, and sorghum) is abolished.[16] The quantification also included a study of the impacts on agricultural production and trade implied by the reform concerning the *ejido* in the Agrarian Law adopted by the Salinas administration. This was done by incorporating into the CGE model two liberalization scenarios, called "LIBl" and "LIB2":

(1) **LIBl** captures what would happen if liberalization of North American trade and of internal agricultural prices was accomplished without *ejido* system land reform. It is therefore assumed that there is no market for rainfed lands dedicated to the production of corn, and it is modeled by fixing the ground rent paid for the use of these lands. This effect illustrates the prereform background inasmuch as an important part of *ejidal* lands are not irrigated and are dedicated to corn production.

(2) **LIB2** quantifies the impacts of trade liberalization and internal reforms in the context of free markets for all lands. This simulates the circumstance that could arise with changes in the Agrarian Law.

Impacts of Liberalization on Exports and Imports of Agricultural Products

Results for exports and imports of agricultural goods are very similar in both scenarios, LIBl and LIB2.[17] Mexico would increase North American imports of products that were subject to tariff and domestic price control—i.e., corn, sorghum, and soybeans (table 12). However, imports of North American corn would increase much more than imports of any other agricultural product. Although there is an expected reduction in imports of wheat, beans, and cattle from North America and of fresh products from the rest of the world, it would not compensate for large imports of corn, sorghum, and soybeans.

Simulated results indicate that Mexican exports to North America, mainly of vegetables and fruits (fresh and processed), would increase considerably (table 13), while agricultural and livestock exports to the rest of the world would decrease slightly. However, increases in exports of fresh agricultural products to North America will not compensate for large increases in the imports of corn, sorghum, and soybeans stimulated by elimination of tariffs and domestic price liberalization (table 14).

Table 12
Results of the Computable General Equilibrium Model: Imports
(millions of pesos at constant prices)

Imports	Values			Change with respect to base case (percentage)	
	Base	LIB1	LIB2	LIB1	LIB2
From North America					
Corn	58,004.0	218,997.0	214,670.2	277.6	270.1
Wheat	8,148.0	7,765.5	7,739.6	-4.7	-5.0
Beans	4,703.0	4,662.8	4,627.4	-0.9	-1.6
Sorghum	51,637.0	73,492.0	72,929.4	42.3	41.2
Soybeans	48,844.0	84,028.9	83,643.4	72.0	71.2
Vegetables & fruits	7,899.0	8,186.9	8,128.6	3.6	2.9
Other agricultural products	42,160.0	43,556.3	43,509.4	3.3	3.2
Bovine cattle	27,087.0	25,450.7	25,428.4	-6.0	-6.1
Other livestock	40,436.0	42,753.5	42,693.3	5.7	5.6
Silviculture, fishing & hunting	5,113.0	6,026.2	6,032.2	17.9	18.0
Processed vegetables & fruits	17,142.0	18,255.7	18,253.2	6.5	6.5
Processed coffee	85,648.0	90,554.3	90,567.4	5.7	5.7
Other processed agriculture & livestock	65,346.0	69,383.5	69,411.5	6.2	6.2
Mining	238,060.0	239,957.3	239,892.7	0.8	0.8
Manufacturing	2,410,181.0	2,581,763.1	2,582,327.1	7.1	7.1
Agriculture & livestock					
Fresh crops	221,395.0	440,689.3	435,248.0	99.1	96.6
Cattle	67,523.0	68,204.2	68,121.7	1.0	0.9
Processed	168,136.0	178,193.5	178,232.0	6.0	6.0
Subtotal	457,054.0	687,087.1	681,601.7	50.3	49.1
From Rest of the World					
Fresh crops	86,248.0	81,999.7	81,723.3	-4.9	-5.2
Cattle	2,306.0	2,379.3	2,375.4	3.2	3.0
Silviculture, fishing & hunting	930.0	945.7	946.2	1.7	1.7
Processed agriculture & livestock*	90,139.0	91,461.1	91,462.9	1.5	1.5
Mining	50,794.0	51,274.0	51,252.6	0.9	0.9
Manufacturing	1,094,380.0	1,093,863.1	1,094,100.2	0.0	0.0

*Excludes textiles and wood and wood products.

Impacts of Liberalization on Agriculture and Livestock Production
Although both scenarios (LIB1 and LIB2) showed very similar results for Mexican imports and exports of agricultural products, results related to agricultural gross domestic product (GDP) diverged notably according to the assumption made about the type of market prevailing in rainfed corn-producing lands.

What would be the effect on crops produced in rainfed lands? When the market for rainfed corn is considered to be absent (LIB1,

Table 13
Results of the Computable General Equilibrium Model: Exports
(millions of pesos at constant prices)

Imports	Values			Change with respect to base case (percentage)	
	Base	LIB1	LIB2	LIB1	LIB2
To North America					
Vegetables & fruits	80,512.0	121,718.2 1	24,364.7	51.2	54.5
Coffee	144,450.0	151,858.0	152,412.9	5.1	5.5
Other agricultural products	7,020.0	8,014.1	8,123.1	14.2	15.7
Bovine cattle	58,570.0	62,802.6	62,879.1	7.2	7.4
Other livestock	8,435.0	10,089.3	10,107.5	19.6	19.8
Silviculture, fishing & hunting	2,208.0	2,341.3	2,337.6	6.0	5.9
Processed vegetables & fruits	16,548.0	24,699.8	24,728.9	49.3	49.4
Other processed agriculture & livestock	85,972.0	97,619.3	97,604.4	13.5	13.5
Mining	1,726,020.0	1,842,092.1	1,838,491.9	6.7	6.5
Manufacturing	3,029,751.0	3,307,940.3	3,300,501.1	9.2	8.9
Agriculture & livestock					
Fresh crops	231,982.0	281,590.3	284,900.6	48.0	51.2
Cattle	67,005.0	72,891.9	72,986.6	8.8	8.9
Processed	102,520.0	122,319.1	122,333.3	11.0	11.2
Subtotal	401,507.0	476,801.3	480,220.5	18.8	19.6
To Rest of World					
Fresh agricultural products	11,919.0	11,801.4	11,858.0	-1.0	-0.5
Silviculture, fishing & hunting	2,627.0	2,596.8	2,595.3	-1.2	-1.2
Processed agriculture & livestock*	59,954.0	59,569.8	59,586.2	-0.6	-0.6
Mining	1,359,918.0	1,342,479.9	1,341,909.0	-1.3	-1.3
Manufacturing	340,843.0	338,535.9	338,342.7	-0.7	-0.7

*Excludes coffee, textiles, and wood and wood products.

which assumes *ejidos* will be maintained), the effect of domestic price liberalization of corn, sorghum, and soybeans (the ones with the largest price distortions) and tariff elimination among NAFTA countries would be a strong reduction in the domestic supply of corn produced in rainfed soil (table 15). However, when a market for lands devoted to produce corn is simulated (LIB2, which assumes a free market for *ejidos*), rainfed production of corn would also diminish, but the reduction would be insignificant. The domestic supply of "other" rainfed crops (see table 14) would be subject to a slight increase under LIB1 and to an abrupt decrease under LIB2. The domestic supply of "other" rainfed crops (see table 14) would be subject to a slight increase under LIBl and to an abrupt decrease under LIB2.

What do the simulation results show for irrigated crops production? The domestic supply of irrigated corn would be subject to a slight increase under the LIB1 scenario and to an abrupt decrease

Table 14
Results of the Computable General Equilibrium Model:
International Trade
(millions of pesos at constant prices)

Imports	Values			Change with respect to base case (percentage)	
	Base	LIB1	LIB2	LIB1	LIB2
With North America					
Fresh crops*	10,827.0	-158,906.2	-150,153.5		
Livestock	-518.0	4,687.6	4,864.9		
Silviculture, fishing & hunting	-2,905.0	-3,684.9	-3,694.6	26.8	27.2
Processed agriculture & livestock**	-281,496.0	-461,619.6	-453,808.9	64.0	61.2
Total agriculture & livestock	78,834.0	95,983.6	96,514.1	21.8	22.4
Mining	1,487,960.0	1,602,134.8	1,598,599.2	7.7	7.4
Manufacturing	619,570.0	726,187.1	718,174.0	17.2	15.9
With Rest of World					
Fresh crops	-74,329.0	-70,198.3	-69,865.3	-5.6	-6.0
Livestock	-2,306.0	-2,379.3	-2,375.4	3.2	3.0
Silviculture, fishing & hunting	1,697.0	1,651.1	1,649.2	-2.7	-2.8
Processed agriculture & livestock**	-74,938.0	-70,926.5	-70,591.5	-5.4	-5.8
Total agriculture & livestock	-30,185.0	-31,891.3	-31,876.6	5.7	5.6
Mining	1,309,124.0	1,291,206.0	1,290,656.4	-1.4	-1.4
Manufacturing	-753,537.0	-755,327.2	-755,757.5	0.2	0.3
Exports					
To North America	5,159,726.0	5,629,367.7	5,621,745.0	9.1	9.0
To Rest of World	1,775,261.0	1,754,983.7	1,754,291.2	-1.1	-1.2
Totals	6,934,987.0	7,384,351.4	7,376,036.2	6.5	6.4
Imports					
From North America	3,110,408.0	3,514,823.7	3,509,853.7	13.0	12.8
From Rest of World	1,324,797.0	1,321,922.8	1,321,860.4	-0.2	-0.2
Totals	4,435,205.0	4,836,746.5	4,831,714.2	9.1	8.9
Balances	2,499,782.0	2,547,604.9	2,544,322.1	1.9	1.8

* Includes coffee.
** Excludes textiles and wood and wood products.

under the LIB2 scenario, as well as a reduction in the production of irrigated sorghum and soybeans. Although the reduction in the production of these crops accompanies a considerable increase in the supply of "other" irrigated crops, this boosting effect is insufficient to balance the overall depressive effect in corn, soybeans, and sorghum. Thus, the production of sorghum and soybeans in irrigated lands showed the same negative effects under the assumption of maintaining or modifying the *ejidal* structure.

Table 15
Results of the Computable General Equilibrium Model:
Gross Domestic Product
(millions of pesos at constant prices)

Imports	Values			Change with respect to base case (percentage)	
	Base	LIB1	LIB2	LIB1	LIB2
Rainfed crops					
Corn	492,145.0	334,181.5	486,651.4	-32.10	-1.12
Beans	53,321.0	53,437.8	53,036.5	0.22	-0.53
Sorghum	17,478.0	17,889.9	16,961.8	2.36	-2.95
Coffee	97,643.0	99,581.2	99,929.6	1.98	2.34
Other rainfed crops	132,790.0	133,147.4	90,131.4	0.27	-32.12
Irrigated crops					
Corn	151,629.0	153,037.4	15,221.9	0.93 -	89.96
Wheat	141,220.0	142,157.5	142,343.1	0.66	0.80
Beans	87,722.0	89,322.1	89,534.4	1.82	2.07
Sorghum	173,387.0	156,676.7	158,502.7	-9.64	-8.58
Soybeans	64,771.0	45,073.5	45,609.8	-30.41	-29.58
Vegetables & fruits	1,136,039.0	1,169,493.9	1,170,158.3	2.94	3.00
Other irrigated crops	97,038.0	98,201.9	138,068.9	1.20	42.28
Bovine cattle	810,387.0	818,605.3	818,913.8	1.01	1.05
Other livestock	469,678.0	472,671.6	472,864.9	0.64	0.68
Total rainfed crops	793,377.0	638,238.0	746,711.0	-19.55	-5.88
Total irrigated crops	1,851,806.0	1,853,963.0	1,759,439.0	0.12	-4.99
Total corn	643,774.0	487,219.0	501,873.0	-24.32	-22.04
Total beans	141,043.0	142,760.0	142,571.0	1.22	1.08
Total sorghum	190,865.0	174,567.0	175,464.0	-8.54	-8.07
Total agriculture	2,645,183.0	2,492,201.0	2,506,150.0	-5.78	-5.26
Total cattle raising	1,280,065.0	1,291,277.0	1,291,779.0	0.88	0.92
Total agroindustry	2,774,327.0	2,800,014.0	2,801,152.0	0.93	0.97
Total agriculture, livestock, & processed foods*	6,699,575.0	6,583,492.0	6,599,081.0	-1.73	-1.50
Silviculture, fishing, & hunting	402,096.0	403,858.0	403,882.0	0.44	0.44
Mining	2,431,814.0	2,465,381.0	2,462,916.0	1.38	1.28
Manufactures	7,300,008.0	7,346,524.0	7,342,677.0	0.64	0.58
Services	24,781,000.0	24,810,000.0	24,806,000.0	0.12	0.10

*Excludes textiles, wood, and wood products.

These results suggest that whether or not there exists a market for rainfed lands for the production of corn (LIBl and LIB2 scenarios), the general effect of trade and price liberalization is to depress Mexico's agricultural production. However, if we take into account that, under the assumption of a free market for *ejido* lands (LIB2), corn rainfed production is less affected, it is possible to argue that domestic price reforms and trade liberalization, together

Table 16
Results of the Computable General Equilibrium Model:
Workers' Income
(millions of pesos at constant prices)

Imports	Values			Change with respect to base case (percentage)	
	Base	LIB1	LIB2	LIB1	LIB2
Rainfed crops					
Corn	319,057.0	216,676.6	315,395.3	-32.09	-1.15
Beans	34,568.0	34,649.1	34,378.8	0.23	-0.55
Sorghum	11,331.0	11,613.8	10,988.5	2.50	-3.02
Coffee	63,302.0	64,743.3	64,403.3	2.28	1.74
Other rainfed crops	86,087.0	86,565.7	58,087.8	0.56	-32.52
Irrigated crops					
Corn	72,311.0	73,010.0	7,255.7	0.97	-89.97
Wheat	67,347.0	67,824.6	67,843.0	0.71	0.74
Beans	41,834.0	42,606.7	42,685.9	1.85	2.04
Sorghum	82,687.0	74,835.7	75,432.3	-9.50	-8.77
Soybeans	30,889.0	21,501.8	21,742.7	-30.39	-29.61
Vegetables & fruits	541,770.0	559,816.5	555,215.1	3.33	2.48
Other irrigated crops	46,277.0	47,007.7	65,511.0	1.58	41.56
Bovine cattle	202,232.0	205,455.5	205,234.9	1.59	1.48
Other livestock	90,473.0	91,612.2	91,506.6	1.26	1.14
Total rainfed crops	514,345.0	414,248.0	483,254.0	-19.46	-6.04
Total irrigated crops	883,115.0	886,603.0	835,685.7	0.39	-5.37
Total corn	391,368.0	289,687.0	322,651.0	-25.98	-17.56
Total beans	76,402.0	77,256.0	77,065.0	1.12	0.87
Total sorghum	94,018.0	86,450.0	86,421.0	-8.05	-8.08
Total agriculture	1,397,460.0	1,300,852.0	1,318,939.0	-6.91	-5.62
Total cattle raising	292,705.0	297,068.0	296,742.0	1.49	1.38
Total agroindustry	497,698.0	505,637.0	505,023.0	1.60	1.47
Total agriculture livestock, & processed foods*	2,187,863.0	2,103,556.0	2,120,704.0	-3.85	-3.07
Silviculture, fishing & hunting	83,611.0	84,486.0	84,362.0	1.05	0.90
Mining	386,421.0	393,162.0	392,146.0	1.74	1.48
Manufactures	1,946,760.0	1,970,596.0	1 ,966,788.0	1.22	1.03
Services	8,579,836.0	8,632,690.0	8,620,490.2	0.62	0.47

*Excludes textiles, wood and wood products.

with property rights' reform, would bring about a more favorable outcome for poor corn rainfed producers.

Impacts of Liberalization on Labor Income
The changes in sectoral labor incomes of the two modeled situations produce outcomes that are very similar to those related to the value of production (compare tables 15 and 16). Therefore, the

comments presented in the previous section about the changes in the composition of supply also apply to labor receipts.[18]

There is, however, a difference between production and labor income that reinforces the previous conclusion that liberalization under the situation represented by LIB2 affects the poor component of Mexico's agricultural sector less. Although there is a reduction of agricultural labor income under both scenarios, the reduction is smaller under LIB2 (table 16), which implies that existence of a market for all types of land, including *ejidos*, is more favorable to the agricultural workers, one of the poorest components of the sector.

Implications of Liberalization on Migration

Although the CGE model does not explicitly include migration, its results on the modifications of sectoral labor income provide clues about the impacts of the modeled policy changes on migration. For this purpose, this chapter focuses on LIB2, which would have the least effect on agricultural labor income and rainfed production. To do this exercise, it is assumed that a negative growth in labor income implies a release of labor, while a positive growth in labor income implies more employment in the sector. Simulated results indicate that a portion of the labor force would be released from the production of corn and sorghum on both types of land, rainfed soybeans, and other rainfed products, while producers of fresh vegetables and fruits, coffee, other irrigated crops and cattle would absorb more labor (table 16).

However, these adjustments in the structure of rural employment are insufficient to employ all of the released agricultural labor force. This is suggested by the result that shows that the reduction of the agricultural workers' income is much higher than the increase of it. Therefore, it would be expected that agroindustry, mining, and manufacturing, which would experience positive growth in labor income, will have to bear the disequilibrium in the agricultural sector.[19] If domestic absorption of displaced workers from the sectors hit by liberalization is insufficient, it is likely that migration to the United States will increase.

Conclusion

The quantitative analysis presented here suggests that NAFTA and domestic price reforms of agricultural products will have significant impacts on the composition of Mexico's agricultural trade, output, and income. The model further both suggests that these policy changes will have an overall negative effect on agriculture and supports government expectations regarding the potential positive effects of reforms of the law concerning the *ejido*.

In order to formulate some policy recommendations, it is important to note that liberalization, although promoting production efficiency and benefiting the consumer, could have negative effects in some components of society. In this analysis, market orientation will affect agriculture, especially rainfed lands and some irrigated crops. One of the consequences of market orientation would be the displacement of labor to other sectors of the Mexican economy.[20] In practice, however, the most likely outcome, at least in the short run, could be the increase in unemployment and/or underemployment in both rural and urban regions in Mexico. A transition policy would be required in order to reduce this risk. Taking into account that the rainfed sector of Mexico's agriculture would be the most affected, that the majority of the rural population works in this sector, and that it is a sector with low productivity of labor, it is suggested in this chapter that policies must be developed toward this portion of the population.

However, an analysis of the actions that the Mexican government must take to ease the movement toward a more market-oriented economy lies outside the scope of this chapter. It is sufficient to say that the design and implementation of an effective policy to increase the productivity of rainfed agriculture is required, that the Mexican government must be convinced that action is necessary and urgent, and that the support from Mexico's North American counterparts and from the international lending institutions must be secured in order to implement this policy.

Notes

1. In order to avoid confusion, the term "agriculture" refers exclusively to crop production. It will be specified when "livestock" or "cattle raising" are incorporated in the analysis. The chapter focuses on crop production inasmuch as information on livestock activities in Mexico is scarce.
2. It was roughly -1.0 percent between 1960–65 and 1983–85 (Yúnez-Naude and Blanno Jasso, 1990, table 7).
3. By contrast, the dynamics of agricultural supply from the 1940s to the mid-1960s were characterized by the boost in irrigation projects and the increase of land use for agricultural purposes (Lamartine-Yates, 1978).
4. Rural units created by the reforms resulting from the 1910 revolution. The government redistributed land to dispossessed farmers.
5. Until a recent change in the Agrarian Law, *ejidatarios* could neither hire labor nor sell or rent their lands. However, these restrictions have not meant that waged labor is not used in *ejidal* production and that *ejidatarios* do not lease out part of the land they received. An analysis of the reasons and processes that led to the change of property rights in Mexico's land is in Pérez Yarahuán (1992).
6. Details are in Yúnez-Naude and Blanno Jasso (1990) and in Yúnez-Naude (1991a).
7. The demand for corn has not decreased in Mexico. It remains the main food for human consumption and it is also used for animal feeding. Population growth and the governmental subsidy schemes for tortilla consumption in urban areas keep the demand high for corn in the country.
8. Canada is not included because Canadian agricultural trade with Mexico is negligible—in 1989–90, it accounted for less than 1 percent of the value of Mexico's total agricultural trade (Yúnez-Naude, 1991b, table 6.2)—and because an important portion of Mexico's agricultural exports to Canada pass through the United States and are included in U.S. data on imports.
9. See Yúnez-Naude (1993b, table 2). The figures of the difference between domestic and international prices take into account transport costs. This is called "nominal implicit protection" (NIP). The elimination of it, as well as tariffs, is used as the basis for the simulations done in the model discussed in the next section of this paper.
10. See Yúnez-Naude (1993b) for details. There are three other recent CGE models that also focus on the agricultural sector: Adelman and Taylor (1991), Levy and van Wijnbergen (1992), and Robinson, et al.

(1991). One of the main differences with respect to my model is that the subdivision of agriculture in these models is less detailed.

11. The assumption implies that the effect of policy changes on gross domestic production is negligible. Evidently, this feature of the model does not mean that we expect no major changes in the composition of output, trade, and sectoral income. So, we have to keep in mind that the model is designed to evaluate the impacts of liberalization on restructuring the economy of Mexico and not on its growth.

12. Although the model has 30 sectors, I concentrate here on the details corresponding to the food-related portions of the Mexican economy. Most of the statistics used are for 1985, which was selected because data for a more recent year are unavailable. However, the information for tariffs and for the nominal implicit protection is for 1989 because they changed considerably during the last half of the 1980s.

13. Notwithstanding this, the consumer does not make any distinction regarding the productive origin of a particular crop.

14. The source is the econometric study done by Barceinas (1992). There are two other sets of elasticities required by the model: one for the composite goods and one for the North American demand for Mexico's exports (the figures and their sources are in Yúnez-Naude, 1993b, table 1).

15. Other exercises have assumed that the only policy change is the elimination of tariffs charged by the three North American countries. However, only the CGE model results of a more comprehensive liberalization process are reported here because, given the current official acceptance of deregulation and the approval of NAFTA, this CGE model represents the more likely scenario. I will just point out that if the change in policy is circumscribed to trilateral tariff elimination, the results of the CGEM show that the production of the agricultural, livestock, and food processing sectors of Mexico will be promoted. As will be seen below, they contrast with the findings when a more liberalized program is simulated.

16. The ad valorem tariff charged by the U.S. government to Mexican exports during 1989, as reported by the U.S. International Trade Commission, are applied. These were nil for corn, beans, soybeans, sorghum, and cattle; 8.6 percent for fresh vegetables and fruits; and 2.2 percent for the remaining agricultural products (the tariffs charged by Mexico and the United States for the remaining products and the NIP for corn, sorghum and soybean are listed [see section entitled "Effects of Trade Liberalization and Price Reforms on Mexican Agriculture"] above).

17. All the figures reported in the three first columns of tables 12 to 16 are presented value form at constant prices, measured in terms of the consumer's price index of Mexico.

18. The resulting changes of sectoral ground rents are also congruous with the modifications corresponding to agricultural production.
19. It is worthwhile to point out that, because labor is considered to be homogeneous and because the CGE model is for a single country, the model does not capture the differences between rural and urban domestic wages and international migration. If we consider the possibility that the gap between sectoral wages increases with liberalization, we may argue that its impacts on rural emigration may be higher than the ones suggested by the results of my model. For example, a parallel study—based on a different CGE model, but comparable to mine—concludes that approximately 12 percent of the rural labor force would migrate to the urban sector of Mexico and to the United States if liberalization includes the abolition of all farm programs prevailing and directed to Mexico's agricultural sector (Robinson et al., 1991, table 7, scenario 3, p. 25).
20. One must keep in mind that my CGE model is static and, at the same time, presents a long-run scenario because it assumes full employment and, hence, that displaced labor will always find productive employment somewhere else. This is the same as saying that the model ignores the problems of transition from the initial equilibrium to after the policy has been changed. The limitation can be overcome by constructing a dynamic CGE model, which is precisely the object of current research. An antecedent is the CGE model of Levy and van Wijnbergen (1992), a model that is focused on questions of transition, but where the variables that make it dynamic are exogenous.

References

Adelman, Irma and J. Edward Taylor, "A computable general equilibrium model for Mexico," mimeo (interim report), University of California, November 1991.

Armington, P., "A theory of demand for products distinguished by place of production," International Monetary Fund Staff Papers 16, 1969, pp. 159–78.

Barceinas, P. Fernando, "Análisis de la estructura productiva agrícola; el caso de México," M.A. thesis, March 1992.

Lamartine-Yates, Paul, El campo mexicano, Editorial El Caballito, México, 1978.

Levy, Santiago and Sweder van Wijnbergen, "Mexican agriculture in the free trade agreement: transition problems in economic reform," OECD, Technical Papers, No. 63, 1992.

Pérez Yarahuán, Gabriela, "El artículo 27: La política pública en torno a los derechos de propiedad," B.A. thesis, Centro de Estudios Internacionales, El Colegio de México, 1992.

Robinson, Sherman, Mary Burfisher, Raúl Hinojosa, and Karen E. Thierfelder, "Agricultural policies and migration in a U.S.-Mexico free trade area: a CGE analysis," Working Paper No. 617, Department of Agriculture and Resource Economics, University of California at Berkeley, December 1991.

Yúnez-Naude, A. and Ramón Blanno Jasso, "Reporte final: el comercio exterior Mexicano de productos agropecuarios," presented to the Commission for the Study of International Migration and Cooperative Economic Development, Washington D.C., January 1990.

Yúnez-Naude, A., "Agricultural trade of Mexico: tendencies and policy options," Food Policy, April 1991a.

———, "El comercio exterior agropecuario de México; evolución y perspectivas frente al acuerdo Norteamericano de libre comercio," presented at the Seminar of the Pacific, November 1991b.

————, "El comercio exterior agropecuario durante el auge y la crisis," *El Trimestre Económico,* 1993a.

————, "El tratado de libre comercio y la agricultura Mexicana; un enfoque de equilibrio general aplicado," *Estudios Económicos,* El Colegio de México, 1993b.

6

Flexible Production and the North American Free Trade Agreement: The Impact on U.S. and Japanese Maquiladoras

Elsie L. Echeverri-Carroll

Introduction

From 1917 to 1964, Mexican citizens were allowed to work on U.S. farms under a series of laws and regulations generally called the Bracero Program. According to Watkins (1994a), the termination of the program was associated with allegations by farm worker unions that use of braceros suppressed wages in the U.S. agricultural sector, stories of abuses of braceros by U.S. farmers, and the development of a mechanical tomato harvester in the early 1960s (preceded by automated cotton harvesters) that reduced the need for braceros. It was in this context that the Mexican government established the Border Industrialization Program (BIP) in 1965 as a way to find jobs for approximately 200,000 unemployed braceros. This program allowed foreign and Mexican investors temporarily to import duty-free all the inputs, machinery, and replacement parts needed for assembly as long as the investors bought a bond that would ensure the eventual reexportation of the assembled good. The government referred to those plants established under the BIP as maquiladoras.[1]

The nature of the maquiladora industry has changed significantly since the initiation of the BIP. The most obvious change has been the increased growth of the industry since 1982. This growth resulted from the devaluation of the peso, which made maquiladora wages more attractive than wages in the Asian countries where labor-intensive production had concentrated in the 1970s. According to statistics published by the Mexican government, the number of maquiladoras increased from 585 plants in 1982 to 2,166 in 1993. The number of people employed by the industry increased from 127,048 in 1982 to 540,927 in 1993 (table 1). According to Watkins (1994a), U.S. companies held controlling ownership of 45 percent of the maquiladoras in 1991. Most of the other maquiladoras, although Mexican-owned, are subcontractors for U.S. companies.

U.S. manufacturers were not the only ones expanding their

Table 1
Maquiladora Industry: Employment and Number of Plants, 1979–1993

Industry	1979		1980		1981		1982		1983	
	Employ	Plants	Employ	Plants	Employ	Plants	Employ	Plants	Employ	Plants
Auto	5,035	38	7,500	53	10,999	44	12,288	44	19,594	47
Electrical	63,461	180	69,401	223	76,187	230	74,116	223	82,690	224
Textile	17,631	122	17,570	117	18,059	117	15,002	107	16,212	94

Industry	1984		1985		1986		1987		1988	
	Employ	Plants	Employ	Plants	Employ	Plants	Employ	Plants	Employ	Plants
Total	111,365	540	119,546	620	130,973	605	127,048	585	150,867	600
Auto	29,378	51	40,150	63	49,050	79	59,280	107	74,380	130
Electrical	108,520	244	100,860	274	113,080	302	129,840	338	152,550	411
Textile	19,888	101	21,473	108	25,311	130	30,070	168	34,710	201
Total	199,684	672	211,970	760	249,830	890	305,250	1,125	369,490	1,396

Industry	1989		1990		1991		1992		1993	
	Employ	Plants	Employ	Plants	Employ	Plants	Employ	Plants	Employ	Plants
Auto	90,520	142	98,920	160	111,960	158	124,350	165	126,610	170
Electrical	166,660	464	169,930	519	161,810	496	177,500	528	188,850	539
Textile	39,080	245	42,040	293	45,730	308	53,490	372	64,510	404
Total	429,730	1,655	460,293	1,938	467,454	1,925	505,053	2,075	540,927	2,166

Sources: INEGI, *Estadisticas de la Industria Maquiladora de Exportacion, 1975-84,* Mexico D.F., 1988. CIEMEX-WEFA, *Maquiladora Industry Analysis,* vol. 7, no. 2, Philadelphia, 1994.

investments in Mexico. The number of Japanese-owned maquiladora plants increased from 8 in 1980 to 70 in 1990 (Echeverri-Carroll 1989, 1990). Japanese participation remains relatively small: 70 plants of about 2,000 maquiladoras, accounting for only about 4 percent of the industry's employment in 1992. However, they represent the largest group after U.S.- and Mexican-owned maquiladoras.

The maquiladora industry is important for both the U.S. and Mexican economies. Access to maquiladoras' low cost assembly has kept numerous U.S. companies from going out of business or losing significant market share because of competition from business in Asia.[2] This is especially true for U.S. industries with highly competitive markets, such as electronics and automobiles. The Big Three (General Motors, Chrysler, and Ford) and Zenith (the only U.S. company producing color televisions) have among the largest maquiladora operations in Mexico. According to Carrillo (1990), in 1987, about 55.2 percent of Ford's employees in Mexico were working for maquiladora plants; the corresponding value for GM was 80.5 percent; for Chrysler, 16.9 percent. Furthermore, the maquiladora industry has been an important source of employment and foreign exchange for Mexico. In 1992, this industry was second only to the petroleum industry and ahead of tourism in foreign exchange contribution to the country (Watkins 1994a), accounting for 20 percent of total manufacturing employment in Mexico.

Manufacturing in a Global Context

Although the statistics published by the Mexican government on the maquiladora industry show industry trends, another set of statistics is needed to analyze the relative importance of maquiladoras in the global assembly industry. The chief source of information on products assembled abroad for the U.S. market is a set of statistics maintained by the U.S. International Trade Commission (ITC). These data track imports entering the United States under tariff item 9802.00.80 (formerly item 807.00), which permits the duty-free entry of U.S. components sent abroad for processing or assembly. However, the importance of production sharing is greater than 9802.00.80 figures indicate. By definition, this tariff item deals with U.S. parts and components that return to the United States, often for further processing and for sale domestically and abroad. The statistics, therefore, do not show complementary intraindustry trade in products that do not return to the United States. Such production-sharing activities may be significant (Grunwald and Flamm 1985). Other omissions are associated with production-sharing trade covered by at least six customs entry provisions that also provide for tariff exemptions (see United States International Trade Commission 1988 for an extensive explanation of these provisions). For instance, the Generalized System of Preferences (GSP) makes available certain duty concessions to developing nation exporters of eligible products. When countries increase local content enough to become eligible for GSP, they may reduce the use of item 9802.00.80. Thus, 9802.00.80 statistics probably underestimate the true importance of such imports.

A study of 9802.00.80 statistics reveals several important features of the global assembly industry:

• The offshore assembly industry has shown dynamic growth. For instance, the value of imports from developing countries under U.S. import item 9802.00.80 increased from $0.3 billion in 1969 to $26.6 billion in 1992 (table 2).

• The offshore assembly industry has concentrated in relatively few countries: the Newly Industrialized Economies (NIEs) of Asia—Korea, Taiwan, Hong Kong, and Singapore—and Mexico. These five countries accounted for 76 percent of total U.S. imports from developing countries under item 9802.00.80 in 1992 (table 2).

• In the 1960s and 1970s, the offshore assembly industry was located mainly in the NIEs, which accounted for 79 percent of imports from developing countries under item 9802.00.80 in 1966 (table 2). However, in the 1980s, Mexico became the most important destination for U.S. labor-intensive facilities (Suarez-Villa 1984; Grunwald and Flamm 1985; Fernandez-Kelly 1987; Gonzales-Arechiga 1988; Hansen 1981; Echeverri-Carroll 1989, 1992, 1994; Sklair 1989). In fact, Mexico increased its participation in the total 9802.00.80 value performed by assemblers in developing countries from 35 percent ($2.2 billion) in 1980 to 61 percent ($16.2 billion) in 1992 (table 2).

• Relatively few products—electronics, automobiles, and textiles—dominate global offshore assembly. For instance, three electronic products—television receivers, electrical conductors, and semiconductors—accounted for more than 40 percent of U.S. imports under provision 9802.00.80 from Korea, Singapore, and Taiwan in 1992 (table 3). These three electronic products and motor vehicles and parts accounted for 55 percent of U.S. imports from Mexico under provision 9802.00.80 in 1992 (table 3). Moreover, statistics from the Mexican government indicate that, in 1993, automobile, textile, and electronics maquiladoras accounted for 70.2 percent employment and 51.3 percent plants in the maquiladora industry (table 1).

What factors determine the location of labor-intensive manufacturing in developing countries? The product cycle theory, developed and popularized by Vernon (1966) and Hirsch (1967), is relevant in explaining the growth of industry in developing countries in order to take advantage of lower wages (Hansen 1981). In the context of the product cycle theory, location in developing countries is closely related to the principle of economic efficiency that runs mass production systems (Abernathy et al. 1981; Piore and Sabel 1984), particularly, the continuous specialization of machines and labor. Adam Smith first observed that the fragmentation of the production process into easily learned, repetitive work steps leads to specialization and greater economic efficiency. His principle governs the organization of production in mass production manufacturing, where the machines and labor are continuously specialized in narrowly defined functions. The product cycle theory suggests that as the division of labor advances in the mass production factory, the demand for labor skills changes, creating the conditions for decentralization. At an early phase of the product cycle, scientific and engineering skills are the key human inputs; in the

Table 2
U. S. Imports Under HTS 9802.00.80, by Country, 1966-1969, 1977-1992
(million dollars)

Country	1966	1967	1968	1969	1977	1978	1979	1980	1981	1982
Mexico		19.3	73.4	145.2	1,106.9	1,489.9	2,001.7	2,276.3	2,655.9	2,804.8
Korea	**	*	*	*	246.2	274.6	322.3	311.2	301.8	375.3
Singapore	—	—	*	6.8	279.1	369.2	547.0	760.4	843.1	836.2
Taiwan	6.6	15.9	45.5	68.1	408.2	489.8	395.9	473.7	536.6	543.0
Hong Kong	41.4	51.4	65.4	90.7	247.8	282.7	326.6	407.8	517.8	508.3
NIEs	**48.0**	**67.3**	**110.9**	**165.6**	**1,181.3**	**1,416.3**	**1,591.8**	**1,953.1**	**2,199.3**	**2,262.8**
Malaysia	**	**	**	**	204.1	397.9	603.5	795.5	900.5	1,096.2
Philippines	0.2	0.8	3.4	5.2	54.0	155.8	264.2	409.9	523.3	660.2
Thailand	**	**	**	**	12.5	52.3	47.6	82.4	106.5	107.3
Near-NIEs	**	**	**	**	**270.6**	**606.0**	**915.3**	**1,287.6**	**1,530.3**	**1,863.7**
Brazil	-0.6	1.0	4.1	119.3	140.8	138.0	110.8	142.1	123.1	
Dom. Rep.	**	**	**	**	45.2	64.2	87.7	97.5	119.7	131.0
Costa Rica	-0.1	0.3	1.8	26.2	33.5	37.0	45.2	53.3	58.9	
Lat. Am.	**	**	**	**	**190.7**	**238.5**	**262.7**	**253.5**	**315.1**	**313.0**
LDCs	60.5	98.2	215.9	366.6	3,002.7	4,081.3	5,194.2	6,232.6	7,192.8	7,795.2

Country	1983	1984	1985	1986	1987	1988	1989	1990	1991	1992
Mexico	3,687.0	4,775.4	5,536.7	6,366.7	8,576.4	10,653.5	11,766.7	12,811.2	14,127.3	16,248.1
Korea	575.0	895.9	397.8	949.5	2,676.1	3,088.7	1,987.0	2,182.3	2,050.7	1,575.7
Singapore	975.6	1,273.8	995.8	365.5	1,697.9	1,856.9	1,376.9	1,334.3	1,263.1	1,205.8
Taiwan	562.5	735.5	518.1	518.5	941.1	1,027.4	1,061.7	957.2	813.8	898.8
Hong Kong	447.9	507.9	393.0	205.7	359.9	369.8	306.4	306.3	324.9	349.5
NIEs	**2,561.0**	**3,413.1**	**2,304.7**	**2,039.2**	**5,675.0**	**6,342.8**	**4,732.0**	**4,780.1**	**4,452.5**	**4,029.8**
Malaysia	1,189.2	1,421.7	427.2	202.5	1,075.2	1,211.7	1,315.6	1,315.2	1,263.1	1,374.9
Philippines	725.2	911.0	297.8	168.4	643.1	639.8	588.9	595.8	621.9	823.4
Thailand	141.2	234.9	63.2	29.7	221.3	397.6	277.7	481.4	395.9	319.1
Near-NIEs	**2,055.6**	**2,567.6**	**788.2**	**400.6**	**1,939.6**	**2,249.1**	**2,182.2**	**2,392.4**	**2,280.9**	**2,517.4**
Brazil	193.0	286.0	289.4	398.7	593.3	820.3	933.5	655.8	478.2	319.4
Dom. Rep.	161.0	204.7	246.6	329.1	428.6	562.4	665.0	704.3	944.5	1,268.3
Costa Rica	78.8	95.8	98.4	133.1	145.8	205.2	277.5	310.5	378.8	500.8
Lat. Am.	**432.8**	**586.5**	**634.4**	**860.9**	**1,167.7**	**1,587.9**	**1,876.0**	**1,670.6**	**1,801.5**	**2,088.5**
LDCs	9,403.1	12,075.2	9,840.9	10,218.9	18,121.5	21,770.3	21,529.0	22,736.0	23,736.9	26,686.3

* = less than 50,000.
** = data not available.
NIEs = newly industrialized economies.
LDCs = less developed countries.
Sources: Compiled from official statistics of the U.S. International Trade Commission.

growth phase of the cycle, management skills become vital; and in the mature phase, cheap labor becomes the critical human input (Hansen 1981). In this process, skilled labor and high technology are commonly assigned to industrialized countries, whereas unskilled routine tasks—especially those that consume large quantities of labor—tend to be shifted to less developed countries. Vernon (1966) also associates spatial decentralization with strong market competition, the engine that propels firms to expand the benefits from continuous specialization of machines and labor in the mass production system. Both strong market competition (mainly from Asia) and an organization of production according to mass production principle characterize the three industries usually associated with the offshore assembly industry: textiles, consumer electronics, and automobiles.

Low wages have been important in attracting manufacturing to developing countries; however, relatively few low-wage countries have attracted labor-intensive assembly. A firm's selection of specific developing countries has to do with cost factors (cost of labor) as well as with government *policies* that affect foreign investment in a direct or indirect way. The decision to locate in a specific developing country is conditioned not only by the cost of labor (although many other developing countries have wages lower than Mexico and the NIEs, the offshore assembly industry has not expanded there), but by other factors much more difficult to measure. Wilson (1992), for instance, points out that one of the key elements of the NIEs' success was labor discipline, a rolling back of many of labor's gains from the period of import substitution. Similarly, since 1982 Mexico has lowered real wage levels (without provoking threatening upheavals), thereby creating the same conditions that led to the success of the Asian offshore assembly industry (Wilson 1992). Even more difficult to measure is the role that large potential markets, politically controlling (even repressive) governments, and relative proximity to industrialized regions play in influencing deci-

Table 3
U.S. Imports Under HTS Provision 9802.00.80 of Six Main Commodity Groups for Selected Countries, 1992
(million dollars)

	Mexico	Korea	Singapore	Taiwan
Textiles, apparel, footwear	1,303.95	447.45	3.01	214.71
Television receivers	1,801.47	0.03*	—	0.45*
Electrical conductors	1,660.07	—	0.63*	51.13
Semiconductors	271.99*	669.36	654.39	397.25
Motor vehicles	3,591.33	380.69	—	—
Motor vehicles parts	1,657.87	20.04*	—	0.03*
Total	16,248.14	1,575.71	1,205.75	898.76

* This item is not among the six largest products for this country, but is among the top six in any of the other countries considered in this table. Note: No similar statistics are published for Hong Kong.
Source: U.S. International Trade Commission, *Production Sharing: U.S. Imports Under Harmonized Tariff Schedule Provisions 9802.00.60 and 9802.00.80, 1989-1992*, January 1994.

sions to locate manufacturing processes in developing countries (Echeverri-Carroll 1994). However, government policies alone are not sufficient to attract manufacturing to developing countries, as indicated by the maquiladora industry. Although provision 98007.00.80 and the BIP were established in the 1960s, the maquiladora industry only began to grow in 1982, reflecting the peso devaluation that made maquiladora wages more attractive than the NIEs' wages.

In accordance with the product cycle theory, most empirical studies associate the growth of the maquiladora industry in Mexico with two variables: (1) the relative cost of labor in Mexico with respect to labor costs in the United States and the NIEs and (2) the growth of the U.S. industrial sector since offshore assembly plants in Mexico are mainly producing components for U.S. companies. Gruben (1989), for instance, found a significant statistical relationship between the growth of maquiladora employment and changes in the ratio of Mexican manufacturing wages to an average of manufacturing wages in the NIEs. Other empirical studies (Navarrete-Vargas and Hernandez 1987; Amozurrutia-Cabrera 1987; Fuentes-Flores 1989) found a positive correlation between increases in U.S. industrial production and the acceleration in the rate of growth of the maquiladora industry. For instance, Navarrete-Vargas and Hernandez's 1987 study shows an elasticity of U.S. industrial production with respect to maquiladora exports of 2.8, indicating that an increase of one unit in U.S. industrial production will increase maquiladora exports by almost three times. The positive correlation between the growth of the maquiladora industry and U.S. industrial production is also observed in the parallel trends tracing the rate of growth of U.S. industrial production and the rate of growth of maquiladora employment (figure 1). The positive correlation is even stronger in the case of the U.S. electronics and automobile industries because these two sectors dominate the maquiladora industry (figures 2 and 3).

Manufacturing is undergoing a revolution in which the mass production model is being replaced by a new form of production organization identified as flexible production. Is spatial decentralization toward developing countries also a feature of this new production organization? Echeverri-Carroll (1994) maintains that Vernon's product cycle theory provides an important explanation of spatial decentralization when production is organized under the principles of mass production, but it is inappropriate in the case of the multifunctional characteristics of machines and labor associated with flex-

Figure 1
U.S. Manufacturing Production and Maquiladora Employment, 1983-1991
(percentage change)

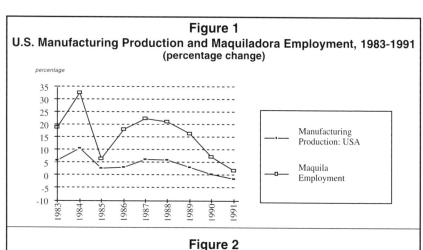

Figure 2
Electronics: U.S. Production Indexes and Maquiladora Employment, 1983-1990
(percentage change)

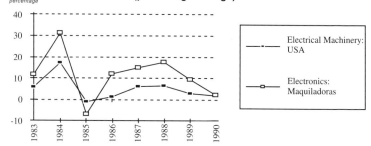

Figure 3
Automotive: U.S. Production Indexes and Maquiladora Employment, 1983-1990
(percentage change)

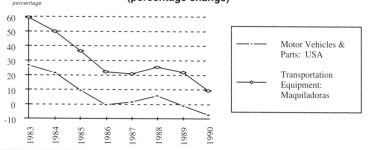

Sources: CIEMEX-WEFA, *Maquiladora Industry Analysis,* Vol. 5, No. 3, 1992.
WEFA Group, *U.S. Long-Term Historical Data,* Second Quarter, 1992.
Board of Governors of the Federal Reserve System, *Federal Bulletin,* monthly.
CIEMEX-WEFA, *Mexican Economic Outlook,* Vol. 24, No. 2, July 1992.
Note: U.S. figures based on 1987 dollars; Mexico figures based on 1980 pesos.

ible production. The differences that distinguish flexible from mass production are apparent in the use of *multipurpose* machines and tools, *multiskilled* labor, and *cooperative partnership* relations between suppliers and assemblers. However, changes in the organization of production are not the only changes affecting firms' decisions to locate in developing countries. Traditional government policies—such as tariff item 9802.00.80 and the maquiladora program—created to stimulate investments in low-skill manufacturing in developing countries have become less attractive under free trade agreements. Therefore, the relevant question should be: How will the process of spatial decentralization toward developing countries change in the context of flexible production and new trade liberalization policies?

Flexible Production and Spatial Decentralization Toward Developing Countries

The mass production model is being replaced by a flexible multi-product firm that emphasizes quality and rapid response to changing market conditions while using technologically advanced equipment and new forms of organization (Milgrom and Roberts 1990). Instead of specialized workers dedicated to fixed assignments as in mass production, labor is flexible. Workers may function according to any one or some combination of flexibilities: functional (production workers are flexible with respect to tasks and are rotated among tasks in team operations or quality circles); numerical (flexible work hours); and pay (flexible wages). (Atkinson 1986 and Ettlinger 1992 provide more detailed descriptions of these types of flexibilities.)

Productivity increases, however, result both from continued incremental improvement in the way existing technology is used and from radical shifts to a new, more efficient technology (Kelley and Brooks 1991). The new paradigm of production involves fundamental reorganization changes both *within* plants and *between* plants—in particular, between suppliers and assemblers—as a direct response to changes in market demand. Thus, competitiveness in manufacturing is determined by two major factors, namely internal efficiency and the management of external relationships, with respect to both customers and suppliers (Turnbull et al. 1992). These reorganizational changes are the response to market and product demands that are changing faster than ever: consumers are demanding greater product choice and customization, product life cycles are getting shorter, and market boundaries are rapidly shifting (Boyton 1993). Production processes within and between firms need to adjust to rapid changes in market demand; in short, they need to be flexible.

Some analysts contend that the adoption of flexible production principles may foster spatial reintegration of production to developed countries, in contrast to earlier decentralization trends toward developing countries associated with mass production (Schoenberger 1987, 1988; Sanderson 1986, 1987; Sanderson et al. 1986; Womack 1987; Jones and Womack 1985; Malecki 1991; Storper and Christopherson 1987). Their predictions are based on two assumptions. The first assumption is that a worker who supports this flexible system will be more knowledgeable, accomplish multitask functions, and participate more in and be more responsible to the production process (Schoenberger 1987). Therefore, this system requires (1) the development of new skills, such as those used by programmers and electronics technicians (Sabel 1982, Shaiken 1984, Piore and Sabel 1984), and (2) workers with more informal and formal education (medium to high skills), both of which are relatively more available in industrialized countries. Labor-related counterarguments to the spatial reconcentration hypothesis attempt to show that there is not necessarily any incompatibility between a cheap labor location and flexible production (Wilson 1992). It can be argued that experienced industrial workers are less flexible or adaptable because of their union history (Shaiken et al. 1986) or that job rotation and worker participation in problem diagnosis and continuous quality control may require a more flexible labor force but not necessarily a more skilled labor force (Wilson 1992).

The second assumption of the spatial reconcentration hypothesis emerges from a new relationship between suppliers and assemblers in the context of flexible production—in particular, from one aspect of this new relationship: the need to deliver components on a just-in-time (JIT) basis. The fact that the JIT *delivery* of components can be more easily accomplished if suppliers cluster around to final assembly has led some analysts to anticipate a reversal of the spatial decentralization process toward developing countries usually associated with mass production (Schoenberger 1987, 1988; Sanderson 1986, 1987; Sanderson et al. 1986; Womack 1987; Jones and Womack 1985; Malecki 1991; Storper and Christopherson 1987). This has been reinforced by the location patterns of the Japanese automobile supplier firms, who are leaders in implementing principles of the new production paradigms. These firms show a marked tendency to cluster around the particular assembly firms they supply in Japan, Europe, and the United States. In Japan, auto assembly and especially parts production is heavily concentrated in the core industrial region of Keihin (Tokyo-Yokohama) (Sheard 1983). The production system of Toyota is located near the cluster of assembly plants in Toyota City (on the periphery of Nagoya City); of Nissan, in the Tokyo-Yokohama region. This same clustering pattern can be observed in the case of Japanese automobile companies located in the United States and Europe (Mair et al. 1988; Glasmeier and McCluskey 1987; Kenney and Florida 1992). Thus, the Japanese automobile industry has provided a useful framework for viewing the organization of economic activities between firms and over space in the context of flexible production.

There is an assumption that the spatial clustering of Japanese firms results from JIT delivery requirements of flexible production (Estall 1985, Holmes 1986, Sayer 1985, Sheard 1983, Kenney and Florida 1992). In fact, it has been noted that Toyota has had much more JIT success than Nissan in Japan precisely because Toyota's suppliers are located closer to the production and are more geographically concentrated than those of Nissan (Cusumano 1985). The assumption that *delivery times* dominate manufacturing location in the context of flexible production has been questioned on grounds of recent empirical evidence that the JIT concept does not necessarily establish a need for geographical proximity to the location of manufacturing facilities in industrialized countries. This evidence can be classified in two groups: (1) spatial decentralization of the automobile industry within industrialized regions and (2) spatial decentralization toward developing countries, mainly in those industries more active in implementing JIT delivery systems. In the first group, the empirical evidence indicates a trend toward spatial decentralization of JIT producers in Japan and in Europe. Linge (1992), for instance, points out that in Japan a major new influence is the growing general shortage of workers. Toyota has been particularly affected because it and other firms have now absorbed the surplus labor in the formerly rural Aichi Prefecture, prompting Toyota to disperse new production facilities to Miyata (Kyushu) and Tomakomai (Hokkaido). Similar spatial dispersion trends are observed in the automobile industry in Europe. Hudson and Sadler (1992) point out that in the European automobile industry, the spatial proximity between assembler and supplier—conceptualized at the local scale rather than in terms of a trans-European or even global set of linkages—appeared increasingly unnecessary, at least for the high-tech core items in which these companies specialized. For example, the major system contracts from Nissan's plant in northeast England went to industry giants such as Lucas and GKN, which have facilities not only outside northeast England (indeed, they have very little production capacity in this sector within the region), but also across Europe.

Empirical evidence from the second group indicates that, contrary to predictions of spatial reconcentration toward industrialized countries, U.S. firms not only actively adopted flexible production principles in their domestic facilities, but also expanded and upgraded their labor-intensive production facilities in developing countries (Echeverri-Carroll 1994). Over time, the comparative advantage of offshore facilities in developing countries has shifted from cheap semiskilled labor performing labor-intensive assembly to more highly skilled and capital-intensive operations. For instance, the average hourly compensation cost for production workers in the NIEs increased from $0.59 in 1975 to $5.00 in 1993 (table 4). Despite the increase in wages, multinationals have not left the NIEs, but rather have diversified, deepened, and expanded their investments in them. Lim and Fong (1991) note that it has become common to relocate design and other capabilities to be close to production, rather than returning production "home" to the industrialized country to be close to these capabilities. While the manufacture of increasingly high-tech and high-value products and their components remains the base of the electronics industry in the NIEs, in recent years the industry has diversified into related non-manufacturing activities. Suppliers to the electronics industry include firms in other sectors, such as glass, engineering, and chemicals. Regional and even some international marketing activities are also relocating there. The result is an emerging spatial division of labor in this region, with more skilled and capital-intensive production processes and design being undertaken in the more sophisticated NIEs, while simpler, more labor-intensive processes are continuing in and being shifted to near-NIEs (Malaysia, Philippines, and Thailand) and China (Lim and Fong 1991, Scott 1987, Yuan and Eden 1992).

Significant changes have also come to the maquiladora industry. The major changes are not only quantitative, but also qualitative, including important changes in the very work processes of the maquiladora plants. Technologically, Mexico has not reached the level of the Asian countries that have been able to develop their own local industry: only 2 percent of the components used by the maquiladora industry are of Mexican origin. However, the maquiladora industry no longer represents simply low productivity, labor-intensive assembly activity. Advanced manufacturing systems have not replaced this industry; rather, they have been applied to it (Koido 1991). Several studies provide empirical evidence that practices related to manufacturing flexibility are part of the maquiladora industry (Carrillo 1989; Brown and Dominguez 1989; Suarez-Villa et al. 1989; Wilson 1989, 1992; Taddei-Bringas 1992; Uchitelle 1993). Carrillo (1989) identifies a dozen auto plants in northern Mexico, several of which are maquiladoras, that use flexible technology, flexible shop floor practices, and JIT, and Mertens and Palomares (1988) and Gonzales-Arechiga and Ramirez (1988) report a tendency toward automation in this industry. Wilson (1992) points out that maquiladoras are avoiding the huge outlays for computer-controlled machinery but adopting some of the soft forms of flexible production more consistent with a low-cost labor location. Regions or countries with relatively abundant labor and appropriate economic and political conditions continue to be attractive places for the location of manufacturing.

The empirical evidence provided by the spatial dispersion of the automobile industry in industrialized regions (Japan, the United States, and Europe) and by the continuous growth and technological sophistication of assembly facilities in developing countries indicates that flexible firms can implement JIT production principles across long distances. But how? One explanation is provided by Linge (1992), who points out that actual delivery arrangements vary, requir-

Table 4
Hourly Compensation Costs for Production Workers
(in U.S. dollars)

Countries	1975	1980	1981	1982	1983	1984	1985	1986	1987	1988	1989	1990	1991	1992	1993
Mexico	1.44	2.18	2.73	1.90	1.42	1.54	1.59	1.09	1.04	1.25	1.48	1.64	1.93	2.29	2.65
Maquiladora	*	1.40	1.68	1.22	0.91	1.05	1.07	0.80	0.81	0.98	1.15	1.26	1.45	1.62	1.62
Taiwan	0.39	0.98	1.18	1.24	1.29	1.42	1.50	1.73	2.26	2.82	3.53	3.95	4.39	5.13	5.23
Korea	0.35	1.02	1.08	1.10	1.17	1.22	1.23	1.31	1.59	2.20	3.17	3.71	4.46	4.93	5.37
Singapore	0.84	1.49	1.79	1.96	2.21	2.46	2.47	2.23	2.31	2.67	3.15	3.78	4.35	4.95	5.38
Hong Kong	0.76	1.51	1.55	1.66	1.51	1.58	1.73	1.88	2.09	2.40	2.79	3.20	3.58	3.92	4.31
Average NIEs	0.59	1.25	1.40	1.49	1.54	1.67	1.73	1.78	2.06	2.52	3.16	3.66	4.19	4.73	5.07
U.S.	6.36	9.84	10.84	11.68	12.14	12.55	13.01	13.26	13.52	13.91	14.32	14.91	15.58	16.17	16.79

* Data not available.
Sources: U.S. Department of Labor, Bureau of Labor Statistics, Office of Productivity and Technology, *Hourly Compensation Costs for Production Workers in Manufacturing*, unpublished data, May 1994. *Hourly Compensation Costs for Production Workers in Manufacturing Industries, Mexico 1975-92*, unpublished data for Mexico and the maquiladora industry.

ing different geographical proximities. Generally, deliveries of large components (e.g., engines, drive shafts, and radiators) have to be made to the assembly plant several times a day at precise times (sometimes known as "open windows"), whereas deliveries of smaller components may be made once every two or three days. In our view, the assumption that delivery times dominate the location decisions of flexible suppliers is narrowly based on the idea that the JIT system is just to deliver on-time. JIT is usually associated with a delivery program in which small quantities of material are transported in correct amounts exactly when and where they are needed. Manufacturers with this view often require their suppliers to make small deliveries at frequent intervals on short notice. This forces the supplier with traditional manufacturing methods to carry increased finished goods inventory and results in consignment inventory, otherwise known as the "hot potato" game (Gottesman 1991). The cost of maintaining inventories will manifest itself in the product and eventually will be passed on to the end user. This scenario does not improve the competitiveness of either the supplier or the finished goods manufacturer. JIT is not the process of shifting inventory to suppliers; in fact, the companies that have made JIT work on the supply end have developed elaborate mechanisms for supplier relations, emphasizing "partnership" rather than impatient demands (Zipkin 1991).

In its purest form, JIT involves both expeditious delivery and cooperative interfirm relations to ensure both reliable production and distribution, as well as zero inventory (Ettlinger 1992). In particular, the system features the formation of closer and more coordinated relations (Ikeda 1987), in contrast to the supply system under mass production, which is based on arm's length relations. The traditional buyer-supplier relationship (emerging in the context of mass production) was one of closed competition, with any new business secured by one supplier at the expense of another; price competitiveness was the primary criterion on which contracts were awarded. In the context of the new paradigm of production, the focus has shifted toward reducing unit costs via a partnership relationship, which has resolved scheduling problems and technical difficulties through a process of *cooperation* rather than competition. In this context, supplier firms are involved in a complex network of input-output relations, in which the suppliers function as extensions of the assembler's plant, resulting in regional production systems that function with the precision approaching that of a single, well organized factory (Sheard 1983). By creating a tight network of suppliers, the system succeeds in extending to a considerable degree the specialization and timing inherent in modern factory production to a wider regional space. Thus, even if suppliers have more flexibility to locate far away from the final assembly because they are producing small components, we still do not know how cooperative supplier-assembler relations are maintained across long distances.

Echeverri-Carroll (1994) points out that only by developing interfirm electronic network systems can suppliers locate far away and maintain JIT production relations with their assemblers. In this sense, the firm's decision to locate suppliers far away in the new production environment will be determined by the existence of an infrastructure that facilitates the movement of information across long distances. The maquiladora industry is an important example of the significance of the relationship between organizational changes and electronic linkages across long distances. According to Barrera (1990), General Motors was the largest user of public telephone networks for transborder communication in the maquiladora industry in 1990, with 30 leased data lines in 27 plants. In 1985, the Mexican telephone company created an office in Ciudad Juarez to manage the demand of the maquiladora industry. GM represented about 40 percent of the total work of this office in 1990. The Ford and Chrysler plants in Ciudad Juarez use the Morelos Satellite System for their data networks with their plants in the United States.

In sum, in the new production environment, a company's decision to spatially decentralize—either within industrialized countries (such as in the case of the automobile industry in industrialized regions) or toward developing countries (such as the case of the maquiladora industry)—will be determined by the existence of an infrastructure that facilitates the movement of information across long distances. If the infrastructure is available, a company's location decision will be determined by the *cost and flexibility of labor* with respect to any one or some combination of flexibilities (functional, numerical, and pay). Spatial decentralization toward developing countries continues to be relevant; however, it is characterized by more flexible production processes and functional integration. This contrasts sharply with the traditional mass production model, which is characterized by global decentralization of "sweatshop" operations that are poorly linked to the parent plant. Despite the importance of these economic variables in the location decisions of flexible producers, firms do not act in a government-less world; their decisions to locate in a developing country must accommodate policies that affect the movement of products and capital between international borders. NAFTA benefits only products of North American origin, adversely affecting maquiladoras (such as the Japanese ones) that use a large percentage of components and machinery from outside the free trade area.

NAFTA and its Implications for the Maquiladora Industry

NAFTA's Tariff Provisions and the Maquiladora Industry

Maquiladoras have traditionally enjoyed tariff privileges from the United States. A major competitive advantage of maquiladora production is the favorable tariff treatment provided by the U.S. government throughout Harmonized Tariff Schedule (HTS) provisions 9802.00.60 and 9802.00.80 and the GSP program. Essentially, item 9802.00.60 (formerly item 806.30) permits the reimport of "fabricated" (but in effect unfinished) metal products into the United States for further processing; 9802.00.80 (formerly item 807.00) permits only the "assembly" of goods for reexport to the United States.

U.S. provisions 9802.00.60 and 9802.00.80 provide import tariff exceptions on U.S. products used by offshore assemblers, but most of these imports come under item 9802.00.80. Products worth $55.3 billion were imported under item 9802.00.80, while products worth only $1.0 billion were imported under item 9802.00.60 in 1992 (United States International Trade Commission, Table B-1, 1994).[3] The importance of HTS provision 9802.00.80 for offshore assembly is evident when considering that duty-free U.S. components accounted for 45.5 percent ($10.8 billion) of total imports from developing countries under this provision in 1992 (United States International Trade Commission 1994). This provision is particularly important for the Mexican maquiladora industry, which accounted for 65.2 percent of total U.S. duty-free products imported to the United States from developing countries under provision 9802.00.80 in 1992 (United States International Trade Commission 1994).

The Generalized System of Preferences makes available certain duty concessions to developing nation exporters of eligible products. Under this system, the entire value of the product returned to the United States can be imported free of duty when the local content increases to at least 35 percent. When possible, importers, including U.S. manufacturers with foreign assembly facilities, will substitute use of the GSP provision for items 9802.00.60 and 9802.00.80 because it provides greater exemption of duties. The higher the share of materials and value added supplied by the exporting nation, the higher are the GSP benefits. By contrast, the higher the share of U.S.-origin materials and components, the greater are 9802.00.60 and 9802.00.80 terms and incentives. There is, however, more substitution of GSP for use of items 9802.00.60 and 9802.00.80 in East Asia than in Mexico because of the greater availability of good quality, locally made components (United States International Trade Commission 1991a).

NAFTA creates new incentives for maquiladoras that use a large percentage of North American components. These new incentives make duty concessions provided by the GSP program and HTS provisions 9802.00.60 and 9802.00.80 irrelevant for most maquiladoras. Hufbauer and Schott (1992) point out that free trade areas are by nature discriminatory: lower tariff and nontariff barriers are enjoyed only by partner countries. To ensure that other countries do not evade the barriers still applied to nonmembers, FTAs necessarily adopt rules of origin to determine which goods actually were produced within the member countries and therefore qualify for preferential treatment. Thus, by 1999, when the implementation of NAFTA will be completed—with all stages of the reduction or elimination of both tariffs and the customs user fee[4] phased in—there will be little or no incentive to import most products from Mexico containing U.S.-made components under the production-sharing provisions 9802.00.60 and 9802.00.80. Because the value of U.S.-made components contained in imports under the production-sharing tariff provisions is exempt from the customs user fee, there will be some incentive to import duty-free products under these provisions until the user fee is phased out under NAFTA by June 1999. According to Watkins (1994a), by 1999, most U.S. imports from Mexico of products that were the result of production sharing will enter free of duty because of the Automotive Products Trade Act or duty-free treatment for certain products from all most favored nation (MFN) suppliers or regular or accelerated phase-in of tariff elimination under the North American Free Trade Agreement. By January 1, 1999, an estimated 62 percent of all otherwise dutiable imports from Mexico will be entering free of duty under NAFTA (Watkins 1994a).

Production-sharing imports from Mexico totaled $16.5 billion in 1992, but should amount to only a small fraction of that figure by the year 2000, the last year before the maquiladora program is eliminated and duty drawback is limited. As a result, imports from Mexico under the production-sharing provisions will drop at the same time that total imports from this country will increase. Although it means that 9802.00.80 statistics will not reflect trends in the offshore assembly industry in Mexico, it certainly does not mean that the industry per se will disappear. On the contrary, low-skilled manufacturing of products (as in maquiladoras) will become even more relevant as elimination of barriers to trade allows each country to specialize more intensively according to their competitive advantages.

The purpose of the North American Free Trade Agreement is to favor the use of components from Canada, the United States, and Mexico. In this sense, NAFTA will most benefit the group of maquiladoras that use a large proportion of U.S. or Mexican components (very few Canadian components are now used) because their products will originate in North America and therefore enjoy preferential treatment. Under HTS provisions 9802.00.60 and 9802.00.80, these maquiladoras pay duties on the value of third-country components (components from outside the free trade area) and the value added in Mexico; under NAFTA, the whole value of the product can be shipped to the United States duty free. A product need not contain 100 percent North American-origin components and materials to be exempted of trade tariffs; it only has to meet certain percentages established by legislation on rules of origin. This opens the possibility that the entire value of the product returned to the United States, including the value of third-country components and the value-added in Mexico, can be imported duty free when the North American content equals at least the minimum percentage required by rules of origin. Maquiladoras with the highest ratio of North American components on a percentage basis are textiles and apparel; scientific instruments, including low-tech instruments and apparatuses; and chemical and related products, including articles of rubber and plastics (table 5).

A second group of maquiladoras will continue to use provision 9802.00.80. This group uses a relatively small percentage of North American components and therefore cannot take advantage of duty exemptions created by NAFTA's rules of origin. Because their products do not contain sufficient North American content to meet the rules of origin necessary to qualify for NAFTA treatment, these maquiladoras will continue to take advantage of tariff exemptions provided by item 9802.00.80, even after NAFTA implementation is completed. The two most important industries in this group are those assembling television sets and those assembling radio equipment, mostly using components imported from Japan. In fact, U.S. compo-

Table 5
Composition of Production Costs of U.S. Imports
Under TSUS Item 807.00, by Industry Group, Mexico, 1986
(value in million dollars)

Industry group	Mexican labor	Mexico	United States	Canada	Europe	Japan	Other East Asia	All other	Total
Agriculture and other forest products	11.6	*	48.8	*	0.0	0.0	0.0	0.0	**61.4**
Shirts and blouses	21.5	*	23.1	*	0.0	0.0	0.0	0.0	**44.7**
Trousers, slacks, and shorts	13.5	*	47.3	0.0	*	0.0	0.0	0.0	**63.4**
Body support garments	3.8	0.0	19.7	0.0	0.0	0.0	0.0	0.0	**23.5**
Footwear	6.1	0.0	30.7	0.0	0.0	0.0	0.0	0.0	**36.8**
Other textile and apparel	14.8	*	48.8	0.0	*	*	0.0	0.0	**94.2**
Chemicals and related products	0.5	0.0	5.8	0.0	0.0	0.0	0.0	0.0	**6.3**
Minerals and metals	9.7	0.0	59.2	0.0	0.0	*	*	0.0	**69.0**
Internal combustion engines	2.1	18.8	31.7	*	*	0.0	0.0	0.0	**58.7**
Office machines	14.5	*	39.7	0.0	0.0	*	0.0	*	**63.8**
Motors and related products	30.0	*	115.9	0.0	0.0	26.7	*	*	**178.9**
Television equipment	78.5	0.0	183.8	0.0	0.0	321.1	*	*	**627.6**
Radio equipment	20.5	7.3	190.0	*	0.0	*	*	256.6	**486.2**
Recording equipment	*	*	*	0.0	0.0	*	*	*	*
Semiconductors	14.2	0.0	113.5	0.0	*	*	*	0.0	**132.4**
Other electrical articles	62.1	7.5	311.4	0.0	4.1	22.6	6.7	37.5	**451.9**
Automobiles, trucks, and buses	*	*	*	0.0	0.0	0.0	0.0	0.0	*
Vehicle parts and other vehicles	169.0	*	502.3	*	23.2	24.2	1.2	1.8	**729.9**
Other machinery and equipment	26.5	3.7	141.9	0.0	*	15.9	*	9.5	**197.6**
Scientific instruments	9.2	*	55.6	**	0.0	*	*	0.0	**68.5**
Furniture and related products	*	*	*	0.0	0.0	0.0	0.0	0.0	*
Miscellaneous manufactures	19.9	16.0	61.4	*	*	*	1.4	0.0	**94.3**
Total	**548.2**	**705.0**	**2,172.1**	**13.4**	**36.9**	**423.4**	**59.0**	**308.4**	**3,631.9**

TSUS=Tariff Schedules of the United States.
* data are suppressed to avoid revealing confidential business information.
** less than $50,000.
Note: Because of rounding, figures may not add up to the totals shown.
Source: U.S. International Trade Commission, "The Use and Economic Impact of TSUS Items 806.30 and 807.00," 1988, pp. 3-12.

nents accounted for only 29 and 39 percent, respectively, of total production costs of these two industries in 1986 (table 5), while Japanese components accounted for 51 percent of the total production costs of maquiladora plants assembling television sets in the same year. Furthermore, television assemblers consumed 75 percent of total components imported from Japan by the maquiladora industry in 1986. The non-North American components used in the assembly of televisions are assessed Mexico's MFN rate of duty for such parts when they enter Mexico.[5] When the assembled televisions enter the United States, they will be assessed the MFN rate of duty applied by the United States toward such products. However, by entering under HTS provision 9802.00.80, the value of the U.S.-made components contained in these televisions will be subtracted from the customs value before applying the MFN rate of duty.

The large number of components imported from Japan for use in the assembly of television sets reflects the strong Japanese presence in this industry in Mexico. The number of Japanese plants increased in the 1980s when Japan significantly increased its capital-intensive investments in the United States and its investments in labor-intensive processing in Mexico (Echeverri-Carroll 1989). These investments resulted from increasing threats of protectionism in the United States and economic policies directed by the Group of Seven (industrially advanced countries). In the fall of 1985, the ministers of finance of the Group of Seven decided to intervene in the international currency market. Consequently, the dollar fell drastically against the yen (from 1:270 in 1984 to 1:150 by mid-1986) as well as against European currencies. The dollar's decline made Japanese exports less competitive, forcing Japan to invest in the United States and Mexico according to the comparative advantages of these countries. By 1987, more than half of the Japanese color television manufacturers had established maquiladora operations along the U.S.-Mexican border (Koido 1991).

During the 1980s, Japanese electronics giants such as Matsushita, Sanyo, Sony, and Hitachi had expanded or started new assembly plants in Tijuana. Toshiba began to produce chassis in Ciudad Juárez for final assembly in its Tennessee plant. The building of Japanese maquiladoras on the U.S.-Mexican border, combined with preexisting U.S. and European maquiladoras, made Mexico a primary export platform of color televisions to the United States. In 1985, Mexico's share of the U.S. color television market was only 1.3 percent: 108,030 units were imported from Mexico from a total of 8.3 million units imported from around the world. Mexico's participation surpassed 58 percent in 1992: 6.2 million units from a total of 10.6 million units imported from all around the world in that year.[6]

A rarer case is the group of maquiladoras that use tariff provisions provided by the GSP. NAFTA will not change the tariff status for maquiladoras using at least 35 percent Mexican components but not enough North American components for their products to be classified as originating in North America. This group of maquiladoras will continue to take advantage of the GSP program that gives the whole value of the product duty-free status as long as the value added in Mexico is at least 35 percent. Under NAFTA and the GSP program, some maquiladora products will be exempted from U.S. import duties on the whole value of the product, even on components that did not originate in North America. However, eligibility for GSP but not for NAFTA is going to be rare and should be treated as hypothetical because Mexico has lost its GSP eligibility for many products.[7] (GSP accounted for only 14 percent of total imports from Mexico in 1992, and most of these imports were from the agricultural sector, which is not represented in the maquiladora industry.[8])

In summary, NAFTA will make maquiladoras that use a large percentage of North American components more competitive because now these maquiladoras will be exempted from duties on the value of the foreign components and the value added in Mexico (these two values do not enjoy preferential treatment under HTS provisions 9802.00.60 and 9802.00.80). On the other hand, those maquiladoras that use a large percentage of third-country components that do not qualify for preferential treatment given by NAFTA's rules of origin will continue to pay duties on third-country components and valued-added in Mexico; therefore, they will continue to benefit from tariff exemptions on U.S. components provided mainly by item 9802.00.80. In terms of tariff provisions, most maquiladoras will benefit under NAFTA, and for a few (mainly the Japanese maquiladoras), the situation will remain unchanged; they will continue to benefit from tariff exemptions on U.S. components provided mainly by item 9802.00.00. However, NAFTA's nontariff provisions will have an opposite effect on Japanese and U.S.-owned maquiladoras.

NAFTA's Nontariff Provisions and the Maquiladora Industry
In the last three decades, most industrialized countries engaging in international trade have undertaken efforts to reduce tariff rates on imported goods. Such duty reductions have been made on a multilateral basis, usually during trade and tariff negotiations sponsored

by the General Agreement on Tariffs and Trade (GATT), or on a bilateral basis between trading partners with a common interest in the liberalized movement of goods across their borders (United States International Trade Commission 1991b). Tariff barriers between Mexico and the United States, for instance, have been dropping significantly in recent years. The effective U.S. tariff on Mexican goods was 1.9 percent in 1991 (compared with a nominal rate of 4 percent from all products from all countries), while the average Mexican tariff on U.S. goods was 7.8 percent (Watkins 1994a).

As tariff barriers have been eliminated, nontariff protection has increased. Thus, the dutiable status or applicable rate of duty on imported goods can be affected by nontariff practices, procedures, and programs. In fact, given the strong reduction on tariffs in Mexico after 1986 and in the United States as a result of GATT negotiations, one of the most important contributions of NAFTA is the *elimination of nontariff barriers*. The United States, for instance, imposes high quotas on the textile industry. NAFTA exempts from quotas all U.S. imports of Mexican textiles and apparel that meet NAFTA's rules of origin. According to the United States International Trade Commission (1993), in 1991, 87 percent of U.S. apparel imports and 36 percent of U.S. textile imports from Mexico were subject to quotas. The Commission estimates that, with NAFTA, about 90 percent of the apparel imports and 65 percent of the textile imports from Mexico subjected to quotas would be quota-free in 1994.

Changes introduced to tariff refund programs for temporary imports as a result of NAFTA will significantly affect the maquiladora industry. Countries have established criteria and procedures that permit the temporary importation of goods without payment of duty pending eventual exportation from the importing country. For instance, under the in-bond arrangement, imported inputs enter Mexico duty free, but the importer posts a bond to guarantee that the finished products will indeed be exported rather than sold on the domestic market; otherwise, appropriate duties are collected from the posted bond. Existing duty refund programs will be terminated by January 1, 2001, for Mexico-U.S. and Canada-Mexico trade. At the time these programs are eliminated, each partner country will adopt the *Limited Duty Exemption Program* to avoid the double taxation effects of payments of duties in two countries. The limitation on conditional duty exemptions applies to all North American trade, not just trade that receives NAFTA benefits (Watkins 1994a). This limitation ensures both that imports from third countries will be subject to ordinary customs duties when imported into North America and that one NAFTA country cannot be used as a platform by third countries for exporting products free of duty to another NAFTA country.[9] NAFTA provides that a duty refund that is contingent on exportation may not exceed the smaller of the following: (1) the total amount of the duties paid on the initial importation of the third country goods into North America, or (2) the total amount of the duties paid on the goods' subsequent shipment to another NAFTA signatory.[10] In other words, maquiladoras importing components in-bond from a third country into Mexico will now pay duties on these components to the Mexican government. Once the components are incorporated into an assembled product that is then sent to the United States, they will again have to pay import duties in the United States on the third-country components and Mexican value-added incorporated in the product if the product does not meet the rules of origin to qualify for NAFTA treatment. To avoid double taxation, the greater amount of these two duty payments will be refunded.

As already indicated, the average effective U.S. tariff on Mexican goods was 1.9 percent in 1991, while average Mexican tariffs on U.S. goods were 7.8 percent in the same year. Although these percentages vary according to product, Mexican duties on U.S. goods—particularly electronics and automobile components—are almost always higher than U.S. duties on Mexican products. Consequently, duty must be paid on foreign content as the product enters the United States, while the Mexican government must refund duties paid in Mexico. This situation is similar to the one existing now in which a maquiladora plant imports components in-bond into Mexico and pays U.S. duties on their value and the value added in Mexico when the already-assembled product enters the United States. Although plants will continue paying duties on foreign components and the value added in Mexico as they had done under the maquiladora program, they are now subject to higher transaction costs because they may present satisfactory evidence of the customs duties to both countries. This measure is equivalent to a nontariff barrier because of the extra cost of dealing with more red tape. These plants will have also higher financial costs, since in essence, they are lending money to the Mexican government between the time when a product is imported into Mexico and duties are paid to the Mexican government and the time when it is sent to the United States and the duty is refunded. The Japanese maquiladoras assembling TV sets may be among the most affected by higher transaction and financial costs because of their reliance on a large percentage of Japanese components.

NAFTA also changes another important provision for the maquiladora industry, the *importation of machinery and equipment free of duty*. The 1989 maquiladora decree established that machinery and equipment brought into Mexico for the maquiladora program are considered temporary imports and are not subject to Mexican import duties. NAFTA eliminates this drawback provision; therefore, maquiladoras will have to pay duties on equipment and machinery that is not considered of North American origin. Maquiladoras that use a relatively large proportion of capital equipment and import most of this equipment from countries outside the free trade area will see their costs increase under NAFTA because they will have to pay duty on such machinery beginning January 1, 2001. According to Kenney and Florida (1994), the vast majority of the Japanese maquiladoras import their production equipment from Japan. Thus, Japanese maquiladoras will be particularly affected by the elimination of the provision allowing them to import machinery free of duty.

Other nontariff provisions given to maquiladoras remain in effect after NAFTA. One such provision, the *special window*, was created to reduce red tape. The 1989 maquiladora decree established that maquiladoras may do all their transactions with an office in the Secretaria de Comercio y Fomento Industrial (SECOFI) instead of dealing with several governmental agencies. Another important NAFTA nontariff provision provides maquiladoras the opportunity to sell in the Mexican market. The 1989 decree established that maquiladoras that show a foreign exchange surplus (export as much or more than they import) can sell at most 50 percent of the total value of their exports in the Mexican market. Thus, access to the internal Mexican market is conditioned on earning an equivalent amount of foreign exchange through exports. Furthermore, they must request a special import permission as well as fulfill the percentage of national integration rule. Thus, at least 2 percent of their components must be of Mexican origin. This percentage increases to 3 percent and 4 percent respectively during the following two years of selling in the Mexican market. NAFTA provides a gradual access to the Mexican market that is not conditioned by surplus foreign exchange, national content requirements, or import permissions. NAFTA establishes that maquiladoras could start selling up to 55 percent of their production in the Mexican market during the first year of the agreement. Complete access to the Mexican market is expected in the year 2001.

In summary, the most important changes prompted by NAFTA relate to nontariff provisions. On the one hand, certain nontariff changes, such as gradual access to the Mexican market will benefit all the maquiladoras. On the other hand, other non-tariff changes, such as the *Limited Duty Exemption Program*, will mean higher transaction and financial costs for maquiladoras that use a small percentage of North American components, such as the Japanese companies assembling televisions. Furthermore, changes in the duty-free importation of machinery will adversely affect Japanese plants using a large proportion of machinery and equipment from Japan; however, the participation of the Japanese maquiladoras in the sector as a whole is small. By facilitating access to the Mexican market and eliminating duties both on Mexican value-added and on the small proportion of components imported from third countries for the large number of maquiladoras that use a large proportion of U.S. components, NAFTA will have a positive impact on the maquiladora industry.

Conclusions

The maquiladora industry is an industry in transition. The transition process is influenced mainly by two forces: first, the challenges and opportunities presented by changes in the relationship between suppliers and assemblers in the new flexible production paradigm and second, by the opportunities and restrictions created by a new set of government regulations under NAFTA. Furthermore, the growth of the maquiladora industry in Mexico will be determined by the expansion of the country's infrastructure and by sound government policies.

In sum, we expect that three variables will mainly influence the growth of the maquiladora industry. The first variable is the capacity to increase flexibility not only within maquiladora plants, but also in the relationship with assemblers. One of the most important variables to influence the growth of the maquiladora industry is changes in the organization of production, in particular, the replacement of mass production by flexible production principles. Some analysts anticipate a spatial reconcentration toward industrialized countries as firms adopt flexible production principles. The assumption of a reversal of spatial decentralization is based on two observations: (1) Japanese automobile supplier firms show a marked tendency to cluster around the particular assembly firms they supply in Japan, Europe, and the United States, and (2) some intrinsic characteristics of flexible production, such as the JIT delivery of components, can be more easily accomplished if suppliers are located close to final assembly in industrialized countries. However, the recent process of spatial decentralization of the automobile industry in Japan and the observation that many of the Japanese automobile industries in the United Kingdom are not buying many of their components locally but importing them from other European countries has led some analysts to anticipate that the JIT concept does not necessarily establish a need for geographical proximity (Linge 1992; Hudson and Sadler 1992). This belief is reinforced by the continuous growth and increasing technological sophistication of assembly facilities in developing countries.

This chapter stresses that JIT systems are not merely the action of delivery on time. In fact, the Japanese automakers' extraordinary performance has been attributed to their supply system, an arrangement based on long-term relationships with suppliers, information exchange, joint problem solving, and "governance by trust" (Helper 1990), not to their "per se" capacity to deliver on time. Unlike Detroit-based firms, which traditionally organize relations with suppliers through a competitive bidding process, Japanese firms maintain long-term, frequently exclusive relations with suppliers (Helper 1990, Cusumano 1985). It is relevant to ask how these partnership relations can be maintained across long distances. In other words, how can the JIT production system be maintained across long distances? The transfer of data and information back and forth between manufacturing facilities across long distances requires the use of facsimile transmission, electronic mail, and especially the development of Electronic Data Interchange (EDI) systems to transfer information *instantaneously* between manufacturing facilities so that assemblers can *coordinate* their actions more closely with those of suppliers in far geographical locations. As Ettlinger (1992) indicates, innovations in communications are permitting and facilitating the coevolution of JIT processes and patterns of nonlocalized linkages.

Although in the context of mass production the decision to locate in a developing country was conditioned by the relative cost of labor, in the new production paradigm this decision is conditioned by new factors available in these countries. In particular, the skill and flexibility of labor, the capacity to develop electronic network systems, and the ability of firms in developing countries to reorganize production processes on more flexible grounds all contribute to location decisions. Thus, maquiladoras must introduce concepts and tools such as quality circles, computer-oriented manufacturing machines, and electronic information systems at the same time they develop partnership relations with buyers so their products can be delivered with the quality, cost, and timeliness required by buyers in industrialized countries. As Kaplinsky and Cooper (1989) point out, changes in the economics of location need not necessarily involve a change in the international division of labor in manufacturing since there is no reason why these clusters of production should not be established in Korea, Brazil, or China. Many developing countries offer a pool of highly skilled labor that could be trained to learn the principles of flexible production.[11] Although there is some skepticism about the possibility of transferring computer-aided manufacturing to developing countries (Gold 1989), there is evidence that flexible production can be implemented in these countries as well as in industrial countries (Womack et al. 1990).

A second variable that will influence the growth of the maquiladora industry is new trade policies, specifically NAFTA's tariff and nontariff provisions. Duties on foreign components and value added in Mexico will be waived for maquiladoras that use a *large* percentage of North American components. Maquiladoras that use a small percentage of North American components will continue to pay duties on foreign components and on value added in Mexico under the 9802.00.80 provision. However, the most important changes introduced by NAFTA are related to nontariff provisions. These changes affect only maquiladoras that use a *small* percentage of machinery and components from the NAFTA region. The substitution of *tariff refund programs* for temporary imports by the *Limited Duty Exemption Program* will impose higher financial and transaction costs for maquiladoras that import a large percentage of components from third countries. Furthermore, the elimination of temporary imports of machinery and equipment will increase duties for maquiladoras that use machinery and equipment from third countries. Japanese maquiladoras, with their significant participation in the assembly of televisions and their use of a large percentage of Japanese components and machinery, could be among the most affected by changes in nontariff provisions. The consequence could be more Japanese investment in North America, as plants already operating in Mexico convince their suppliers to locate either in the United States or in Mexico, according to the comparative advantages of these countries.

Despite higher financial and transaction costs for some maquiladoras, foreign investment in maquiladoras still looks favorable, not only because of the administrative agility provided by the *special window*, but also because of the possibility of 100 percent ownership. Mexico's 1973 foreign investment law, still in effect, basically regulates foreign investment and promotes domestic investment. Although the 1989 foreign investment decree introduced important changes that created an environment more open to foreign investment, liberalization of the foreign investment regime has been implemented through executive decrees while the restrictive 1973 law remains intact. Maquiladoras will continue to offer the possibility of 100 percent foreign ownership, while some changes will still have to be made to the 1989 foreign investment decree before liberalization of foreign investment can be effective.

A third variable that will influence the growth of the maquiladora industry is the capacity of the Mexican government to provide the infrastructure that will facilitate the movement of goods between countries. Mexico's road and highway infrastructure is about 240,000 kilometers, only 19 percent of which are main highways, while 25 percent are feeder roads and 56 percent are rural roads. In 1991, Mexico's federal government estimated more than 16,000 km of highway with four or more lanes were needed by the year 2000 to be able both to integrate the nation's diverse regions through a modern and rapid transportation system and to satisfy the demands of international trade in terms of punctuality, capacity, cost, and safety.[12] Although availability and quality of the highway system is a priority for international trade, border formalities on the U.S. side have been one of the biggest obstacles to the flow of goods. U.S. efforts to reduce contraband traffic, such as drugs and undocumented workers, cause most of the delays. Waits of more than an hour are not uncommon. One answer to border delays has been the run-through container train with special customs inspection arrangements: maquiladora products are inspected at the factory, placed in sealed containers, and then passed through border customs without being inspected again there. Moreover, evidence suggests that constraints on social infrastructure (housing, electricity, urban transportation, and telecommunication systems) have also slowed the growth of the maquiladora industry considerably (Watkins 1994a).

Finally, given the importance of labor costs for the maquiladora industry, it is relevant to ask what impact NAFTA will have on Mexican wages. As more investment (both foreign and domestic) is generated in Mexico because of NAFTA, the demand for Mexican labor will rise, which will tend to raise wages. Most of the increase in Mexican wages, however, will be the result of increases in productivity that will occur as Mexican firms become increasingly rationalized under NAFTA. To the extent that increases in wages will be created by gains in productivity as maquiladoras become more integrated with firms in industrialized countries, maquiladoras will be better off even if free trade produces wage increases. Nevertheless, Mexican wages will not increase *significantly* for a number of reasons. First, significant increases in labor demand from new, labor-intensive, foreign-owned facilities are not expected; most such enterprises have probably been attracted into the maquiladora program already. Second, as Lustig (1992) points out, the extent of labor dislocation and its effect on unemployment and real wages in Mexico will be more affected by the performance of the economy than by the impact of trade liberalization. The evolution of fiscal and monetary policies—the exchange rate in particular—could have a far greater impact on aggregate employment and wage levels than changes caused by the removal of tariff and nontariff trade barriers.

Our analysis suggests that factors such as relative labor costs that conditioned mass producers' location decisions are of limited value in the new production system that emphasizes flexible linkages and flexible production as key factors in the location decision. Ettlinger (1992) denotes that unlike the spatial patterning of traditional American production, which essentially capitalizes on the uneven development of core and peripheral areas, flexible production lacks a distinct spatial logic; interfirm linkages may be localized or nonlocalized. Echeverri-Carroll (1994), however, points out that firms *still* capitalize on uneven local economic developments, but this process is conditioned not only by quantitative factors such as the relative cost of labor, but also by qualitative factors such as regional differences in labor flexibility and in the capacity of local suppliers to become flexible producers and develop cooperative linkages. Thus, empirical studies concerned with the growth of the maquiladora industry should not focus only on the traditional variables, such as the cost of labor or the growth of the U.S. economy as determinant variables, but also on other factors that are more relevant for the growth of the industry in the context of the new flexible production paradigm and NAFTA. The flexibility of labor, the use of electronic networks, the origin of components, and the availability of transportation infrastructure play a more significant role than the traditional labor costs and duty exemptions provided by HTS item 9802.00.80. Future research should focus on measur-

ing the implications of these variables for spatial patterns of manufacturing activities, in particular for offshore assembly.

The author appreciates the valuable comments from Ralph Watkins, International Trade Commission, Washington, D.C. The views presented in
this article are strictly those of the author.

Notes

1. The term maquiladora is derived from the Spanish word for the amount of corn paid by a farmer to the miller to grind the corn. Similarly, the maquiladora industry uses inputs provided by the client and returns the output to the same client. This is also called the in-bond industry because the industry imports in-bond components and machinery. Both names are used interchangeably in this chapter.
2. Watkins (1994b) mentions that of 323 companies responding to an International Trade Commission survey, 62 firms (19 percent) said they would have gone out of business if they had not been able to use low-cost maquiladora assembly plants.
3. Given the relative importance of provision 9802.00.80, this chapter focuses hereafter mainly on trends related to this provision.
4. The customs user fee, established in 1986, requires that merchandise formally entered, or withdrawn from the warehouse for consumption, be subject to an ad valorem fee. The fee was not intended to be permanent, but it has been continued to help defray costs of Customs Service administration. The user fee is applied to the value of the dutiable (foreign value added) portion of imports under HTS 9802.00.60 and 9802.00.80, but not to the nondutiable (U.S. origin) portion.
5. Such parts are usually shipped from Asia to California and trucked under bond to Tijuana. Such imports will continue to be accorded duty-free treatment while in transit through the United States to Mexico (Watkins 1994a).
6. Data obtained from the Consumer Electronics Division of the U.S. International Trade Commission, Washington, D.C.
7. Conversation with Ralph Watkins, U.S. International Trade Commission.
8. *Ibid.*
9. For a more extensive discussion regarding the changes to duty drawbacks agreed to in NAFTA, see U.S. International Trade Commission (1993).
10. An example taken from U.S. International Trade Commission (1993) illustrates how this measure works. Assume a company imports $100 of non-NAFTA components that are dutiable at 15 percent. The company would pay $15 in duties at the time of importation. The company uses the component to manufacture a finished product valued at $200 and the finished product is exported to another NAFTA signatory. Assume further that the finished product is dutiable at 5 percent by the other NAFTA signatory, either because

the product fails to satisfy the NAFTA rule of origin or because the NAFTA staged rate reductions are still being phased in. The importer of the finished product would pay a duty of 5 percent of $200, or $10. Under the *Limited Duty Exemption Program*, the company would be eligible for a refund of $10, which is the lesser of the two duty amounts.

11. The Ford plant in Hermosillo, Mexico, employs 100 licensed engineers and 700 production workers. The production workers are high school or technical school graduates, trained by Ford to work up to electrician, machinery repair person, computer programmer, or mechanic (Uchitelle 1993).

12. Highway infrastructure needs are in sharp contrast with significant decreases in public sector investments (from 0.75 percent of GDP in the 1970s to 0.3 percent in the 1980s) (Secretaria de Comunicacion y Transporte 1990).

References

Abernathy, W.J., K.B. Clark, and A.M. Kantrow. 1981. "The New Industrial Competition." *Harvard Business Review* 59: 68–81.

Amozurrutia-Cabrera, J. 1987. "La Generacion de Empleo por Maquiladoras en Mexico y los Ciclos Economicos de Estados Unidos, 1978-1985." In *Maquiladoras*, edited by A. Garcia Espinosa. Universidad Autonoma de Nuevo Leon, Mexico.

Atkinson, J. 1986. "Employment Flexibility in Internal and External Labour Markets." Working paper, Institute for Manpower Studies, University of Sussex.

Barrera, E. 1990. *Telecommunications in Industrial Enclaves: The Maquiladora Industry on the United States-Mexico Border.* Center for Research on Communication Technology and Society, University of Texas at Austin.

Boyton, A.C. 1993. "Achieving Dynamic Stability through Information Technology." *Management Review* 35: 58–77.

Brown, F. and L. Dominguez. 1989. "Nuevas Tecnologias en la Industria Maquiladora de Exportacion." *Comercio Exterior* 39: 215–223.

Burns, G. and R. Watkins. 1993. *Industry Trade and Technology Review.* Washington, D.C.: U.S. International Trade Commission.

Carrillo, J.V. 1989. "Reestructuracion en la Industria Automotriz en Mexico: Politicas de Ajuste e Implicaciones Laborales." Working paper, El Colegio de la Frontera Norte, Tijuana, Mexico.

————. 1990. "Maquilinizacion de la Industria Automotriz en Mexico: De la Industria Terminal a la Industria de Ensamble." In *La Nueva Era de La Industria Automotriz en Mexico*, edited by J. Carrillo. El Colegio de la Frontera Norte, Tijuana, Mexico.

CIEMEX-WEFA. 1992. *Maquiladora Industry Analysis*, Vol. 5, No. 1, January.

Cusumano, M. 1985. *The Japanese Automobile Industry.* Cambridge: Harvard University Press.

DRI/McGraw-Hill. 1992. *Review of the U.S. Economy—Ten Year Projections.* Lexington, Massachusetts.

Echeverri-Carroll, E. 1989. "Maquilas: Economic Impacts and Foreign Investment Opportunities: The Japanese Maquilas, A Special Case." Paper presented at Maquila Seminar, Latin American Study Program, Wilson Center, Washington D.C.

————. 1990. "La Inversion Japonesa en Mexico: Perspec-tivas Industriales y de Comercio." In *Subcontratacion y Empresas Trans-nacionales,* edited by B. Gonzales-Arechiga. Friedrich Ebert Foundation, El Colegio de la Frontera Norte, Tijuana, Mexico.

————. 1992. "La Industria Maquiladora en un Contexto de Libre Comercio y de Cambios Tecnologicos en las Plantas Matrices." *Estudios Sociales* 3: 81–98.

————. 1994. "Flexible Linkages and Offshore Assembly Facilities in Developing Countries." *International Regional Science Review* 17.

Estall, R.C. 1985. "Stock Control in Manufacturing: The Just-in-time System and Its Locational Implications." *Area* 17: 129–133.

Ettlinger, N. 1992. "Modes of Corporate Organization and Geography of Development." *Papers in Regional Science: The Journal of the RSAI* 2: 107–126.

Fernandez-Kelly, P.M. 1987. "Technology and Employment Along the U.S.-Mexican Border." In *The United-States and Mexico Face to Face with New Technology,* edited by Cathryn L. Thorup. Overseas Development Council, New Brunswick.

Fuentes-Flores, N.A. 1989. "Ciclos Economicos Estadounidenses y Actividad Maquiladora." Paper presented at Maquiladora Seminar, El Colegio de Mexico, Mexico, June 5–7.

Glasmeier, A.K. and R.E. McCluskey. 1987. "U.S. Auto Production: An Analysis of the Organization and Location of a Changing Industry." *Economic Geography* 63: 142–159.

Gold, B. 1989. "Computerization in Domestic and International Manufacturing." *Management Review* 31: 129–143.

Gonzales-Arechiga, B. 1988. "Analisis de las Fuentes de Crecimiento y el Cambio en la Composicion Laboral de la Maquiladora." Working paper, Colegio de la Frontera Norte, Tijuana, Mexico.

Gonzales-Arechiga, B. and J.C. Ramirez. 1988. "Productividad sin Distribucion: Cambio Tecnologico en la Maquiladora Electronica." Working paper, Colegio de la Frontera Norte, Tijuana, Mexico.

Gottesman, K. 1991. "JIT Manufacturing Is More Than Inventory Programs and Delivery Schedules." *Industrial Engineering* 23: 19–20, 58.

Gruben, W. 1989. "Do Maquiladoras Take American Jobs?" Federal Reserve Bank, Dallas, Texas.

Grunwald, J. and K. Flamm. 1985. *The Global Factory.* The Brookings Institution, Washington, D.C.

Hansen, N. 1981. "Mexico's Border Industry and the International Division of Labor." *The Annals of Regional Science* 15: 1–12.

Helper, S. 1990. "Comparative Supplier Relations in the U.S. and Japanese Auto Industries: An Exit/Voice Approach." *Business and Economic History* 19: 153–162.

Hinojosa-Ojeda, R. and S. Robinson. 1991. *Altenative Scenarios of a U.S.-Mexico Integration: A Computable General Equilibrium Approach.* Working Paper No. 609. Department of Agriculture and Resource Economics, Division of Agriculture and Natural Resources, University of California.

Hirsch, S. 1967. *Location of Industry and International Competitiveness.* Clarendon Press: Oxford.

Holmes, J. 1986. "Industrial Change in the Canadian Automotive Products Industry, 1973-1984: The Impact of Technical Change in the Organization and Locational Structure of Automobile Production." Working paper, Department of Geography, Queens University, Ontario, Canada.

Hudson, R. and D. Sadler. 1992. "'Just-in-time' Production and the European Automotive Components Industry." *International Journal of Physical Distribution & Logistics Management* 22: 40–45.

Hufbauer, G.C. and J.J. Schott. 1992. *North American Free Trade: Issues and Recommendations.* Institute for International Economics, Washington, D.C.

Ikeda, M. 1987. *Production Network of Big Firms and Smaller Subcontractors in Japan.* Chuo University, Tokyo.

Jones, D.T. and J.P. Womack. 1985. "Developing Countries and the Future of the Automobile Industry." *World Development* 13: 404–405.

Kaplinsky R. and C. Cooper. 1989. *Technology and Development in the Third Industrial Revolution.* Frank Cass, Savage, Maryland.

Kelley, M.R. and H. Brooks. 1991. "External Learning Opportunities and the Diffusion of Process Innovations to Small Firms: The Case of Programmable Automation." *Technology Forecasting and Social Change* 39: 103–125.

Kenney, M. and R. Florida. 1992. "The Japanese Transplants—Production Organization and Regional Development." *Journal of the American Planning Association* 58: 21–38.

————. 1994. "Japanese Maquiladoras: Production Organization and Global Commodity Chains." *World Development* 22: 27–44.

Koido, A. 1991. "The Color Television Industry: Japanese-U.S. Competition and Mexico's Maquiladoras." In *Manufacturing Across Borders and Oceans*, edited by G. Szekely. Center for U.S.-Mexican Studies, University of California, San Diego.

Lim, L. and P.E. Fong. 1991. *Foreign Investment and Industrialization in Malaysia, Singapore, Taiwan, and Thailand.* Development Centre of the Organization for Economic Cooperation and Development, France.

Linge, G.J.R. 1992. "Just-in-Time: More or Less Flexible?" *Economic Geography* 67: 316–332.

Lustig, N. 1992. *Mexico: the Remaking of an Economy.* The Brookings Institution, Washington, D.C.

Mair, A., R. Florida, and M. Kenney. 1988. "The New Geography of Automobile Production: Japanese Transplants in North America." *Economic Geography* 64: 352–373.

Malecki, E. 1991. *Technology and Economic Development.* New York: John Wiley & Sons, Inc., copublished with Longman Scientific & Technical.

Mertens, L. and L. Palomares. 1988. "El Surgimiento de un Nuevo Tipo de Trabajador en al Industria de Alta Tecnologia: El Caso de la Electronica." In *Testimonios de Crisis I*, Siglo XXI, edited by Estela Gutierrez, Mexico.

Milgrom, P. and J. Roberts. 1990. "The Economics of Modern Manufacturing: Technology, Strategy, and Organization." *American Economic Review* 6: 511–528.

Navarrete-Vargas, R. and J. L. Hernandez. 1987. "Determinantes del Crecimiento del Empleo en la Industria Maquiladora de Exportacion en Mexico." In *Maquiladoras,* edited by A. Garcia Espinosa, Universidad Autonoma de Nuevo Leon, Mexico.

Ojeda-Lajud, O. 1992. "NAFTA to End Maquiladora Program." *El Financiero International.* September 7, p. 4.

Piore, M.J. and C.F. Sabel. 1984. *The Second Industrial Divide.* New York: Basic Books.

Sabel, C.F. 1982. *Work and Politics.* Cambridge: Cambridge University Press.

Sanderson, S.W. 1986. "American Industry Can Go Home Again. " *Across the Board* 23: 38–43.

———. 1987. "Automated Manufacturing and Offshore Assembly in Mexico." In *The United-States and Mexico Face to Face with New Technology,* edited by Cathryn L. Thorup. *U.S. Third World Policy Perspectives,* No. 8. Overseas Development Council, New Brunswick.

Sanderson, S.W., G. Williams, T. Ballenger, and B.L. Berry. 1986. "Impacts of Computer-Aided Manufacturing on Offshore Assembly and Future Manufacturing Locations." *Regional Studies* 21: 131–142.

Sayer, A. 1985. *New Developments in Manufacturing and Their Spatial Implications.* Working Paper 49, School of Urban and Regional Studies, University of Sussex, Brighton, England.

Schoenberger, E. 1987. "Technological and Organizational Changes in Automobile Production: Spatial Implications." *Regional Studies* 21: 199–214.

———. 1988. "From Fordism to Flexible Accumulation: Technology, Competitive Strategies, and International Location." *Environmental and Planning D: Society and Space* 6: 245–262.

Scott, A. J. 1987. "The Semiconductor Industry in South-East Asia: Organization, Location and the International Division of Labour." *Regional Studies* 21: 143–160.

Secretaria de Comunicacion y Transporte. 1990. *Programa Nacional de Modernizacion de la Infraestructura de Transporte 1990–1994.* Mexico D.F.

Shaiken, H. 1984. *Work Transformed: Automation and Labor in the Computer Age.* New York: Holt, Rinehart and Winston Press.

Shaiken, H., S. Herzenberg, and S. Kuhn. 1986. "The Work Process Under More Flexible Production." *Industrial Relations* 25:167–183.

Sheard, P. 1983. "Auto Production Systems in Japan: Organizational and Locational Features." *Australian Geographical Studies* 21: 49–68.

Sklair, L. 1989. *Assembling for Development: The Maquila Industry in Mexico and The United States*. Boston: Unwin Hyman Press.

Storper, M. and S. Christopherson. 1987. "Flexible Specialization and Regional Industrial Agglomerations: The Case of the U.S. Motion Picture Industry." *Annals of the Association of American Geographers* 77: 104–117.

Suarez-Villa, L. 1984. "The Manufacturing Process Cycle and the Industrialization of the United States-Mexico Borderlands." *Annals of Regional Science* 28: 1–23.

Suarez-Villa, L., B. Gonzales-Arechiga, and J.C. Ramirez. 1989. *Mexico's Border Electronics Industry: International Competitiveness and Regional Impacts*. Colegio de la Frontera Norte, Tijuana, Mexico.

Taddei-Bringas, C. 1992. "La Inversion Japonesa en el Norte de Mexico. Centro de Investigacion en Alimentacion y Desarrollo, A.C." Working paper, University of Sonora, Mexico.

Turnbull, P., N. Oliver, and B. Wilkinson. 1992. "Buyer-Supplier Relations in the UK Automotive Industry: Strategic Implications of the Japanese Manufacturing Model." *Strategic Managment Journal* 13: 159–168.

Uchitelle, L. 1993. "Northern Mexico Becomes a Big Draw for High-Tech Plants—and U.S. Jobs." *New York Times,* March 21: F1, F14.

United States International Trade Commission. 1988. *Imports Under Items 806.30 and 807.00 of the Tariff Schedules of the United States, 1984-87.* USITC Publication 2144, Washington, D.C.

————. 1991a. *Production Sharing: U.S. Imports Under Harmonized Tariff Schedule Provisions 9802.00.60 and 9802.00.80, 1986–89.* USITC Publication 2349, Washington, D.C.

————. 1991b. *Rules of Origin Issues Related to NAFTA and the North American Automotive Industry.* USITC Publication 2460, Washington, D.C.

————. 1993. *Potential Impact on the U.S. Economy and Selected Industries of the North American Free-Trade Agreement.* USITC Publication 2596, Washington, D.C.

————. 1994. *Production Sharing: U.S. Imports Under Harmonized Tariff Schedule Provisions 9802.00.60 and 9802.00.80, 1989–1992.* USITC Publication 2729, Washington, D.C.

Vernon, R. 1966. "International Investment and International Trade in the Product Cycle." *Quarterly Journal of Economics* 80: 190–207.

Watkins, R. 1994a. "Implications of the North American Free Trade Agreement for Mexico's Maquiladora Industry and the Use of the Production Sharing Tariff Provision." In *Production Sharing: U.S. Imports Under Harmonized Tariff Schedule Provisions 9802.00.60 and 98.00.80, 1989–1992,* U.S. International Trade Commission, Washington, D.C.

————. 1994b. "Nafta and Mexico's Maquiladora Industry." In *Industry Trade and Technology Review,* U.S. International Trade Commission, Washington, D.C.

Wilson, P. 1989. "The New Maquiladoras: Flexible Production in Low Wage Regions." *Community and Regional Planning Working Paper Series No. 9,* University of Texas at Austin.

————. 1992. *Exports and Local Development Mexico's New Maquiladoras.* Austin: University of Texas Press.

Womack, J.P. 1987. "Prospects for the U.S.-Mexican Relationship in the Motor Vehicle Sector." In *The United States and Mexico Face to Face with New Technology,* edited by Cathryn L. Thorup. Overseas Development Council, Washington D.C.

Womack, J., D. Jones, and D. Roos. 1990. *The Machine that Changed the World.* New York: Rawson Associates.

Yuan, J. and L. Eden. 1992. "Export Processing Zones in Asia: A Comparative Study." *Asian Survey* 32: 1026–1045.

Zipkin, P.H. 1991. "Does Manufacturing Need a JIT Revolution?" *Harvard Business Review* 69: 40–46.

Part III

Trade Liberalization in the Americas

7

The Economic Integration of Argentina and Brazil, MERCOSUR, and the Regionalization of the Southern Cone Market

María Beatriz Nofal

Introduction

As of January 1995, MERCOSUR ("Mercado Comun del Sur," or Common Market of the South) is an integrated large regional market formed by Argentina, Brazil, Paraguay, and Uruguay, and an *imperfect customs union.* (The initial objective of forming a common market has been postponed to a later date.) The *customs union* implies the establishment of a trade bloc among the member countries. There is free intraregional trade between partner countries and a unified trade policy vis-à-vis the world or third countries.

In reality, because MERCOSUR will function as an imperfect customs union, the only element of a common trade policy that is in place starting in January 1995 is a common external tariff, which is applied to the majority of goods (except capital goods), some sensitive items, and informatics and telecommunications that will converge to the level of the agreed common external tariff in the years 2001 and 2006. The implication of this common external tariff, with a maximum level of 20 percent, is that it may, in fact, lower protection levels of the two larger economies of the trade bloc: Brazil and Argentina.

Intraregional trade among MERCOSUR partners has been substantially liberalized and, since January 1995, free from any tariff barriers, except in the case of sugar; some national lists of sensitive items, which have another four years for complete tariff elimination; and the automotive industry, which is freed from tariff barriers, but still subject to regulation until 1999, given national automotive regimes.

The expectations for MERCOSUR increased after July 1994 because of the initial success of the stabilization plan, known as the "Plan Real," implemented in Brazil. Brazil is the largest economy in MERCOSUR, and therefore its macroeconomic performance is of utmost importance for the economic evolution of the other MERCOSUR partner countries. After a three-year period of stagnation and high spiralling inflation, the economy of Brazil has experienced since July 1994 a sharp reduction in monthly inflation rates (from 45 and 49 percent in May and June 1994, to 6.4 percent in July and 1.8 percent in October 1994), a strong domestic demand recovery, a significant reduction of fiscal disequilibrium, and a remonetization of the economy.

Based on 1993 data, MERCOSUR countries have a total population of about 200 million inhabitants, a combined GDP (gross domestic product) of U.S.$702 billion, and a total amount of trade with the world (exports plus imports) of U.S.$100 billion. Estimates for 1995 indicate a combined regional GDP of more than U.S.$900 billion. (Brazil projects a GDP of U.S.$610 billion for 1995, taking into account the growth recovery of 1994 and the appreciation of the domestic currency in relation to the dollar.)

In our opinion, the process of regionalization in the Southern Cone region of South America is irreversible. The formation of a large regional market in the context of greater unilateral openness constitutes a strategic option for growth recovery and for strengthening the prospects of economic development. Subregional integration possesses the potential to enhance the competitive advantages of each country, as well as to facilitate integration of the Southern Cone region into the world economy, insofar as regionalism and multilateralism remain the global approach to trade policy.

Also, the process of regionalization in the Southern Cone is of hemispheric interest for the United States, important for the building of a free trade area in the Americas by 2005, and of global interest for both the European Union and for Japan. MERCOSUR will extend geographically throughout South America by the means of signing free trade agreements with other countries in the region or with groups of countries. Chile, Bolivia, and Peru probably will be the first countries to negotiate free trade agreements with MERCOSUR. The final objective is to establish a free trade area in South America ("Asociacion de Libre Comercio de Sudamerica," or ALCSA) by 2005. Additionally, MERCOSUR will be crucial for the achievement of a hemispheric free trade area in the year 2005, as agreed at the "Summit of the Americas" in December 1994. Finally, MERCOSUR and the European Union have already initiated talks to establish a free trade area between these trade blocs (although the process is likely to be slow, and the time horizon is set for around the year 2015).

In this chapter, we analyze the process of regionalization in the Southern Cone, paying special attention to the economic integration of Argentina and Brazil as the founding pillar of MERCOSUR. We examine how the process of integration has worked, what changes and/or adjustments are needed, and what challenges await.

Economic Integration of Argentina and Brazil and MERCOSUR

The process of economic integration between Brazil and Argentina has played a key role in the creation of an integrated regional market in the Southern Cone. Bilateral integration between Argentina and Brazil began in 1986; integration in MERCOSUR (Argentina, Brazil, Paraguay, and Uruguay), in 1991—both have resulted in a significant increase in intraregional trade flows.

For instance, during the period 1985–1994, Argentina's total trade with MERCOSUR grew 610.6 percent, while total trade with the rest of the world, excluding MERCOSUR, grew 147 percent. The expansion of intraregional trade was also facilitated by the unilateral liberalization of the economies of Argentina and Brazil beginning in 1987, with additional reductions in tariff barriers implemented since 1991 (including Uruguay).

In the case of Argentina and Brazil, however, the process of regional integration stimulated the process of unilateral liberalization, rather than vice versa, as is usually suggested in the literature.

The growth trend in intraregional trade remains stable, but there is volatility in the bilateral trade balances of the major partners, Brazil and Argentina. The following section demonstrates that two major determinants of volatility in the intraregional trade balances are macroeconomic divergence (particularly, when instability and recession affects the largest economy, Brazil) and the divergent movements of the exchange rates.

In what follows we analyze the evolution and the determinants of intraregional trade flows, focusing mainly on the bilateral Argentina-Brazil trade inasmuch as it represents about 80 percent of total MERCOSUR trade. (Tables 3, 6, and 7 present intraregional trade figures in MERCOSUR and trade figures of Argentina and Brazil, respectively, with Uruguay and Paraguay.)

The evolution of Argentina-Brazil trade in the post-1986 period developed in two phases. These two phases are divided by distinctive trade agreements, earmarking different stages in the integration process, and by the changes in trade results.

Phase One: Linking Economies
The *first phase* (1986–1990) was defined by the initial efforts of Argentina and Brazil to link their economies. This process was driven by *free trade sectoral agreements* (the Capital Goods and the Food Indus-

try Agreements) and a renegotiated Preferential Trade Agreement Nº 1 (AAP Nº 1)[1] between Argentina and Brazil in the Latin American Association of Integration (LAIA). Both countries agreed to reduce tariffs further on some goods and to eliminate nontariff barriers for all the goods included in the agreement. The Preferential Trade Agreement, in particular, represented an important commitment from Brazil to facilitate market access for Argentine goods. In November 1988, the Integration Treaty was signed.[2] Its aim was to free trade between Brazil and Argentina from all existing tariff and nontariff barriers in a ten-year period, constituting then a free trade area. In 1990, the treaty was substituted for another bilateral agreement to form a common market by the year 1995.

The initial trade liberalization agreements produced three positive economic results for Argentina:

• First, bilateral trade (exports plus imports) doubled from U.S.$1.1 billion in 1985 to U.S.$2.1 billion in 1990 (figure 1 and table 1). This bilateral trade growth was mainly spurred by the increases in Argentine exports. In the 1985–1990 period, the cumulative rate of growth of exports from Argentina to Brazil was 186.6 percent while exports from Brazil to Argentina increased only 17.4 percent (table 1).

• Second, Argentina's bilateral trade composition became more balanced due to the increase in the exports of manufactured goods of industrial origin. While in 1985 only 21 percent of total Argentine exports to Brazil were industrial manufactures, in 1990 these represented 38.7 percent of total exports (table 4). Brazil became the most important foreign market for Argentina not only for exports of industrial manufactures but also for exports of manufactured goods of agricultural origin, particularly nontraditional agricultural exports such as processed and/or canned fruits and vegetables, cheeses, and wines.

• Third, the capital goods sector that opened early to free trade shows an *intra*sectoral pattern of trade specialization. This means that each country specializes in and exports certain types of capital goods. Neither country is the exclusive exporter of the sector's goods at the expense of the other one.[3] Consequently, on the one hand, the adaptation process induced by trade liberalization is less costly than an *inter*sectoral specialization pattern. On the other hand, welfare gains can be obtained through a decrease in costs due to economies of scale and specialization and to an increase in the variety of goods available.

The relation between rates of exchange explains part of the favorable trade results for Argentina during the 1986–1990 period. An analysis of the real exchange rate evolution of each country, relative to the U.S. dollar and the evolution of the austral-cruzeiro exchange parity, indicates that from 1986–1988 there was a somewhat stable relation among the currencies (figures 2 and 3). In 1989, the Argentine currency became relatively more undervalued in relation to the U.S. dollar than did the Brazilian currency. In 1990, the Argentine currency experienced a revaluation relative to the dollar, and, although still advantageous (figures 2 and 3), the parity relation with the Brazilian cruzeiro deteriorated (by 24.5 percent if deflated by the consumer price index and by 1.1 percent if deflated by the wholesale price index) (figure 4).

In fact, the relation between rates of exchange explains only one part of the Argentina-Brazil trade results during the 1986–1990 period. The positive change in trade results and relations for Argentina has to be attributed mainly to the integration efforts that began in 1986, which opened the Brazilian market to Argentine exports (Brazil's market was almost closed before 1986).

Phase Two: Creation of MERCOSUR and Transition to a Customs Union

The *second phase* (1991–1994) in the Southern Cone regionalization process began with the announcement of a new *common market* program between Argentina and Brazil and, accordingly, the implementation of an automatic progressive tariff reduction schedule on intraregional trade (LAIA Agreement AAP-CE[4] Nº 14, November 1990) to phase out tariffs by December 1994. In March 1991, the "Treaty of Asunción" was signed, forming a common market, MERCOSUR, among Argentina, Brazil, Uruguay, and Paraguay. With the implementation of the treaty (LAIA Agreement AAP-CE Nº 18, November 1991) in December 1991, Uruguay and Paraguay also began to apply the intraregional progressive tariff reduction schedule. Regarding the industrial sector, the Automotive Free Trade Agreement, signed in 1988 and implemented in 1991, was another important step in the economic integration of the Southern Cone.

In fact, by January 1995, after completing a transition period of four years, MERCOSUR became a *customs union*, although in an imperfect fashion. This means that partner countries have almost completely liberalized intraregional trade at the same time as a new common external tariff was implemented. The customs union is imperfect because, on the one hand, there is a reduced list of goods excepted from the common external tariff and, on the other hand, progress still needs to be made to formulate a common trade policy, both regarding exports and protection from unfair import competition. The objective of creating a common market was postponed, given both the difficulties encountered and the necessity to advance further in the coordination and harmonization of economic policies.

During this second phase, Argentina's trade flows with Brazil and other MERCOSUR countries underwent the following changes:

• First, bilateral trade between Argentina and Brazil increased 253 percent, from U.S. $2.1 billion in 1990 to an estimated U.S. $7.5 billion in 1994. The average annual bilateral trade growth rate was 38 percent during the 1990–94 period, which was significantly higher than the 11.7 percent average annual growth rate of the 1985–90 period (figure 1 and table 1).

• Second, contrary to Argentina's experience in the first phase, growth in bilateral trade was prompted mainly by the increase in Brazil's exports to Argentina, while exports from Argentina to Brazil grew at a slower pace. While the volume of Brazilian exports to Argentina grew at an annual average rate of 64.3 percent from 1991 to 1994, Argentine exports to Brazil grew at an annual average rate of 25.7 percent (table 1).

• Third, the unbalanced growth of trade flows led to a large Argentine trade deficit with Brazil in 1992 of U.S.$1.7 billion. That was reduced by half to U.S.$755.6 million in 1993 and increased again slightly to an estimate of U.S.$900 million in 1994 (table 1).

• Fourth, in terms of trade composition, there was a decrease in high value-added exports from Argentina to Brazil. This affected the exports of both manufactures of industrial origin (except motor vehicles and parts and components) and manufactures of agricultural origin (particularly nontraditional exports, such as processed and canned fruits and vegetables) (table 4). At the same time, there was an increase in Brazilian exports to Argentina of high value-added products: capital goods, consumer goods, and motor vehicles (table 5). Thus reappeared the traditional problem of a qualitative imbalance in the bilateral trade with Brazil—a problem that had been substantially overcome during the 1986–1990 period.

• Fifth, Argentina's total trade (exports and imports) with all other MERCOSUR members exhibited strong growth between 1991 and 1994 (tables 2 and 6). This growth, however, resulted from the large increase in Argentine imports from these countries. In fact, intra-regional trade growth in MERCOSUR, during the transition period, was mainly fueled by the expansion of Argentina's import demand. Argentine imports from MERCOSUR grew 381.5 percent in 1993 compared to 1990, while Brazilian imports from MERCOSUR only grew 4.4 percent in the same period. Consequently, Argentina's relative share in total imports from MERCOSUR increased from 21.4 percent in 1990 to 45.6 in 1993, while Brazil's relative share went down from 56.6 percent in 1990 to 36 percent in 1993 (table 3).

The unbalanced growth for Argentina in trade with Brazil in the 1991–mid-1994 period can be attributed to two main factors. One is the divergent macroeconomic evolution in both countries: economic recession, high inflation, and high real interest rates in Brazil; demand recovery, moderately low inflation, and lower real interest rates in Argentina. The other is the divergent movements in the exchange rates: the real devaluation of the cruzeiro and real appreciation of the peso in this period (figures 2, 3, 4). Both factors help explain, on the one hand, the slow growth of the Brazilian market for Argentine exports. Demand for these exports decreased given the domestic recession and high inflation, as did the competitiveness of Argentine exports due to the real appreciation of the peso. They also explain the large increase in Brazilian exports to Argentina. The economic recovery in Argentina created a demand "pull" effect; the recession in Brazil, a "push" effect. Also, the peso/cruzeiro parity (figure 4) was favorable to Argentine imports from Brazil.

Although in the first phase of the integration process, the relation between real exchange rates movement, or the exchange parity relation between both currencies, was but one factor influencing trade results. In the next phase, the exchange rate became a more important causal factor, given the speed with which intraregional trade was liberalized. The initial minimum tariff reduction was 47 percent in the second semester of 1991, followed every six months by another cumulative 7 percent reduction, reaching 100 percent tariff reduction by December 1994.

As previously stated, these changes in trade results are associated, in part, with changes in the relationship between the Argentine and Brazilian exchange rates. For instance, in the period from March 1991[5] to December 1992[6] the peso-cruzeiro exchange rate parity deteriorated 33.6 percent (figure 4). This was the result of two divergent moves on the value of the respective currencies. On the one hand, the Brazilian currency was undervalued with respect to the U.S. dollar (i.e., in the period from March 1991 to December 1992 the rate of devaluation of the cruzeiro, 4,702.7 percent, was higher than the rate of consumer price inflation, 3,903.7 percent in Brazil). On the other hand, the Argentine peso appreciated relative to the U.S. dollar (i.e., from March 1991 to December 1992 the peso/dollar rate remained fixed while there was a moderate rate of domestic consumer price inflation of 42.4 percent) (figures 2 and 3). During this period, the peso appreciation relative to the U.S. dollar was 11 percent, measured by the combined consumer price/wholesale index, or 23 percent, measured by the consumer price index. Later, in the period January 1993–June 1994, the divergence in the movements of the value of respective currencies started to narrow, and exchange rates followed a parallel path. As a result of a slight appreciation of the Brazilian currency and of a smaller appreciation of the Argentine currency (than that experienced in the previous period), the exchange parity relation of the Argentine peso improved 8.3 percent from January 1993–June 1994, although in June 1994 the peso/cruzeiro exchange rate parity showed a 26 percent deterioration with regard to March 1991 (figure 4).

After the implementation of the "Real Plan" in Brazil, in July 1994, the movement of the value of the respective currencies increasingly converged, mainly because the new Brazilian currency, the real, appreciated with regard to the dollar. Consequently, the exchange parity relation of the peso/real by December 1994 improved, reaching a level slightly above that of March 1991 (the improvement was about 2.9 percent when deflated by the consumer price index and 13.3 percent when deflated by the wholesale price index) (figure 4).

Clearly, Brazil's lackluster macroeconomic performance in the period 1991 to mid-1994 cannot be the only cause of trade imbalances. The 311.7 percent increase in total Argentine imports in 1993 compared to 1990—with increases in imports from the United States and Chile of 347.8 percent and 530 percent respectively in this period—show that demand recovery in Argentina and relative prices, as determined by the exchange rate, are also influencing trade results (table 6). But an economic recovery in Brazil can produce striking results in terms of the rebalancing of trade flows and the improvement of Argentine export performance. This was shown in the second half of 1994 by the increase in Argentina's exports to Brazil following Brazil's expansion of domestic and import demand after the implementation of the "Real Plan."

Finally, the unbalanced growth of trade between Argentina and Brazil could also be influenced by the slow progress in policy coordination and harmonization relative to the fast pace of intraregional and bilateral trade liberalization as prescribed by the automatic tariff phase-out mechanism. The slow progress in the reduction of "asymmetries" in competitive conditions, due to the differences in national economic policies, worked to the disadvantage of firms in Argentina, as did the fact that external regulatory factors, not controlled by the firms, resulted in production costs that were higher than those in Brazil. In Argentina, these external factors included higher taxes on labor (later reduced in 1994); a greater cumulative tax burden resulting, in part, from specific taxes on electrical energy, gas and fuels;[7] and less government assistance (on exports and investment).

MERCOSUR: Challenges and Prospects

The governments involved in the integration of the Southern Cone face important challenges of economic policy coordination and harmonization. These challenges must be met in order to promote competitive conditions that will allow for fairness in the distribution of costs and benefits among the parties. If the distribution of costs and benefits is perceived as unfair by any of the partners, there will either be a reluctance to participate or a credibility loss that will affect participation in the integration efforts.

As of January 1995, MERCOSUR functions as an *imperfect customs union*—not as a common market as was proposed by the Treaty of Asunción—and this makes imperative advancement in macroeconomic coordination and the harmonization of other economic policies.

It is important to make clear that, in our opinion, a *free trade area* (FTA) is a better option at present for Southern Cone countries than a *customs union* (CU) or a *common market* (CM).[8] These three alternative forms of regional integration allow free trade of goods and services between member countries (discriminating geographically against countries outside the region). But one key difference between a FTA and a CU or a CM is that the FTA allows for free intraregional trade, but leaves each country with the freedom to formulate its own trade policy, while the CU and CM options require a unified trade policy vis-à-vis the world and a joint negotiation of any changes on that policy. One other key difference is that the CM option also entails free movement of production, labor, and capital, in addition to the free trade of goods and services. Insofar as regional integration advances from the form of an FTA to that of a CU and that of a CM, it increases the necessary degree of coordination and harmonization of economic policies at the same time as it lowers the degree of individual freedom of each country in the formulation of economic policies.

Consequently, a FTA is a better option for the following main reasons:

• First, the Southern Cone countries are in different stages of stabilization and economic reforms (e.g., deregulation, privatization, trade and investment liberalization). For example, Argentina is far more advanced than Brazil in market-oriented reforms. The different degrees of advancement in stabilization and economic reforms complicate the process of policy harmonization, particularly in issues that are central to a customs union and a common market, such as compatible competition policies and subsidies restraint.

•Second, Chile, another possible partner in Southern Cone regionalization, formally declined a full partnership in the present customs union option basically because the announced MERCOSUR common tariff will have a maximum level of 20 percent.[9] Chile's uniform tariff is 11 per cent. Consequently, if, after joining MERCOSUR, Chile must raise external tariffs, the costs of trade diversion (displacement of low cost imports from outside the common market to less efficient sources of supply within the common market) will outweigh the beneficial effects of trade creation (replacement of inefficient domestic production by low cost imports). For this main reason, Chile now seeks access to MERCOSUR, but through signing a free trade area agreement. There is, however, an inconsistency here: while the smaller economies in MERCOSUR will have to pay trade deviation costs to have access to Brazil's large domestic market and to conform to a wider regional market, other competing countries in the region, like Chile, by striking an FTA, will benefit from free market access without having to pay trade deviation costs.

• Finally, a free trade area in the Southern Cone would reduce the degree of exclusivity of MERCOSUR (inasmuch as countries do not have to sign a common trade policy) and, thus, speed progress toward a Western Hemisphere Free Trade Area (WHFTA)—as envisioned at the Summit of the Americas—and the linking of subregional integration efforts, such as NAFTA and MERCOSUR.

Under the customs union option, the top priorities in the MERCOSUR negotiating agenda for policy coordination and harmonization in 1995 should be:

• First, to advance in the coordination of macroeconomic and exchange rate policies step-by-step, adopting commitments on fiscal and monetary discipline. Mutually agreed-upon, compulsory targets for fiscal and monetary equilibrium are required to assure the region's success in increasing macroeconomic convergence and attaining sustained stability and growth.

• Second, to adopt compatible competition policies and subsidies restraint. At the minimum, countries must avoid implementation of new subsidies that distort competition. Also, an evaluation of the existing subsidies at the country level is required to determine which are compatible with the customs union and which are not compatible and should be phased-out. Additionally, common criteria should be formulated for any future regional incentive schemes (e.g., investment- or technology- related incentives).

• Third, to incorporate the basic national obligation of national treatment of the GATT into MERCOSUR so as to avoid discrimination once goods are imported into any member country. Such an obligation is absent in the Treaty of Asunción, although it should be an essential part of any trade agreement that eliminates tariff and nontariff barriers because it prevents their replacement by domestic measures favoring national goods over imports.

• Fourth, to advance in the harmonization of export policy and import policy so as to perfect the customs union in MERCOSUR.

• Fifth, to prevent the use of standards-related measures as obstacles to trade and to promote compatibility, either through harmonization or through mutual recognition of national standards (when based on international standards).

• Sixth, to facilitate open access in the markets of public procurement and services of all the member countries. Establishing the principle of reciprocity in market access in the negotiations may be a useful mechanism to promote openness.

• Seventh, to formulate a social agenda to assist restructuring and adjustment efforts, particularly with regard to the labor market and to the less developed regional economies. Probably, external and catalytic financing, as in the Multilateral Investment Fund (MIF), will be needed to support pro-market policy reforms, adjustment in the labor market, and the adaptation of small and medium enterprises to free intraregional trade. Also, as a counterpart to the provision of external financing, new multilateral rules for adjustment measures could be developed.

The difficulties in the coordination and harmonization of economic policies, added to the persisting "asymmetries" in policies (particularly, those related to tax policy, export and investment incentives, industrial and regional policies, product standards) can entail a delay in the medium term in the perfection of the *customs union* or in the construction of the *common market*. The MERCOSUR governments, however, have not yet made a decision regarding the new time frame for completing the customs union and then forming the common market.

Nevertheless, the risk of reversal of the present regionalization process in MERCOSUR is extremely low. The difficulties that may be encountered will not result in a return to the closed border situation, although they may slow down the deepening and broadening of MERCOSUR.

Notwithstanding, it is imperative in the context of the MERCOSUR *customs union* to make effective progress in macroeconomic and exchange rate coordination, on the one hand, and in the harmonization of policies that affect the conditions of competition to eliminate asymmetries and build more transparent open markets, on the other. This is in order to promote an equitable distribution of the gains from free intraregional trade and a sustainable development process for all the member countries.

Given the differences in size and levels of industrial development in MERCOSUR, it is only in the context of macroeconomic convergence—with sustainable stability and growth in the member countries, including Brazil's economy—that a balanced pattern of specialization (intrasectoral and sectoral) and complementation will develop as flows of productive investment and technology modernization will be encouraged. Such an environment will enhance productivity gains—based on economies of scale, specialization, and technological modernization—improvements in competitiveness, and real income gains.

MERCOSUR and NAFTA

Do MERCOSUR and NAFTA represent divergent or convergent

roads on the way to Western Hemisphere free trade? Does accession to NAFTA and the linkage of subregional integration agreements constitute alternative or complementary means to a Western Hemisphere Free Trade Agreement? In our opinion, MERCOSUR and NAFTA are complementary efforts. MERCOSUR has so far contributed to the process of multilateral trade liberalization and market-oriented policy reforms.

MERCOSUR and the initial bilateral trade agreements between Argentina and Brazil have had a strong, liberalizing effect on the Brazilian economy, making it less inward-looking. This is a result of intraregional trade liberalization, which, on the one hand, facilitated the process of unilateral reduction of both tariff and nontariff barriers by Brazil and, on the other hand, set some limits to the new implementation of subsidies that will overtly distort competition and trade (both regionally and globally).

Consequently, NAFTA and MERCOSUR offer parallel paths to a WHFTA. Insofar as subregional integration deepens and remains outward-oriented and consistent with multilateral trade liberalization, an interdependency of liberalization efforts will likely occur between subregional groupings. It is rather unlikely that a WHFTA will be achieved solely by extending the NAFTA model. This does not seem to be the efficient way to incorporate Brazil and to promote that country's progress toward domestic liberalization and unilateral reduction of trade barriers. And, without Brazil, the largest market in South America, there cannot be a WHFTA.

In fact, the differences between NAFTA and MERCOSUR transition schemes with regard to trade liberalization schedules and trade rules were not that substantial, as noted below:

• NAFTA's trade liberalization schedule—implemented since 1994—phases outs tariffs in stages over a period of up to ten years for most goods; up to fifteen years for sensitive items. In MERCOSUR, an automatic progressive tariff reduction schedule phased out tariffs over a period from 1991 until December 1994. Tariff reductions were across-the-board, and there was a list of goods excepted, which, in the case of Brazil and Argentina, were reduced by 20 percent annually to disappear by December 1994. (Paraguay and Uruguay have to eliminate the list of goods excepted by the end of 1995.) Presently, in MERCOSUR's customs union another four years were granted to all member countries to eliminate existing tariffs on the remaining list of goods excepted.

The time span (up to fifteen years) of the NAFTA phase-outs

seems more reasonable than the short initial schedule set for MERCOSUR trade liberalization. On the one hand, the MERCOSUR across-the-board, progressive tariff reduction schedule was simpler to negotiate and implement than the phase-out approach of NAFTA. On the other hand, the NAFTA example may provide a schedule of trade liberalization more tailor-made for the requirements of each country and, thus, may constitute a better political alternative for governments.

• Rules of origin, so far, were and are less restrictive in MERCOSUR than in NAFTA. Now, in MERCOSUR's customs union, rules of origin are only applied to those goods excepted from the common external tariff.

• NAFTA bilateral safeguards are tariff-based and can be extended up to four years. MERCOSUR safeguards in the transition period were quota-based and could be extended up to two years. At present, in MERCOSUR's custom union, no safeguard mechanisms have been formulated.

• Dispute settlement procedures are better spelled out in NAFTA.

Of course, NAFTA's liberalization efforts go beyond the elimination of tariff and nontariff barriers and include elimination of investment barriers, as well as provisions on service trade (including land transport specialty air services), financial services, and intellectual property. It also includes environmental provisions. With the exception of land transport, none of these issues have yet been addressed in MERCOSUR.

At the same time, the intention of MERCOSUR is the creation of a common market. In contrast, the goal of NAFTA is a comprehensive free trade area. However, so far, MERCOSUR progress toward the common market objective has led to the formation of a customs union. The common external tariff is therefore, at present, the main difference between MERCOSUR and NAFTA liberalization efforts, insofar as forms of integration are concerned. This instrument cannot present an obstacle for future negotiations of a free trade area agreement between MERCOSUR and NAFTA. What is clear, however, is that because MERCOSUR became a customs union as of January 1995, none of the individual countries could, in principle, seek individual access to NAFTA.

Conclusion: Trade Liberalization in the Americas

More discussion is needed to find compatibilities and points of linkage among existing subregional integration efforts and to anticipate and solve problems. This is the logical next step in promoting hemispheric trade liberalization.

An extension of the NAFTA dispute settlement procedures to be granted by the United States to the other countries in the region could be an effective second step.

The success of trade liberalization and market-oriented policy reforms in Latin America requires wider and more predictable access to U.S. markets and those of other industrial countries (e.g., Japan and the European Union) through multilateral and regional frameworks.

At the same time, the progress of outward-oriented regionalization in the Southern Cone of the Americas will enhance the advancement of economic integration and free trade. The success of MERCOSUR will serve both to broaden the regionalization process, incorporating other countries in the region (Chile) and converging with other subregional trade arrangements in the Western Hemisphere (such as the Andean Pact and NAFTA), and to strengthen the possibilities for establishing in the near future the "Free Trade Area of the Americas," as agreed upon at the December 1994 Summit of the Americas. Similarly, the success of MERCOSUR will encourage cooperation with other regions to build more open and integrated markets (such as the European Union and Asean Pacific Region).

In the particular case of MERCOSUR-NAFTA, the time factor will favor complementarity between both integration efforts and bringing the agreements together. In 1995, MERCOSUR almost completed the process of intraregional trade liberalization with the elimination of barriers to trade, while the NAFTA transition period started in 1994 and requires another nine to fourteen years for the complete phaseout of trade barriers. Therefore, it is very likely that in MERCOSUR integration will deepen and intraregional trade liberalization will be completed before effective negotiations are entertained to access NAFTA.

In light of the preceding, it can be safely concluded that the progress already realized in intraregional trade liberalization in MERCOSUR will only strengthen the prospects of free trade and integration in the hemisphere and thereby contribute to raising the standards of living in the region. From this standpoint, MERCOSUR is a building block, and not a stepping stone, for the integration of the Americas.

Table 1
Bilateral Trade, Argentina-Brazil, 1980–1994

	Argentina's exports to Brazil		Argentina's imports from Brazil		Total bilateral trade		Bilateral trade balance
	millions of U.S.$	percentage change	millions of U.S.$	percentage change	millions of U.S.$	percentage change	
1980	765.0	—	1,072.3	—	1,837.3	—	-307.3
1981	595.1	-22.2	893.3	-16.7	1,488.4	-19.0	-298.2
1982	567.7	-4.6	687.7	-23.0	1,255.4	-15.7	-120.0
1983	358.3	-36.9	666.8	-3.0	1,025.1	-18.3	-308.5
1984	478.2	33.5	831.2	24.7	1,309.4	27.7	-353.0
1985	496.3	3.8	611.5	-26.4	1,107.8	-15.4	-115.2
1986	698.1	40.7	691.3	13.0	1,389.4	25.4	6.8
1987	539.3	-22.7	819.2	18.5	1,358.5	-2.2	-279.9
1988	607.9	12.7	971.4	18.6	1,579.3	16.3	-363.5
1989	1,124.1	84.9	721.4	-25.7	1,845.4	16.8	402.6
1990	1,422.5	26.6	717.9	-0.5	2,140.4	16.0	704.6
1991	1,488.6	4.6	1,526.3	112.6	3,014.9	40.9	-37.7
1992	1,617.4	12.3	3,338.8	118.8	5,010.2	66.2	-1,667.4
1993	2,814.3	68.4	3,569.9	6.9	6,384.2	27.4	-755.6
1994	3,312.7	17.7	4,249.5	19.0	7,562.2	18.5	-936.8
1985/90	186.6%		17.4%		93.2%		
1990/94	132.9%		491.9%		253.3%		

FOB = free on board.
Source: Based on INDEC (Argentina). Note: Trade figures differ according to whether they are based on Argentine statistics (INDEC) or Brazilian statistics (DTIC).

Table 2
Argentina-MERCOSUR Trade, 1980–1994
(FOB values)

	Argentina's exports to MERCOSUR		Argentina's imports from MERCOSUR		Argentina/MERCOSUR total trade		Argentina/ MERCOSUR trade balance
	millions of U.S.$	percentage change	millions of U.S.$	percentage change	millions of U.S.$	percentage change	
1980	1,136.7	—	1,304.7	—	2,441.4	—	-168.0
1981	892.4	-21.5	1,105.9	-15.2	1,998.3	-18.1	-213.5
1982	828.3	-7.2	827.0	-25.2	1,655.3	-17.2	1.3
1983	522.4	-36.9	794.5	-3.9	1,316.9	-20.4	-272.1
1984	655.5	25.5	979.7	23.3	1,635.2	24.2	-324.2
1985	667.5	1.8	697.6	-28.8	1,365.1	-16.5	-30.1
1986	894.8	34.1	831.7	19.2	1,726.5	26.5	63.1
1987	768.6	-14.1	1,003.3	20.6	1,771.9	2.6	-234.7
1988	875.3	13.9	1,169.9	16.6	2,045.2	15.4	-294.6
1989	1,428.1	63.2	869.0	-25.7	2,297.1	12.3	559.0
1990	1,832.5	28.3	875.2	0.7	2,707.7	17.9	957.3
1991	1,977.4	7.9	1,804.2	106.1	3,781.6	39.7	173.2
1992	2,327.1	17.7	3,754.9	108.1	6,082.0	60.8	-1,427.8
1993	3,684.3	58.3	4,213.6	12.2	7,897.9	29.9	-529.3
1994	4,391.4	19.2	5,097.5	21.0	9,488.9	20.1	-706.1
1985/90	174.5%		25.5%		98.4%		
1990/94	139.6%		482.4%		250.4%		

FOB=free on board.
Source: ECO-AXIS S.A., based on INDEC (Argentina).

Table 3
Intraregional and Total Exports and Imports
of MERCOSUR Countries
(millions of U.S. dollars and percentages)

1990	1991	1992	1993		1990	1991	1992	1993
Exports to				**Argentina**	**Imports from**			
1,832.5	1,977.4	2,327.1	3,684.3	MERCOSUR	875.2	1,804.2	3,754.9	4,213.6
12,352.6	11,977.7	12,235.0	13,117.6	Total	4,077.4	8,275.5	14,871.7	16,783.4
14.8%	16.5%	19.0%	28.1%	MERCOSUR/total	21.5%	21.8%	25.2%	25.1%
Exports to				**Brazil**	**Imports from**			
1,320.2	2,309.4	4,097.5	5,394.3	MERCOSUR	2,319.6	2,268.4	2,249.6	3,334.0
31,413.8	31,620.5	35,862.0	38,610.0	Total	20,661.0	21,041.0	20,554.0	25,655.0
4.2%	7.3%	11.4%	14.0%	MERCOSUR/total	11.2%	10.8%	10.9%	13.0%
Exports to				**Paraguay**	**Imports from**			
379.3	259.5	246.4	287.3	MERCOSUR	367.3	396.9	475.0	570.7
958.7	737.1	656.6	725.2	Total	1,352.0	1,460.3	1,421.8	1,688.8
39.6%	35.2%	37.5%	39.6%	MERCOSUR/total	27.2%	27.2%	33.4%	33.8%
Exports to				**Uruguay**	**Imports from**			
590.8	551.5	622.0	698.8	MERCOSUR	535.2	662.6	882.5	1,125.1
1,692.9	1,604.7	1,702.5	1,645.3	Total	1,342.9	1,636.4	2,045.1	2,324.4
34.9%	34.4%	36.5%	42.5%	MERCOSUR/total	39.9%	40.5%	43.2%	48.4%
Exports to				**MERCOSUR**	**Imports from**			
4,122.9	5,097.7	7,293.0	10,064.6	MERCOSUR	4,097.3	5,132.1	7,362.0	9,243.4
46,417.9	45,940.0	50,456.1	54,098.1	Total	27,443.3	32,413.2	38,892.6	46,451.6
8.9%	11.1%	14.5%	18.6%	MERCOSUR/total	14.9%	15.8%	18.9%	19.9%

Sources: ECO-AXIS S.A., based on INDEC (Argentina) and Central Banks of Brazil, Paraguay, and Uruguay.

Table 4
Composition of Argentine Exports to Brazil

	1985	1986	1987	1988	1989	1990	1991	1992	1993	Jan-Sep 94
					Millions of U.S. dollars					
Primary products	178.7	317.4	218.1	210.4	346.8	560.0	592.0	711.2	865.5	733.5
Manufactures of agricultural origin	148.7	206.7	113.1	93.7	259.3	306.2	335.0	242.3	343.3	311.9
Industrial manufactures	104.1	150.3	207.8	299.3	498.7	550.2	533.1	596.4	1,088.2	860.1
Fuels & energy	64.5	23.4	0.1	4.1	18.5	5.7	28.4	121.5	493.7	422.9
Total exports	496.3	698.1	539.3	607.9	1,124.4	1,422.7	1,488.5	1,671.4	2,790.7	2,328.4
					Percentages					
Primary products	36.0	45.5	40.4	34.6	30.8	39.4	39.8	42.6	31.0	31.5
Manufactures of agricultural origin	30.0	29.6	21.0	15.4	23.1	21.5	22.5	14.5	12.3	13.4
Industrial manufactures	21.0	21.5	38.5	49.2	44.4	38.7	35.8	35.7	39.0	36.9
Fuels & energy	13.0	3.3	0.0	0.7	1.6	0.4	1.9	7.3	17.7	18.2
Total exports	100.0	100.0	100.0	100.0	100.0	100.0	100.0	100.0	100.0	100.0

		Growth rates in percentages							
	85/86	86/87	87/88	88/89	89/90	90/91	91/92	92/93	Jan-Sep 93/94
Primary products	77.6	-31.3	-3.6	64.9	61.5	5.7	20.1	21.7	-0.4
Manufactures of agricultural origin	39.0	-45.3	-17.2	176.8	18.1	9.4	-27.7	41.7	21.4
Industrial manufactures	44.4	38.2	44.0	66.6	10.3	-3.1	11.9	82.5	9.6
Fuels & energy	-63.7	-99.6	4,731.8	349.7	-69.1	397.0	327.0	306.3	41.3
Total exports	40.7	-22.7	12.7	85.0	26.5	4.6	12.3	67.0	12.1

Source: ECO-AXIS S.A., based on INDEC (Argentina).

Table 5
Composition of Argentine Imports from Brazil

	1990	1991	1992	1993	Jan-Sep 1994
	Millions of U.S. dollars				
Capital goods	64.1	167.4	414.4	472.8	547.2
Intermediate goods	474.7	801.1	1,333.9	1,346.1	1,257.6
Fuels	0.6	5.1	23.4	89.4	76.2
Parts of capital goods	129.9	291.4	721.9	874.7	725.4
Consumer goods	41.2	171.9	480.0	567.4	453.4
Motor vehicles*	0.1	87.3	360.7	214.0	125.5
Others	7.3	2.4	4.4	5.5	2.5
Total imports	717.9	1,526.6	3,338.7	3,569.9	3,187.8
	Percentages				
Capital goods	8.9	11.0	12.4	13.2	17.2
Intermediate goods	66.1	52.5	40.0	37.7	39.5
Fuels	0.1	0.3	0.7	2.5	2.4
Parts of capital goods	18.1	19.1	21.6	24.5	22.8
Consumer goods	5.7	11.3	14.4	15.9	14.2
Motor vehicles*	0.0	5.7	10.8	6.0	3.9
Others	1.0	0.2	0.1	0.2	0.1
Total imports	100.0	100.0	100.0	100.0	100.0
		Growth rates in percentages			
		1990/91	1991/92	1992/93	Jan-Sep 93/94
Capital goods		161.2	147.6	14.1	87.5
Intermediate goods		68.8	66.5	0.9	29.2
Fuels		750.0	358.8	282.1	-8.3
Parts of capital goods		124.3	147.7	21.2	14.7
Consumer goods		317.2	179.2	18.2	15.9
Motor vehicles*		87,200.0	313.2	-40.7	-30.6
Others		-67.1	83.3	25.0	-44.4
Total imports		112.6	118.7	6.9	24.6

*Fully assembled cars only. Argentine imports of motor vehicles and parts from Brazil in 1992 were more than U.S.$880 million.
Source: ECO-AXIS S.A., based on INDEC (Argentina).

Table 6
Argentina Exports and Imports, 1988–1994

	Exports (millions of U.S. dollars)							Export destinations, relative shares (percentages)			
	Brazil	Paraguay	Uruguay	MERCOSUR	Chile	LAIA*	U.S.	Total	Brazil / total	MERCOSUR / total	LAIA / total	U.S. /total
1988	607.9	79.9	187.4	875.3	259.3	1,760.6	1,185.5	9,134.8	6.7	9.6	19.3	13.0
1989	1,124.4	96.3	207.7	1,428.4	350.3	2,388.0	1,151.8	9,579.3	11.7	14.9	24.9	12.0
1990	1,422.7	147.4	262.6	1,832.6	462.3	3,128.1	1,665.2	12,352.5	11.5	14.8	25.3	13.5
1991	1,488.5	178.0	311.0	1,977.5	487.7	3,368.7	1,210.1	11,977.8	12.4	16.5	28.1	10.1
1992	1,671.3	271.9	383.6	2,326.8	580.9	3,917.6	1,349.4	12,234.9	13.7	19.0	32.0	11.0
1993	2,790.5	357.8	512.7	3,661.0	590.8	5,262.4	1,273.4	13,090.4	21.3	28.0	40.2	9.7
J-S 94**	2,328.4	325.6	460.7	3,114.7	674.4	4,692.8	1,307.9	11,546.0	20.2	27.0	40.6	11.3

	Imports (millions of U.S. dollars)							Import origin, relative shares (percentages)			
	Brazil	Paraguay	Uruguay	MERCOSUR	Chile	LAIA*	U.S.	Total	Brazil / total	MERCOSUR / total	LAIA / total	U.S. /total
1988	971.4	67.6	130.9	1,169.9	146.8	1,774.5	908.2	5,321.6	18.3	22.0	33.3	17.1
1989	721.4	48.8	98.9	869.1	111.3	1,389.2	880.2	4,203.2	17.2	20.7	33.1	20.9
1990	717.9	41.6	116.1	875.6	111.9	1,403.3	861.6	4,076.7	17.6	21.5	34.4	21.1
1991	1,526.3	42.8	235.2	1,804.3	381.4	2,748.4	1,845.2	8,275.5	18.4	21.8	33.2	22.3
1992	3,338.8	64.7	351.2	3,754.7	645.8	4,981.3	3,226.3	14,871.8	22.5	25.2	33.5	21.7
1993	3,569.9	72.9	570.8	4,213.6	706.0	5,434.2	3,858.6	16,786.0	21.3	25.1	32.4	23.0
J-S 94**	3,188.0	47.9	562.2	3,798.1	605.5	4,856.0	3,652.2	15,870.5	20.1	23.9	30.6	23.0

* Latin American Association of Integration.
** January-September.
Source: Based on DTIC (Brazil) and NTDB (United States).

Table 7
Brazilian Exports and Imports, 1988–1994

	Exports (millions of U.S. dollars)							Export destinations, relative shares (percentages)			
	Argentina	Paraguay	Uruguay	MERCOSUR	Chile	LAIA*	U.S.	Total	Argentina / total	MERCOSUR / total	LAIA / total	U.S. /total
1988	976.5	340.8	321.2	1,638.5	—	—	—	33,789.0	2.9	4.8	—	—
1989	725.0	321.0	333.6	1,379.6	694.4	3,487.9	—	34,383.0	2.1	4.0	10.1	—
1990	645.2	380.5	294.6	1,320.3	483.7	3,193.7	7,762.1	31,414.0	2.1	4.2	10.2	24.7
1991	1,476.2	496.1	337.1	2,309.4	677.3	4,938.7	6,760.5	31,620.0	4.7	7.3	15.6	21.4
1992	3,039.8	543.3	514.2	4,097.3	922.6	7,591.9	7,058.6	35,861.5	8.5	11.4	21.2	19.7
1993	3,661.5	960.6	774.8	5,396.9	1,110.4	9,144.0	8,023.8	38,782.7	9.4	13.9	23.6	20.7
J-S 94**	1,907.2	472.3	345.5	2,725.0	455.4	4,506.9	4,145.2	20,123.7	9.5	13.5	22.4	20.6

	Imports (millions of U.S. dollars)							Import origin, relative shares (percentages)			
	Argentina	Paraguay	Uruguay	MERCOSUR	Chile	LAIA*	U.S.	Total	Argentina / total	MERCOSUR / total	LAIA / total	U.S. /total
1988	706.0	117.4	313.9	1,137.3	—	—	—	14,605.0	4.8	7.8	—	—
1989	1,248.0	358.8	596.1	2,202.9	515.1	3,391.8	—	18,263.0	6.8	12.1	18.6	—
1990	1,412.4	329.7	584.6	2,326.8	485.4	3,805.9	4,876.5	20,661.0	6.8	11.3	18.4	23.6
1991	1,614.7	219.6	434.1	2,268.4	493.6	3,667.6	5,945.1	21,041.0	7.7	10.8	17.4	28.3
1992	1,687.1	184.6	342.9	2,214.6	474.5	2,672.7	5,441.6	20,542.0	8.2	10.8	13.0	26.5
1993	2,626.0	272.0	431.0	3,329.0	438.0	4,290.0	6,028.0	25,655.0	10.2	13.0	16.7	23.5
J-S 94**	1,119.0	79.5	163.8	1,362.3	135.0	1,898.0	2,578.0	10,639.0	10.5	12.8	17.8	24.2

* Latin American Association of Integration.
** January-September.
Source: ECO-AXIS S.A., based on DTIC (Brazil) and NTDB (United States).

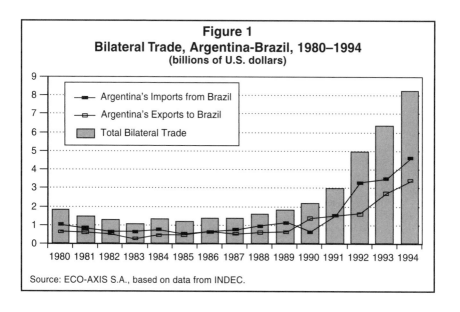

Figure 1
Bilateral Trade, Argentina-Brazil, 1980–1994
(billions of U.S. dollars)

Legend:
- Argentina's Imports from Brazil
- Argentina's Exports to Brazil
- Total Bilateral Trade

Source: ECO-AXIS S.A., based on data from INDEC.

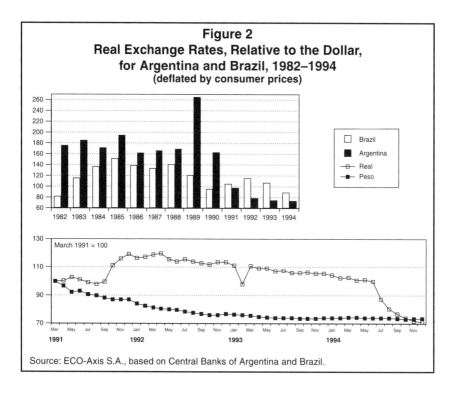

Figure 2
Real Exchange Rates, Relative to the Dollar,
for Argentina and Brazil, 1982–1994
(deflated by consumer prices)

Legend:
- Brazil
- Argentina
- Real
- Peso

March 1991 = 100

Source: ECO-Axis S.A., based on Central Banks of Argentina and Brazil.

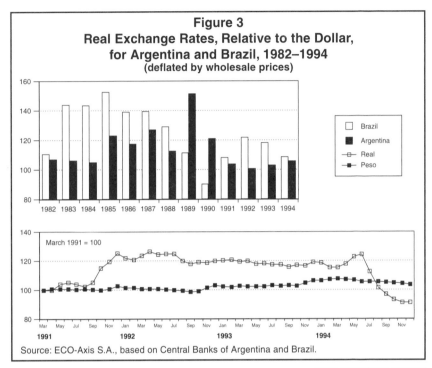

Figure 3
Real Exchange Rates, Relative to the Dollar,
for Argentina and Brazil, 1982–1994
(deflated by wholesale prices)

March 1991 = 100

Source: ECO-Axis S.A., based on Central Banks of Argentina and Brazil.

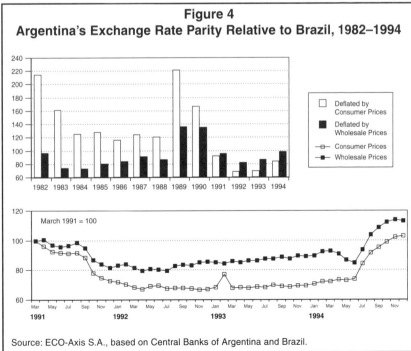

Figure 4
Argentina's Exchange Rate Parity Relative to Brazil, 1982–1994

March 1991 = 100

Source: ECO-Axis S.A., based on Central Banks of Argentina and Brazil.

Notes

1. *Acuerdo de Alcance Parcial*, or Partial Preferential Trade Agreement.

2. The Integration Treaty between Argentina and Brazil, signed by President Raul Alfonsin from Argentina and President Jose Sarney from Brazil, was approved by the congress of both countries in August 1989, but it was not implemented. The goal—to free bilateral trade in a ten-year period—was modified by the decision to constitute a common market between Argentina and Brazil by the year 1995 and adopted in mid-1990 by the newly elected governments of President Carlos Menem in Argentina and President Fernando Collor de Melo in Brazil.

3. As trade opens more, this pattern of intrasectoral trade specialization is likely to be observed. Recent research shows evidence of a growing intraindustry trade pattern (Lucángeli, 1993; Sourrouille and Lucángeli, 1992).

4. *Acuerdo de Alcance Parcial de Complementación Económica* or Economic Complementation Agreement.

5. March 1991 is a good base from which to evaluate exchange rate evolution: during this month the "Treaty of Asunción" confirming MERCOSUR was signed, and Argentina, in an effort to stabilize the economy, launched the "Convertibility Plan," making the peso convertible with the dollar at an almost fixed one-to-one rate.

6. From the Brazilian standpoint, the cruzeiro-peso exchange parity improved 50 percent from March 1991–December 1992.

7. In a sectoral analysis of "Competitiveness in the Steel Industry of Argentina Relative to Brazil" (Nofal, 1990), it was found that taxes on electrical energy, gas, and fuels (at the federal, state, and local levels) imposed a greater burden in Argentina. Due to its cumulative nature, the tax burden was comparatively higher in the case of export sales and high value-added products.

8. The opinion that a free trade area was a better option than a customs union or a common market prompted the Integration Treaty signed between Argentina and Brazil in 1988. As Under-Secretary of the Secretariat of Industry and Trade in 1988, I corrected the preliminary

version of the Integration Treaty and eliminated all references to a common external trade policy. In the same fashion, the reference to a common market was set in a medium- to long-term horizon, requiring previous examination of its impact upon human resources development. Historically, Brazil was the supporter of the common market option for regional integration; Argentina, of the free trade area option. In 1990, the agreement between President Carlos Menem of Argentina and President Fernando Collor de Melo of Brazil tipped the balance toward the common market option.

9. Chile initially formally declined to be a full partner in MERCOSUR, but has advanced *de facto* toward integration with Argentina through direct investment (acquisitions of Argentine firms in manufacturing and services) and increased bilateral trade. Also during 1994, Chile expressed interest in negotiating a *free trade agreement* with MERCOSUR, although still declining to be a full member of the *customs union* in MERCOSUR.

References

Field, Peter B. (1993). "Getting to a Western Hemisphere Free Trade Area," presented at the Conference on Designing the Architecture for a Western Hemisphere Free Trade Area, North-South Center, University of Miami, January 28-29.

Field, Peter B. (1992). "Free Trade Areas, Common Markets and Competitiveness in the Americas: A U.S. Perspective." North-South Center, University of Miami, September.

Hufbauer, Gary C. and Jeffrey J. Schott (1992). *North American Free Trade: Issues and Recommendations.* Institute for International Economics, Washington, D.C.

Lipsey, Richard G. (1993). "Laying the Foundations: The Main Paths to Hemispheric Free Trade," presented at the Conference on Designing the Architecture for a Western Hemisphere Free Trade Area, North-South Center, University of Miami, January 28-29.

Lucángeli, Jorge (1993). "Integración Comercial, Intercambio Intra-Industrial y Creación y Desvío de Comercio: El intercambio comercial entre Argentina y Brasil en los años recientes." Secretaría de Programación Económica, Subsecretaría de Estudios Económicos-PNUD, Buenos Aires.

Nofal, María Beatriz (1993). "Comercio Exterior de Brasil en 1992." *Revista IDEA.* Instituto para el Desarrollo de Empresarios en la Argentina, N° 172, March/April.

———— (1993). "Brasil no es Unico Culpable del Desequilibrio Comercial." *Ambito Financiero.* Buenos Aires, December 24, 1992.

———— (1992). "El Problema no es el Déficit sino los Flujos de Comercio." *Ambito Financiero.* Buenos Aires, February 11, 1993.

———— (1992). "Integración Argentina-Brasil y Regionalización de los Mercados en el Cono Sur." *Valores en la Sociedad Industrial.* Universidad Católica Argentina, October.

———— (1991). "Integración Argentina-Brasil." *Contribuciones.* CIEDLA, October/December.

———— (1991). "Argentina y Brasil: Asimetrías de Política Industrial y de Comercio Exterior." *Revista IDEA*. Instituto para el Desarrollo de Empresarios en la Argentina, N⁰ 159, November.

———— (1990). "The Argentine-Brazilian Integration Process: Achievements, Problems and Prospects." *The Wilson Center Working Papers N⁰ 181* (22-33). Washington, D.C.

———— (1990). "Industria Siderúrgica Argentina: Competitividad Respecto de Brasil y Políticas de Integración." *Competitividad y Alternativas Estratégicas de Desarrollo para la Industria Siderúrgica Argentina (1900-2000)*. Parte II (STRAT), November.

Sourrouille, Juan V. y Jorge Lucángeli (1992). "El Intercambio Comercial Argentino-Brasileño. Un Examen del Comercio Intraindustria." Instituto para la Integración de América Latina (INTAL). Buenos Aires.

Weintraub, Sidney (1992). "Western Hemisphere Free Trade: Getting from Here to There." *Working Papers on Trade in the Western Hemisphere* N⁰ 13, Document IDB-ECLAC, November.

Wilson Center (1990). "The Argentine-Brazilian Integration Program: An Early Assessment." *Working Papers N⁰ 181*. Washington, D.C.

8

Trade Liberalization in Chile: Lessons for Hemispheric Integration

Raimundo Soto

Introduction

In the last decade, most Latin American countries have been transformed. From a group of debt-burdened, inflationary, stagnating economies with few international economic links—especially with their neighbors—they have become dynamic economies in which reforms are being implemented and capital has become abundant and for which the word "integration" conveys an important message of hope for sustained development. During the 1990–93 period, macroeconomic stability was reestablished, per capita GDP grew by 4.3 percent—as opposed to the 8.9 percent reduction in the previous decade—and exports increased from U.S.$78 billion to U.S.$133 billion.[1] Inflation declined from an annual average rate of 75 percent in 1985 to 19 percent in 1993.

This metamorphosis, perhaps the most important economic phenomenon in decades, has been greatly influenced by a global tendency toward market deregulation and government retrenchment. An important influence can be found in the successful transformation of Chile, once the most conservative import substitution regime, into a dynamic export-oriented economy. Chile has become a leading example of the widespread benefits, as well as the difficulties, of unilateral trade liberalization and market reform. The pioneering program of trade liberalization and structural adjustment, implemented in 1975, led to rapid growth, expanding exports, and increased productivity in the tradable and nontradable sectors in the late 1970s. This early start, however, was dramatically interrupted in 1982 when the cumulative effects of exchange rate mismanagement, falling terms of trade, and the debt crisis induced a severe downturn in the economy. After a brief reverse in the reforms during the 1983–84 period, the authorities renewed their efforts to modernize and transform the economy, reshaping incentives toward export markets. In the decade 1985–1994, this strategy paid off: the economy experienced a remarkable period of sustained growth, exports expanded and diversified, inflation remained under control, and unemployment and poverty declined markedly.

This chapter examines the Chilean experience with trade reform. The first section reviews the Chilean experience with structural reforms and discusses some of the most important implications for countries in the early stages of their own reform processes. Congruency in the implementation of trade liberalization and its consistency with other macroeconomic policies emerge as crucial elements for the success of a reform program, hastening the yield of benefits. The need to bolster and maintain the credibility of reform policies becomes a crucial element in inducing private investment, critical to maintaining high rates of growth, to seize the opportunities emerging from the reform process. The fact that the costs of the reforms, especially the cost of policy mistakes, can be quite high in the transition period, particularly in terms of unemployment and/or worsening income distribution, introduces a note of caution.

The next section of the chapter analyzes the main weaknesses of the current economic situation in Chile, the extent to which unilateral trade liberalization can overcome these limitations, and Chile's incentives to join trade agreements, such as MERCOSUR, NAFTA, and CACM.[2] In the Chilean case, trade is not the main incentive for joining a pact, as the reforms have already accomplished a high degree of integration into world markets; rather, nontrade factors, such as the reduction in the country's financial risk, prompt access to new technologies, and a defense against further protectionism in developed countries, appear to be more important determinants in the decision to join trade agreements.

The discussion on integration is extended in the next section to consider the formation of a Western Hemisphere free trade agreement (WHFTA), as that proposed in the December 1994 summit of Latin American, Canadian, and U.S. leaders in Miami. The creation of a WHFTA has been widely discussed since the launch of the Enterprise for the Americas Initiative (EAI) in 1990. Nevertheless, the lack of U.S. involvement in the region during the 1990–92 period provoked some disillusionment among several Latin American countries, which was only mildly dissipated by Mexico's entry into NAFTA in 1993. The unexpected announcement of a deadline of as early as 2005 for the formation of the free trade area radically changed the perception regarding the commitment of the United States and the major Latin American countries—in particular,

Mexico and Brazil—toward free trade. Although the schedule for the implementation of the agreement was not delineated at the summit, indications point to two strategies that could be used to achieve full integration. First, existing trade agreements among Latin American countries, once fully implemented, are expected to merge in order to form large blocs of countries that would, in turn, negotiate accession to NAFTA. Second, the invitation of NAFTA members to Chile to initiate negotiations for admission in May 1995 also suggests that the incremental expansion of NAFTA might be possible. This section discusses the advantages and drawbacks of each strategy, as conditioned by political and economic forces at the country and international levels.

The last section summarizes the main findings and brings a word of caution regarding the current wave of trade opening and reforms. Although the outlook for Latin America is promising, recent events suggest the necessity for a prudent assessment of the situation. Financial flows have eased the implementation of reforms, and current account deficits, to be expected as a consequence of trade liberalization, have been easily financed with foreign saving. The increasing instability of the Mexican stock market, the large current account deficit of Argentina, and the financial crisis in Venezuela, however, are signs that the situation in Latin America remains to be consolidated.

Lessons from Trade Liberalization and Economic Reforms in Chile

In recent years Chile has experienced the most successful period of economic growth since the depression of the 1930s. In 1993, the economy completed its ninth year of continuous growth at an average rate of 6.6 percent per year, and per capita GDP reached U.S.$3,200, more than doubling its 1983 level. This vigorous expansion in production has been accompanied both by reduced levels of unemployment—which bottomed at 4.6 percent in 1993—decreasing inflation and poverty levels, and by a buoyant external situation, characterized by a sound balance of payments, vigorous exports, and a solid inflow of foreign direct investment. Table 1 presents a set of selected macroeconomic indicators for the 1960–1993 period.

The engine of the spectacular transformation of the Chilean economy has undoubtedly been the trade liberalization program initiated in the mid-1970s.[3] The radical transformation prompted by the trade reforms was brought about by the clear failure of the

Table 1
Chile: Selected Macroeconomic Indicators, 1960-1993

	GDP growth (percentage)	Inflation (percentage)	Govern-ment deficit (percentage)	Unemploy-ment rate (percentage)	Gross in-vestment (percentage of GDP)	Current ac-count deficit (percentage of GDP)	Exports (millions 1993 U.S.$)	Terms of trade (1980=100)	Average tariff (percentage)
1960-64	3.6	23.5	4.7	7.5	15.3	3.9	2,377	83.7	103.9
1965-70	4.1	26.6	2.1	5.6	14.5	1.4	3,891	192.0	66.7
1971-73	0.7	152.1	16.1	4.1	13.5	2.9	3,596	175.2	90.9
1974-81	3.6	163.9	1.6	15.1	15.8	5.0	6,072	121.6	28.4
1982-84	-3.6	19.0	8.5	28.9	13.0	8.4	5,393	83.7	17.3
1985-93	6.6	19.7	1.5	10.0	21.5	3.6	8,160	99.8	16.0

Source: Central Bank of Chile (1994). (Complete data are presented in the appendix table.)

import substitution strategy to provide the basis for sustained growth. The import substitution scheme, implemented in Chile since the 1940s, included high and very differentiated import tariffs (ranging from 0 for capital goods to 750 percent for luxury goods), quotas and import prohibitions, the requirement of a 90-day non-interest-bearing deposit of 10,000 percent of the cost, insurance, and freight (CIF) value of imported goods, and administrative approval of all import operations. In addition, a system of multiple exchange rates prevailed, reaching, at the collapse of the economy in 1973, a proportion of 52 to 1 (Corbo and Fischer, 1994).[4]

By the late 1960s, trade restrictions had practically isolated the Chilean economy, exacerbating its dependence on copper exports and confining imports to intermediate and capital goods (see table 2). The structure of relative prices was characterized by important distortions in favor of industrial goods at the expense of agricultural, mining, and other tradable activities. Differential import duties exempted capital goods and levied high taxes on final goods, creating a largely inefficient capital-intensive industrial sector. On the macroeconomic front, reliance on money printing to finance large fiscal deficits[5] caused inflation to become a chronic phenomenon; despite several stabilization plans implemented in the 1952–1970 period, average inflation remained at 34 percent per year with a maximum of 84 percent per year in 1955.[6]

Unusually favorable terms of trade during the second half of the 1960s (see table 1) allowed very expansive fiscal policies, increasing the average growth rate of GDP to 4 percent per year, reducing unemployment, and expanding real wages at an annual rate of 11.2 percent, well above productivity increases. When the Allende administration took office in 1970, the economy was already out of balance. Fueled by the electionary process, government expenditures had expanded 21 percent in real terms and the fiscal deficit increased to 2.7 percent of GDP. Annual inflation reached 32 percent, and the foreign trade balance deteriorated markedly, despite increasing quantitative controls. During the next three years, the Allende administration attempted a transformation of the economy along socialist lines: land reform, bank nationalization, and a further expansion of public expenditures were financed by a massive injection of credit. Under increasing social instability, the populist strategy rapidly sent the economy out of control: the fiscal deficit reached 24.7 percent of GDP in 1973; inflation spiralled, surpassing 360 percent in 1973; black markets multiplied as price controls increased; and GDP, which had grown by 9 percent in 1971, stagnated in 1972 and collapsed in 1973. In September 1973, the military overthrew the government in a violent coup d'etat.

The crisis of 1973 marked the culmination of a period of widespread government intervention and generalized lack of confidence in the role of the market, and particularly in foreign trade, as a mechanism to allocate resources and develop a sustainable growth strategy. In the following fifteen years, trade liberalization policies were to be the cornerstone of the transformation of the inward-oriented Chilean economy into a dynamic export-oriented country. (A brief chronology of the trade reform is presented in table 3.)

The initial set of measures—including price liberalization, exchange market unification, and the elimination of most nontariff barriers (quotas and prohibitions)—was designed primarily to stabilize inflation, eliminate black markets, and reduce speculation. The

Table 2 Chile: Composition of Trade by Goods (percentage)						
	1970	1975	1980	1985	1990	1993
Exports:						
Copper	75.5	57.4	46.1	46.1	45.7	35.5
Other minerals	9.9	11.9	13.3	14.8	9.7	7.5
Fisheries*	0.1	2.3	6.2	8.8	10.1	4.0
Agriculture	2.7	8.1	12.7	8.2	11.4	10.9
Forestry**	0.9	4.9	6.0	11.8	3.8	8.0
Industrial goods	10.8	15.4	15.7	10.3	19.3	34.1
Imports:						
Consumption goods	15.0	28.0	33.7	23.0	13.6	18.1
Intermediate goods	40.8	52.9	45.6	57.1	55.1	54.7
Capital goods	44.2	19.0	20.7	19.9	31.3	27.2
* Includes fishmeal. ** Includes processed derivatives (pulp). Source: Central Bank of Chile.						

Table 3
Chronology of the Trade Liberalization Process in Chile, 1973-1993

1973   Price controls on more than 3,000 goods and quota and other restrictions on 2,278 importable goods are eliminated. The multiple exchange rate system is reduced to two rates and a crawling peg mechanism is enacted.

1974   Average tariffs are reduced from 105 percent to 57 percent, while the maximum rate drops from 750 percent to 120 percent. The administrative approval of imports is eliminated.

    The foreign investment statute is enacted to encourage capital inflow and repatriation.

    The Central Bank announces that tariffs will adjust downward to locate in the 10 to 35 percent range (the higher rate for manufactured goods) in a two-and-a-half year period.

    The cascade sales tax is replaced by the value-added tax (VAT). Exporters are entitled to rebates on VAT and duties on imported inputs.

1975   Import restrictions and quotas on 3,212 goods are eliminated; only five items remain controlled (gold, jewels, color TV sets, furs, and whiskey).

1976   Chile withdraws from the Andean Pact, to allow a further trade liberalization. Tariffs on imputs, intermediate goods, tools, and machinery not produced in the country are, unexpectedly, lowered to 10 percent.

1977   The tariff adjustment planned for 1978 is enacted in advance. Tax surcharges on tobacco, perfumes, and other "luxurious" goods are eliminated.

    The govenment takes advantage of discontent with the 10–35 percent tariff structure, proposing a 10 percent flat rate and an 18-month phaseout period for the existing structure.

1978   Import duty exemptions are eliminated.

1979   Tariffs are reduced to a flat rate of 10 percent. The exchange rate is fixed at $39 per U.S.$.

1982   To confront the crisis, the exchange rate is devalued, tariffs are temporarily increased to 35 percent, and trade and exchange controls are reinstated.

1986   Tariffs are reduced to 15 percent and controls lifted. The capital account is increasingly opened and capital inflows resumed.

resistance of inflation to the stabilization effort, despite the substantial decline in the fiscal deficit, led the government to institute a drastic program of austerity and monetary restraint in mid-1975, which effectively reduced inflation from 70 percent in the second quarter to less than 25 percent in the third. On the productive side, however, the stabilization effort, coupled with a severe downturn in terms of trade, induced a drastic recession: in 1975, GDP fell by 13.3 percent and unemployment rates sharply rose to 17 percent.

During the 1976–80 period, the economy recovered at high speed. GDP grew at an average rate of 7 percent, the availability of foreign goods expanded markedly, and the government deficit became a surplus. In addition, important reforms were initiated to complement and reinforce the change in relative prices induced by trade deregulation. A large number of public enterprises were privatized, labor markets were deregulated, social security was reformed, and health and public education responsibilities were transferred from the ministries to the county levels. Despite these reforms, two major problems remained unsolved: unemployment levels were not significantly reduced and inflation remained high. One of the instruments used to control inflation, the fixing of the nominal exchange rate in June 1979, proved to have a devastating effect. The highly indexed nature of the Chilean economy,[7] in combination with the fixed exchange rate, induced an increasing overvaluation in the real exchange rate, fostering imports and discouraging exports and leading to large current account deficits (see table 4).[8] In 1981, the deficit reached 14.5 percent of GDP. Large amounts of foreign loans financed the trade imbalance and, as a consequence, the foreign debt increased from U.S.$6 billion in 1977 to U.S.$14.8 billion in 1981. Two additional elements augmenting the level of indebtedness were the resistance of the real interest rate to converge to world levels and the deregulation of the financial market in 1981. The former generated a continuous flow of short-term lending. The lack of adequate supervision of the quality of the portfolio of banks in the latter led to a generalized miscalculation of risk levels and imprudent domestic lending.

With such a large trade imbalance, confidence in the Chilean economy faltered and foreign lending ceased. In June 1982, the authorities were forced to devalue the peso by 19 percent, but "it was too little, and too late" (Edwards and Cox-Edwards, 1987). The economy fell into a deep recession as GDP dropped by 13.4 percent in 1982 and then by a further 3.5 percent in 1983; unemployment, already high, skyrocketed to 34 percent of the labor force (including emergency employment programs), and the government deficit increased to almost 9 percent of GDP when the Central Bank had to rescue the financial sector from bankruptcy. Foreign debt reached 130 percent of GDP in 1983.

During much of the 1983–84 period economic policy drifted. Exchange controls were reintroduced, trade restrictions multiplied, and subsidies for financial and industrial firms were allocated on a very discretionary basis. Despite the military stronghold, political turmoil emerged. After expansive fiscal policies, enacted in 1984 to cope with the hardness of the recession, increased inflation and the foreign trade alarmingly, the government returned to a market-based approach in early 1985, engineered a large real devaluation (30 percent), and set the economy firmly into its current export-oriented strategy. Tariffs and restrictions were scheduled to be shortly phased-out, tax incentives for exporters expanded, and government expenditures were reduced, aiming at both fiscal austerity and exchange rate support.

The story of Chile in the 1986–1993 period is one of marked success, in which a dynamic tradable sector has become the source of sustained development. Moreover, Chile completed a very difficult transition from military rule to democracy, without a contraction in output or private investment. A crucial element in this transition has been the firm commitment of the newly elected democratic government to maintain and deepen the reforms. As a result, GDP has grown at very high rates (7 percent), inflation remains under control,[9] exports continue to expand and diversify, and unemployment has declined to historical lows. Foreign direct investment increased to U.S.$1.5 billion in 1993, while Chilean in-

Table 4
Chile: Balance of Payments, 1975–1993
(in millions U.S.$)

	1975–1978	1979–1981	1982–1984	1985–1989	1990–1993
Exports	2,088	4,125	3,729	5,670	9,107
Imports	-2,008	-5,391	-3,259	-4,270	-8,452
Trade balance	80	-1,265	470	1,400	655
Current account balance	-495	-2,631	-1,844	-869	-782
Capital account balance	716	3,370	1,221	1,071	2,385
Foreign direct investment	52	291	205	802	1,070
Chilean investment abroad	14	26	10	8	223
Net capital flows	664	3,115	1,026	277	1,579
Reserves accumulation	207	786	-563	178	1,671
Foreign debt	5,550	12,667	17,767	18,400	18,170

Source: Central Bank of Chile (1994).

vestment abroad reached significant levels (U.S.$400 million in 1992 and 1993). As of today, Chile stands as one of the most open economies in Latin America and, probably, among the developing countries. With a level of tariffs as low as 11 percent and the absence of nontariff barriers, it has become a paradigm of trade liberalization.

Lessons of the Chilean Experience

Probably the most significant lesson to be drawn from the Chilean experience is the importance of *a systematic effort to implement and deepen the reforms*, despite the natural resistance of those who might be adversely affected by them and the uncertainty—due to shocks to domestic and international markets—of the outcome of the reforms. As noted above, the early reforms were interrupted abruptly in the early 1980s; amidst the chaos induced by the collapse of the financial sector, import tariffs were increased to 30 percent, and foreign exchange controls were reenacted. Critics of the reform process multiplied, and even within the military regime there were voices calling for a return to the import substitution strategy (Velasco, 1994). The de facto nationalization of an important part of the banking and financial sector also signalled a reversal of the privatization process and the government's return to productive activities. Nevertheless, the authorities persisted in their attempts to keep the economy as open and deregulated as it had been before the crisis and declared their intention to reprivatize banks and financial institutions (this time under strict regulation). Tariff surcharges, defined as temporary, were rescheduled to decrease in short time to a level of 15 percent. Once the foreign debt was renegotiated, exchange controls were lifted. The privatization of public enterprises, which had been suspended during the crisis, was reinvigorated by a generous subsidy to acquire property using foreign debt bonds.[10]

A second important lesson from the Chilean experience is that *a comprehensive program of reforms is necessary* to complement and reinforce the benefits of trade liberalization. The benefits in terms of efficiency and increased growth potential from expanding trade require a sound macroeconomic environment, factor markets freed of restrictions, and an institutional setup that reduces risk for private investment and provides an adequate structure of incentives.[11] The Chilean experience also shows that regulation and supervision of financial activities are crucial to avoid negative externalities and mismanagement of the newly created opportunities.

The Chilean experience also shows that *the costs of the reforms can be very high.* Consequently, measures to ameliorate their adverse effects on vulnerable groups are required to maintain support for the reforms. Although not binding in the Chilean case, political support for the reforms can become a significant constraint in the context of democratic regimes. Labor markets appear to be very sensitive to the massive reallocation of resources stemming from changes in relative prices; unemployment rates in Chile remained high (more than 15 percent between 1975 and 1985) during most of the reform period, inducing a severe cost for the most vulnerable groups in society and severely deteriorating income distribution (Marcel and Solimano, 1994). Likewise, downsizing governmental activities involves reducing important subsidies to health, education, and housing, which are not usually covered by the private sector.

Structural adjustment, by nature, includes redesigning the role of the government. Along with the retrenchment of the government from productive activities, the liberalization of goods and factor markets, and the elimination of administrative controls usually comes the risk that the private sector will deviate toward noncompetitive practices. Therefore, *adequate regulation is important.* This becomes a very difficult balancing act between market supervision and outright intervention. In the Chilean case, financial deregulation in the early 1980s was not accompanied by the proper supervision and led to a fragile and highly indebted financial sector. The direct cost of the financial collapse and bailout of financial institutions by the Central Bank has been estimated at around 10 percent of GDP (Larrañaga, 1989).

Reform strategy credibility and the government's ability to implement it is another element that plays a crucial role in the success of trade liberalization and structural transformation. The success of reforms hinges, to a great extent, on inducing the private sector to move away from low profit, inefficient, or socially nonproductive activities (such as rent seeking) toward highly efficient areas. In order to accomplish this, investors need to be sure that reforms are credible. As Chile and other developing countries have learned, however, this is a slow process.[12] Private investment in Chile did not expand as the economic authorities expected in the mid- and late 1970s and most of the 1980s (see table 1). Only after 1989 did investment rates reach a level compatible with high long-run growth rates. In this respect, policy mistakes can be very costly: the use of the nominal exchange rate to control inflation in Chile in the 1979–82 period proved a disastrously myopic policy, as the cost in terms of export competitiveness and credibility largely outweighed the benefit of reducing inflation. Once capital is installed, it usually becomes irreversible. Pindyck and Solimano (1994) show that the slow response of private investment after stabilization can be understood as an option (i.e., a wait-and-see strategy) to reduce the investment risk.

A final, and perhaps obvious, lesson from the Chilean experience is that *foreign trade can be a source of sustained growth* for Latin American countries, as it has been for East Asian economies. Between 1975 and 1993 total exports expanded from U.S.$1.5 billion to U.S.$10 billion, despite the largely depressed terms of trade. Non-copper exports increased from less than U.S.$600 million to U.S.$6 billion, at an average real growth rate of 9.5 percent per year. Moreover, diversification in terms of partners has also been achieved (see table 5). Asian markets, beyond Japan, are currently an important destination for exports and an increasingly attractive source of imports.

To assess the importance of trade opening in the Chilean case, Krueger (1994) suggests the following counterfactual exercise. Imagine that, instead of reforming the economy along the lines described above, the authorities had engaged in a successful stabilization program and undertaken most reforms, except trade liberalization. Would the same dynamic growth rates within the bounds of a mostly closed, import substitution economy have been as likely?

The Weaknesses of the Chilean Economy and the Role of Foreign Trade

Despite its successful experience with reforms, important weaknesses remain in the Chilean economy. These can be overcome by an appropriate trade policy. First, the capacity of the economy to

Table 5
Chile: Composition of Trade by Partner
(percentage)

	Exports		Imports	
	1970	1992	1970	1992
United States	140.3	16.3	6.9	20.5
European Community	60.9	29.0	35.3	19.0
Asia	12.1	30.5	3.1	18.1
—of which, Japan	12.0	16.9	3.0	10.0
Latin America	11.4	16.0	22.1	24.7
—of which, MERCOSUR	8.5	10.1	13.4	18.3
Other	1.4	8.3	0.6	17.6

Source: Central Bank of Chile (1994).

grow, based on the expansion of the domestic demand, is limited by its reduced size and the absence of important scale economies. Therefore, in order to sustain high growth rates, a further deepening of the integration with international markets is necessary, in particular to diversify exports in terms of goods and partners. Diversification of the structure of exported goods is necessary to reduce terms of trade dependency on the fluctuations in the price of copper. As of 1993, copper still accounted for more than 35 percent of total exports (see table 2), so the large fluctuations in copper prices induced a marked variability on the terms of trade, as can be seen in table 1.[13] To reduce the dependence of foreign trade on the fluctuations of commodity markets, it is necessary to increase exports of manufactures and, in particular, to expand the volume of financial and nonfinancial services (e.g., tourism and computer software) that can be sold abroad. Exports of nonfinancial services have increased at an average rate of 17 percent per year since 1984. As of 1993, they amounted to U.S.$2.6 billion (25 percent of total exports), and, for the first time in history, the balance in nonfinancial services exhibited a surplus in that year.

Diversification in terms of commercial partners is also desirable. Concentrating on a few trade partners, as was the case in Chile during the 1960s and 1970s, is excessively risky and impedes profiting on the expansion of other regions or countries. Chilean exports have diversified markedly since trade liberalization, and the ability of exporters to penetrate East Asian markets and benefit from the rapid expansion in this geographic area has been remarkable (see table 5). In 1970, 12 percent of total trade (U.S.$145 million) was directed to Japan and East Asia, increasing to 31 percent of total trade (U.S.$3.1 billion) in 1992; on the other hand, the share of exports of European countries declined from 60 percent to only 29 percent in the same period. Nevertheless, the large concentration of some goods into specific areas (e.g., fruits to the highly regulated markets of the United States and the Organization for Economic Cooperation and Development [OECD]) produces a certain degree of instability and fragility to exports, in particular for agricultural goods.[14]

Second, inadequate levels of human capital and physical infrastructure have been identified as another important limitation to sustained growth. The Frei administration, which took office in 1994, declared its commitment to a large effort in education and training, as well as to an aggressive program of public works to improve transportation (only 10,000 miles of roads are paved), ports and airways, and communications (Jadresic, 1994). The limited physical infrastructure is, to an important extent, the consequence of the structural adjustment of the economy during the reform period and after the 1982–83 crisis. It is important to note that for most of the reform period, investment rates were generally below 15 percent of GDP (see table 1), and public investment, which corresponds mostly to infrastructure, did not reach 5.5 percent in the 1978–85 period.[15] To maintain the dynamism of the tradable sector, it is important to develop infrastructure and to provide an adequate support for the private sector to allocate resources to profitable activities.

A third element that would hamper high growth levels in Chile is the insufficient investment in technology and know-how. It is well known that developing countries benefit from the technological "catch-up" of developed countries by acquiring successfully applied technologies and avoiding the cost of testing others that are inadequate. Nevertheless, once these scale economies are exhausted, investment in research and development (R&D) becomes an important determinant of the country's long-run growth. Although scale economies may not have been fully used in the case of Chile, investment in R&D (around 1 percent of GDP) is still very low for international standards or compared to most high-growth economies, in which it is usually over 3 percent of GDP. The lack of technological renovation, combined with a relatively unskilled labor force, limits the diversification of Chilean exports into goods of higher value added and can lower growth rates.

Given the limited availability of human and financial resources to develop new markets and products, the selection of potential "winners" becomes a key element in sustaining high growth rates. To date, the Chilean authorities have opted for a hands-off approach, leaving all initiative to the private sector. Although this strategy has been successful, the above mentioned exhaustion of technological catch-up suggests an increasing cost of wrong decisions. The successful experience of East Asian countries with technological innovation, however, needs to be examined in order to determine the extent to which it is possible to combine public and private effort to develop new export markets. Contrary to the historic Latin American experience, some East Asian governments (e.g., Korea, Taiwan) have been able to identify and take advantage of windows of opportunity to develop specific industrial areas, such as electronics and ship building (World Bank, 1993). It remains to be seen whether the current Chilean policy is optimal or if it is nec-

essary to design a mechanism that allows the private sector to reduce the expected cost of developing new export markets.

The Role of Trade Agreements for Chile

Foreign commerce plays a crucial role in the Chilean development
strategy. Noneconomic determinants of trade appear to be on the
rise, indicating a need to secure export and import markets beyond
what unilateral trade liberalization alone can achieve. This can be
accomplished through trade agreements, as long as they do not
derive their benefits mainly from trade diversion.[16] In recent years,
these agreements have become increasingly important, as two
seemingly opposite tendencies have emerged in world markets.
First, as more countries (Argentina, Mexico, East Asian and East
European countries) reduce protection and liberalize their economies, and technological improvements allow fast and cheap communications, there has been a general tendency toward globalization of international markets. On the other hand, trade has
become increasingly concentrated in geographic areas, such as the
European Community, North America, and Japan and East Asia
(Frenkel, Stein, and Wei, 1995). The first tendency indicates that
world markets are becoming more competitive, hence Chilean exporters must increase their efforts to maintain their competitiveness and share of the markets. (The prices of the principal export
goods, in fact, have declined significantly since 1989: copper
dropped 33 percent; fishmeal, 20 percent; and pulp, 52 percent).
The second tendency suggests that the privileges granted to those
countries already members of a trade bloc may eventually displace
Chilean exports.

The latter effect is probably more worrisome to the Chilean
authorities, and it explains their willingness to enter into lengthy
negotiations and lobbying with neighboring countries and members of NAFTA, MERCOSUR, and, more recently, the Asian Pacific
Economic Cooperation forum (APEC). Since 1990, Chile has
signed a significant number of trade agreements with other Latin
American countries (Mexico, Argentina, Colombia, and Venezuela),
and, although it may be premature to try to assess the effect of
these pacts, early evidence suggests an important response in trade
volumes. (Chilean exports to Mexico increased from U.S.$44 mil-
lion in 1992 to U.S.$131 million in 1993.) MERCOSUR could guar-
antee access to a large market (190 million inhabitants and a combined GDP of approximately U.S.$400 billion). However, unless
Chile is granted special status, it is unlikely that it will join the re-

gional pact because of the macroeconomic situation and trade status of MERCOSUR members. First, reform remains uncertain in the two major country members, Brazil and Argentina, and macroeconomic stability has not been achieved. Although the situation appears promising, Argentina has a long way to go before reforms are consolidated, and more structural adjustment in the economy may be required to overcome the fragile external situation (in 1993, the increasingly overvalued real exchange rate pushed the current account deficit above 6.5 percent of GDP). Brazil is in an even earlier stage as it just begins to stabilize its economy (after a dramatic decline, inflation picked up in the last quarter of 1994) and consider reforms (in particular, trade liberalization and fiscal restructuring have not been undertaken). Chilean authorities fear that closer economic ties with these countries might prove short-lived and induce instability in the economy.

Secondly, the benefits to Chile from a trade agreement with MERCOSUR may be substantially outweighed by its costs. Tariffs with the rest of the world would increase from the current level of 11 percent to the common MERCOSUR level of 30 percent. Because trade with MERCOSUR countries is reduced (10 to 15 percent of total trade), such an increase in tariffs would also substantially increase average protection levels in Chile. In addition, it is not clear that the agreement would cover all goods (e.g., automobiles are excepted from the common tariff), which, in turn, could create major domestic price distortions. Furthermore, Argentina and Brazil may not be willing to give Chilean exports access to their markets at a zero tariff rate because the subsequent impact on specific domestic producers would be significantly negative, due to the higher efficiency of Chilean producers in areas such as fruits, fishmeal, or pulp.

The most important reason for not joining MERCOSUR, however, is that it will not address what Chile needs from a trade agreement. Massive technological transfer is unlikely to be obtained from Brazil or Argentina, except in selected sectors and probably not in manufactures or services. Likewise, as the demand for Chilean industrial goods will probably be reduced, MERCOSUR will produce neither a more diversified portfolio of exports nor a reduction in the risk accompanying volatile terms of trade.

At the same time there are important reasons to maintain links with MERCOSUR without joining it. By the end of 1994, most privileges granted to Chilean exports by MERCOSUR members in the context of the *Asociación Latino Americana de Integracion*

(ALADI) will phase out, and Chilean producers will lose an important concession. Under the special status of "non-member commercial partner," Chile may in part retain these advantages. A second incentive for maintaining a fluid relationship with Argentina and Brazil is to ensure the security of the important volume of Chilean investment in these countries: during 1992 and 1993, more than U.S.$800 million was invested abroad, mostly in Argentina, Brazil, and Peru. A third, and more strategic reason to leave the option open on becoming an important partner of both countries is the possibility that reforms in MERCOSUR countries may consolidate and the general economic situation may improve.

The case of NAFTA differs significantly from that of MERCOSUR. Casual evidence from the large effort undertaken by the Chilean government and private sector to join NAFTA and/or sign a free trade agreement (FTA) with the United States would suggest that there are important direct gains from entering into these pacts. On the contrary, it is estimated that Chile has little to gain directly and in the short run from an FTA with the United States because Chilean exports are subject to an average import tariff of only 1.8 percent and 60 percent of total exports are affected by a tariff of less than 0.7 percent (Butelmann and Frohman, 1992). A study by Valdés (1992) calculates that the welfare impact of a Chile-U.S. FTA would amount to slightly more than U.S.$300 million, or 1 percent of GDP in present value. Exports would increase by as much as 4.5 percent (U.S.$60 million), while imports would increase by 27 percent (U.S.$376 million). Manufactures exported to the United States (30 percent of total) would benefit from avoiding the step-tariff system already in use; it is estimated that they might expand by 8 percent.

The advantages of joining NAFTA are mostly strategic and concern (1) the fear that a protectionist wave in the United States might reduce access to U.S. markets; (2) a likely decline in the country's risk premium, which, in turn, would make credit and investment less expensive; (3) a potential reduction in the cost of technology; (4) an eventual expansion of foreign investment in the form of joint ventures; and (5) possible important dynamic advantages in the form of developing new markets for goods that currently face increasing tariffs and nontariff restrictions and that, consequently, do not export significant amounts to the United States.

Trade Liberalization: A Hemispheric Perspective

In December 1994, leaders of 33 Latin American countries and the United States met in Miami for what was, doubtlessly, the most significant step toward hemispheric integration in history. Unexpectedly and despite the initial reluctance of the three largest economies (Brazil, Mexico, and the United States[17]), the participants set a date—the year 2005—for achieving a free trade agreement that includes all Latin American countries (except Cuba), Canada, and the United States. As a demonstration of its commitment to this goal, the Clinton administration announced that it would initiate negotiations to admit Chile to NAFTA in May 1995.

Although the announcement of a deadline to achieve a Western Hemisphere Free Trade Area (WHFTA) came as a surprise, the idea that the current wave of trade liberalization and market reforms might lead to the creation of a large trade union had been taking form since the launch of the EAI in 1990 (Bouzas and Lustig, 1992). Despite its failure to establish a large umbrella for regional trade, the EAI sparked the enthusiasm of Latin American countries for forming new trade unions (such as MERCOSUR and the Colombia-Venezuela-Mexico Trade Accord) or for revitalizing existing arrangements (e.g., the CACM). The relatively short horizon—ten years—set for reaching full integration reflects the realization on the part of Latin American governments that integration to an increasing global economy provides a window of opportunity for modernizing their economies.

Two additional elements have played an important role in accelerating integration. First, the current international situation is perhaps the most favorable scenario for opening the economy, as substantial foreign resources are available to counterbalance potential trade deficits arising from the implementation of reforms (Calvo et al., 1993). Second, political support for reforms, both domestic and international, may be at its highest point in decades. The completion of the Uruguay round of the General Agreement on Tariffs and Trade (GATT) negotiations and its swift approval in the U.S. Congress in November 1994 are clear signs of the willingness of developed countries to reduce protection and engage in free trade. On the Latin American front, the experiences of Argentina, Costa Rica, and Peru, all of which have succeeded in maintaining popular support for reforms, amply demonstrate the feasibility of making trade and structural reforms a politically attractive strategy. Despite this politically favorable scenario, the successful formation of a regional trade agreement depends mostly on economic factors. First, though several Latin American countries have initiated trade reforms, other structural reforms (such as privatization of public enterprises and market deregulation) either have not been implemented or remain to be consolidated. Chile's experience with economic transformation shows that comprehensive reforms are necessary to achieve a lasting liberalization of foreign trade. If comprehensive reforms at the country level are not undertaken, trade liberalization will be unsustainable in the long run, and trade agreements in Latin America will probably be as inconsequential as previous pacts have been.[18] In this sense, subregional pacts or NAFTA should not be expected to provide an impulse for trade integration that would substitute for the need for comprehensive trade reforms.

Second, the lack of a schedule for negotiations and the heterogeneity of Latin American countries in terms of the implementation of reforms and the removal of trade barriers suggest that important obstacles to integration remain. Despite the political willingness of Latin American leaders, the necessary harmonization of economic interests among countries will certainly require lengthy negotiations. Likewise, merging existing trade agreements will probably be cumbersome, as they differ markedly in terms of objectives and programmed schedules. Free trade agreements (such as the Chile-Mexico pact) require only the setting of a common tariff level for those goods traded among members of the pact; trade unions (e.g., the Andean Pact), in addition, oblige country members to set a common tariff for other nonmember countries, while common markets (such as the initial proposal for MERCOSUR) include the liberalization of factor (such as labor and financial) markets. Moreover, existing agreements have different schedules for implementation. For example, while MERCOSUR countries are expected to abolish tariffs in early 1995, the CACM and Andean Pact are to be fully implemented much later.

If, on the other hand, integration is to be achieved by the incremental expansion of NAFTA, the requirements for admission remain to be determined. The eventual entry of Chile clearly sets a high standard for the rest of the Latin American economies; most countries will have to undertake important measures to achieve this "floor" before applying for admission. Even if the requirements are eased, this strategy for achieving integration may be inefficient as it allots a large proportion of the costs to Latin American countries, most of which have limited resources available to finance the liberalization of their economies. As such, this strategy assigns a very passive role to NAFTA members—in particular, the United States—which mainly have to wait for Latin American countries to reach the required level of maturity in their reforms to be able to meet the standard.

Third, the creation of a successful WHFTA depends to a large extent on the participation of the three largest Latin American economies (Argentina, Brazil, and Mexico) and the provision of temporary relief for small economies. Mexico, of course, is already a member of NAFTA, and Argentina has implemented an important number of trade and structural reforms to become an attractive commercial partner. The current performance of Brazil suggests, however, that the likelihood of a hemispheric trade union is remote in the short run. The Brazilian economy, which accounts for one-half of Latin America's GDP, has long been under fiscal mismanagement and suffering from hyperinflation and heavy government intervention. A successful reversal in this trend will likely require a lengthy period of time.

In the case of the small countries, a successful hemispheric integration necessitates provisions for those economies that cannot openly compete with more developed countries in a fully integrated market. Signs that Caribbean countries fear that their economies could suffer greatly from the WHFTA were already present at the Miami Summit. The Prime Minister of Barbados warned that "a rising tide can also overturn small boats."[19] Exports from most small Caribbean economies currently enjoy preferential access to the U.S. market, an advantage that will disappear after the WHFTA is implemented. Consequently, temporary relief for these economies will probably be necessary for a smooth transition.

A final element that will be crucial in achieving the WHFTA is the development of political events within the United States. The 1994 Miami Summit eased most apprehensions regarding the political will of the United States—and in particular of the Clinton administration—toward fostering free trade with Latin America. By inviting Chile to initiate discussions to join NAFTA, the Clinton administration displayed confidence that swift ratification from Congress can be achieved. As discussed earlier, the small Chilean economy does not represent a threat to American producers or workers. On the other hand, the narrow ratification in the case of Mexico demonstrates that negotiation with Congress can become quite cumbersome when the pact is expected to have significant effects.

Summary

Trade reform and market deregulation have become important features of economic policy in Latin American countries in recent years. After several decades of pursuing import substitution strategies, which confined growth to the expansion of the domestic demand, Latin American countries have turned toward foreign trade as a source for sustained growth. In turn, this new strategy has raised a number of issues regarding integration to world markets and the role of regional trade agreements in fostering the transition period.

Chile is, undoubtedly, a pioneer among Latin American countries in trade liberalization and market reforms. The path to this achievement, however, has been a lengthy and "rocky" road (Taylor, 1993). After a successful start in the late 1970s, the economy fell into distress during the 1982–83 crisis; high unemployment, contracting output, financial collapse, and a surge in inflationary pressures led reform critics to suggest a return to protective practices. A firm commitment to the reforms and confidence in the ability of the private sector to overcome the crisis, however difficult in the short run, produced important long-run benefits. In the last decade, with economic growth at almost 7 percent per year, exports doubling, and unemployment rates receding to less than 5 percent, a dynamic, export-oriented economy emerged.

This chapter explored the Chilean experience with trade liberalization and structural reforms and addressed two broad issues. First, we analyzed the lessons to be drawn from almost two decades of market reforms that could be useful for countries at the beginning of the reform process. In particular, we discussed the extent to which foreign trade can become a source for sustained growth. Second, we analyzed the pattern of integration with world markets and neighbor countries that is achieved through a unilateral trade liberalization process. We explored the incentives Chile has to join trade agreements and what role it could play in the formation of an ample trade agreement in the region, inclusive of the United States and Canada, as those that have recently been proposed.

Among the lessons to be derived from the Chilean experience, the need for a systematic effort to implement and deepen the reforms, the important complementary effect of other reforms (financial, labor markets, etc.), and the crucial role of credibility in reform measures appear to be most important. In addition, the cost of the reforms for the most vulnerable groups in the society and the political repercussions are an important consideration when assessing the support for change.

Regarding integration with international markets, the Chilean case is a remarkable success. Sustained trade expansion and adequate diversification of exports in terms of goods and partners, however, reduce the number of incentives to join trade agreements. As the short-run gains for Chile from trade pacts are small, dynamic considerations (such as securing long-run foreign investment, easing the adoption of technology and know-how, and declining country risk) become key aspects of its trade strategy. Regional pacts, such as MERCOSUR, do not address Chilean interests in these considerations, and this explains Chile's lack of interest in joining them.

The December 1994 Summit of the Americas produced two important results regarding integration in Latin America and the eventual formation of a Western Hemisphere free trade zone: a 2005 deadline for the integration of all Latin American countries (except Cuba), Canada, and the United States and an invitation to Chile to initiate negotiations for admission to NAFTA in 1995. The mechanism and schedule to achieve full integration were not delineated at the summit, but there were indications that it could be achieved by incremental expansion of NAFTA and/or by merging existing trade pacts. The incremental expansion of NAFTA is possible, as exemplified by Chile. The Chilean case, nevertheless, is not representative of the situation of Latin American economies, and, because Chile sets a high standard, it is unlikely that it will become the benchmark for other Latin American countries seeking to join NAFTA. As for merging with other trade agreements, this strategy involves the formidable task of harmonizing the heterogeneous status of Latin American countries in terms of economic interests, reform implementation, and degree of trade liberalization. No matter which strategy is chosen, the structure of the WHFTA will certainly be influenced by the political environment within the United States at the moment of negotiations.

A final caveat on the current regional integration wave: care should be taken when assessing the robustness of the process. It is possible that a significant part of the enthusiasm for implementing trade openness is a response to a rather unusual availability of foreign exchange, due in part to the reform process of Latin American countries, but also importantly to the international situation. The massive inflow of capital to Latin America has allowed countries to lessen restrictions on imports and to finance large trade imbalances.

Were these flows to revert, several countries would find themselves in a very unfavorable external situation that would raise incentives to increase protection and halt the reforms. The Chilean experience in this respect is explicit: after benefiting from cheap foreign saving in the late 1970s, the subsequent 1982–83 crisis led to a partial reversal of reforms and increased protection. An important effort had to be devoted to undertake the structural reforms required to rescue the economy from the crisis and, at the same time, to return to the correct trade liberalization path.

Comments and suggestions by Hernán Cortés, Elsie Echeverri-Carroll, Fernando Fuentes, Norman Loayza, and Claude Montenegro greatly improved the quality of this chapter, part of which was written while the author was with the Macroeconomics and Growth Division of the World Bank. Remaining errors are, of course, the author's responsibility.

Notes

1. Includes all Latin American countries, except Cuba, as reported by ECLAC (1994). Inflation figures exclude countries with hyperinflationary processes: Bolivia in 1985 (8,170 percent) and Brazil in 1993 (2,244 percent).
2. MERCOSUR is the *Mercado Común de América del Sur* (South-America Common Market) formed by Argentina, Brazil, Paraguay, and Uruguay. The North American Free Trade Agreement (NAFTA) includes Canada, the United States, and Mexico. CACM is the acronym for Central American Common Market.
3. The Chilean economic transformation has been extensively documented by Sjaastad and Cortés (1981), Edwards and Cox-Edwards (1987), de la Cuadra and Hachette (1991), and Bosworth, Dornbusch, and Labán (1994).
4. A thorough description of the structure of foreign trade before reforms is presented in de la Cuadra and Hachette (1991).
5. The fiscal deficit includes, in addition to the deficit of the government, the deficit of public enterprises. It is a more appropriate measure of the public sector stance when, as in the Chilean case in the 1960–79 period, most public enterprises received large subsidies from the government to cover losses.
6. Only one stabilization plan, in 1959, included wide-range trade liberalization measures. Expansionary government policies led to overvaluation of the exchange rate, a large increase in imports, and an unsustainable current account deficit and balance of payments crisis in 1962. In turn, it prompted a large devaluation and a return to capital and trade controls (Velasco, 1994).
7. Indexation is a mechanism by which prices and wages are automatically adjusted by past inflation to keep their real level constant.
8. It has been estimated that by 1981 the exchange rate was overvalued by 21 percent (Elbadawi and Soto, 1994).
9. Inflation, though still high for OECD standards, has been slowly receding, reaching single-digit levels only in 1994.
10. Servén, Solimano, and Soto (1994) present an analytical discussion of the macroeconomic effects of privatization, with emphasis on the cases of Argentina, Chile, and Mexico.
11. The appropriate sequence of reforms and the speed at which these should be implemented is an area in which agreement has not been reached. Conventional wisdom (McKinnon, 1973, and, more recently, Corbo and Fischer, 1994) argue the need to undertake trade reforms in advance of other reforms (financial, labor markets, etc.). On the

contrary, Lal (1984) indicates that financial opening is required first, while Krueger (1994) suggests that a simultaneous path increases the ability to cope with the political pressures imposed by trade liberalization and structural reforms.

12. Meller (1994) notes that, although reforms can boost credibility, the link is far more subtle. The massive reforms of the 1970s did not bolster credibility in the government's ability to control inflation, even after most reforms had been undertaken and fiscal surplus achieved. On the contrary, the financial collapse of the early 1980s did not lead agents to inflationary expectations, despite the massive devaluation and fiscal imbalances on the order of 8 percent of GDP.

13. The large fluctuations of copper prices have important effects on the government budget, for which copper taxes and profits are a crucial source of revenue. Chile has implemented a stabilization fund that ameliorates, in part, these adverse fluctuations; as of 1993, the fund had reached a level over U.S$700 million.

14. In 1989, U.S. imports of Chilean fruits were suspended for two months after allegations that a shipment of grapes had been poisoned. Losses for Chilean exporters have been estimated at 1.5 percent of GDP.

15. In comparison, public investment in East Asian countries was, on average, 10.5 percent of GDP in the same period (World Bank, 1993).

16. Trade agreements between two countries have a positive outcome (trade "creation," or the increase in trade resulting from lowering barriers) and a negative outcome (trade "diversion," or the cost of eliminating competition from more efficient third countries not included in the agreement).

17. U.S. administration officials acknowledged that they were reluctant to set a date. The change in U.S. policy, undertaken within a week of the summit, was motivated, in part, by the tardy ratification of the GATT in the U.S. Congress, but also as a response to pressures by Latin American countries (*New York Times*, p. A8, 7 December 1994).

18. For a thorough analysis of the failure of trade pacts in Latin America in the 1955–1990 period, see Rosenthal (1993).

19. *New York Times*, p. A35, 12 December 1994.

References

Bosworth, Barry, Rudiger Dornbusch, and Raul Labán, eds. (1994), *The Chilean Economy: Lessons and Challenges*, The Brookings Institution, Washington, D.C.

Bouzas, Roberto and Nora Lustig, eds. (1992), *Liberalización Comercial e Integración Regional: De NAFTA a MERCOSUR*, FLACSO, Buenos Aires.

Butelmann, Andrea (1993), "Acuerdo de Libre Comercio: ¿qué se negocia?" in Andrea Butelman and Patricio Meller, eds., *Estrategia Comercial Chilena para la década del 90: Elementos para el Debate*, CIEPLAN.

Butelmann, Andrea and Alicia Frohman (1992), "Hacia un acuerdo de libre comercio entre EEUU y Chile," in Roberto Bouzas and Nora Lustig, eds., *Liberalización Comercial e Integración Regional: de NAFTA a MERCOSUR*, FLACSO, Buenos Aires.

Butelmann, Andrea and Patricio Meller (1993), "Tópicos Centrales en una Estrategia Comercial Chilena para la Década de los 90," in Andrea Butelman and Patricio Meller, eds., *Estrategia Comercial Chilena para la Década del 90: Elementos para el Debate*, CIEPLAN.

Calvo, Guillermo, Leonardo Leiderman, and Carmen Reinhart (1993), "Real Exchange Rate Appreciation in Latin America," *IMF Staff Papers*, vol. 40, No. 1, March.

Central Bank of Chile (1994), *Monthly Bulletin*, various issues.

Corbo, Vittorio and Stanley Fischer (1994), "Lessons from the Chilean Stabilization and Recovery," in Barry P. Bosworth, Rudiger Dornbusch, and Raul Labán, eds., *The Chilean Economy: Lessons and Challenges*, The Brookings Institution, Washington, D.C.

de la Cuadra, Sergio and Dominique Hachette (1991), "Chile: Trade Liberalization since 1974," in G. Sheperd and C.G. Langoni, eds.,*Trade Reforms: Lessons from Eight Countries*, International Center for Economic Growth, San Francisco, California.

ECLAC (1994), *Balance Preliminar de la Economía de América Latina y el Caribe, 1993*, Santiago, Chile.

Edwards, Sebastián and Alejandra Cox-Edwards (1987), *Monetarism and Liberalization: the Chilean Experiment*, 2nd edition, The University of Chicago Press, Chicago.

Edwards, Sebastián and Rudiger Dornbusch (1994), "Exchange Rate Policy and Trade Strategy," in Barry P. Bosworth, Rudiger Dornbusch, and Raul Labán, eds., *The Chilean Economy: Lessons and Challenges*, The Brookings Institution, Washington, D.C.

Elbadawi, Ibrahim and Raimundo Soto (1994), "Capital Inflows and Long-Term Equilibrium Real Exchange Rates in Chile," *PRD Working Papers* #1306, The World Bank, Washington, D.C.

Frankel, Jeffrey, Ernesto Stein, and Shang-Jin Wei (1995), "Trading Blocs: the Natural, the Unnatural and the Super-Natural," *Journal of Developing Economics.*

Fritsch, Winston (1992), "Integración Económica: ¿Conviene la Discriminación Comercial?" in Roberto Bouzas and Nora Lustig, eds., *Liberalización Comercial e Integración Regional: De NAFTA a MERCOSUR*, FLACSO, Buenos Aires.

Hakim, Peter (1992), "La Iniciativa para las Américas: Qué Quiere Washington?" in Roberto Bouzas and Nora Lustig, eds., *Liberalización Comercial e Integración Regional: De NAFTA a MERCOSUR*, FLACSO, Buenos Aires.

Jadresic, Esteban (1994), "Factores Estratégicos y Escenarios Futuros de Comercio Exterior," *Monthly Bulletin* # 798, Central Bank of Chile.

Krueger, Anne O. (1994),"Comments on 'Lessons from the Chilean Stabilization and Recovery,' by V. Corbo and S. Fischer," in Barry P. Bosworth, Rudiger Dornbusch, and Raul Labán, eds., *The Chilean Economy: Lessons and Challenges*, The Brookings Institution, Washington, D.C.

Lal, Deepak (1984), "The Real Aspects of Stabilization and Structural Adjustment Policies: An Extension of the Australian Model," *Staff Working Papers* #636, The World Bank, Washington, D.C.

Larrañaga, Osvaldo (1989), *El Déficit Público y la Política Fiscal en Chile: 1978–1987*, ECLAC, Santiago, Chile.

Marcel, Mario and Andrés Solimano (1994), "Thirty Years of Income Distribution in Chile," in Barry P. Bosworth, Rudiger Dornbusch, and Raul Labán, eds., *The Chilean Economy: Lessons and Challenges*, The Brookings Institution, Washington, D.C.

McKinnon, Ronald (1973), *Money and Capital in Economic Development*, The Brookings Institution, Washington, D.C.

257

Meller, Patricio (1994), "Comments on 'Lessons from the Chilean Stabilization and Recovery,' by V. Corbo and S. Fischer," in Barry P. Bosworth, Rudiger Dornbusch, and Raul Labán, eds., *The Chilean Economy: Lessons and Challenges*, The Brookings Institution, Washington, D.C.

Pindyck, Robert and Andrés Solimano (1993), "Waiting and the Option to Invest: Theory and Evidence," *NBER Macroeconomics Annual*.

Rojas, Francisco (1993), "El Cono Sur Latinoamericano y la Iniciativa para las Américas,"*Estudios Internacionales*, vol. 26, no. 101.

Rosenthal, Gert (1993), "Treinta Años de Integración en América Latina: Un Examen Crítico," *Estudios Internacionales*, vol. 26, no. 101.

Sanger, David E. (1994), "U.S. Envisions an Expansion of Free Trade in Hemisphere," *New York Times*, 7 December, sec. A.

——— (1994), "Chile is Admitted as North American Free Trade Partner," *New York Times*, 12 December, sec. A.

Servén, Luis, Andrés Solimano, and Raimundo Soto (1994), "The Macroeconomics of Public Enterprise Reform and Privatization: Theory and Evidence from Developing Countries," presented at the conference on "The Changing Role of the State: Strategies for Reforming Public Enterprises," The World Bank, Washington, D.C., February.

Sjaastad, Larry and Hernán Cortés (1981), "Protección y el Volumen de Comercio en Chile: la Evidencia," *Cuadernos de Economía*, vols 54–55, pp. 263–292.

TASC (1993), "Chile y los acuerdos comerciales," *Bulletin* # 45, Graduate Program in Economics, ILADES-Georgetown University, Santiago, Chile, July.

Taylor, Lance (1993),*The Rocky Road to Reform: Adjustment, Income Distribution and Growth in the Developing World*, MIT Press, Cambridge, Massachusetts.

Valdés, Rodrigo (1992), "Una Metodología para Evaluar el Impacto Cuantitativo de una Liberalización Comercial: Aplicación al ALC entre Chile y E.U.," in Andrea Butelmann and Patricio Meller, eds., *Estrategia Comercial Chilena para la Década del 90: Elementos para el Debate*, CIEPLAN.

Velasco, Andres (1994), "The State and Economic Policy: Chile, 1952–1992," in Barry P. Bosworth, Rudiger Dornbusch, and Raul Labán, eds.,

The Chilean Economy: Lessons and Challenges, The Brookings Institution, Washington, D.C.

World Bank (1993), *The East Asian Miracle*, Oxford University Press for The World Bank, Washington, D.C.

Appendix Table
Chile: Selected Macroeconomic Indicators, 1960–1993

	Real GDP (billions 1990 U.S.$)	GDP growth (percentage)	Inflation (percentage)	Fiscal deficit* (percentage)	Unemploy-ment** (percentage)	Investment*** (percentage of GDP)	Current account deficit (percentage of GDP)	Exports % of GDP	Exports 1993 U.S.$	Terms of trade	Nominal tariffs (percentage) Average	Nominal tariffs (percentage) Maximum
1960	3,525	—	5.5	4.6	7.1	14.7	3.8	—	2,343	76.0	102.0	NA
1961	3,694	4.8	7.7	4.5	8.0	15.1	5.5	12.5	2,144	75.0	135.0	NA
1962	3,869	4.7	14.0	5.8	7.9	15.2	3.0	12.4	2,312	76.3	94.1	NA
1963	4,114	6.3	44.1	4.9	7.5	16.1	4.3	12.7	2,326	76.5	94.1	NA
1964	4,205	2.2	46.0	3.9	7.0	15.3	2.7	12.2	2,757	114.7	94.1	NA
1965	4,239	0.8	28.8	4.1	6.4	14.7	1.3	13.6	3,170	152.9	94.1	NA
1966	4,712	11.2	23.1	2.5	6.1	14.2	1.4	11.4	3,825	185.2	76.2	NA
1967	4,865	3.2	18.8	1.3	4.7	14.2	1.6	14.5	3,822	176.4	76.2	NA
1968	5,039	3.6	26.3	1.5	4.9	14.7	2.0	14.1	3,771	188.6	76.2	NA
1969	5,227	3.7	30.4	0.4	5.5	14.3	0.6	16.7	4,617	222.8	38.6	NA
1970	5,334	2.1	32.5	2.7	5.7	15.0	1.2	14.8	4,141	226.1	38.6	NA
1971	5,812	9.0	20.0	10.7	3.9	14.6	2.1	10.9	3,568	172.3	56.7	NA
1972	5,741	-1.2	74.8	13.0	3.3	13.1	3.9	9.6	2,940	166.2	111.0	NA
1973	5,422	-5.6	361.5	24.7	5.0	12.8	2.7	12.0	4,280	187.2	105.0	750.0
1974	5,475	1.0	504.7	10.5	9.5	17.0	0.4	20.4	6,301	197.8	75.0	160.0
1975	4,747	-13.3	374.7	2.6	16.8	17.7	5.2	25.5	4,267	118.5	49.0	108.0
1976	4,898	3.2	211.8	2.3	20.1	17.3	-1.7	25.1	5,371	127.8	36.0	66.0
1977	5,305	8.3	91.9	1.9	16.2	13.3	3.7	20.6	5,210	114.4	22.0	43.0
1978	5,719	7.8	40.1	0.9	16.1	14.7	5.2	20.6	5,447	111.0	15.0	20.0
1979	6,125	7.1	33.4	-1.7	15.3	14.9	5.4	23.3	7,632	118.5	10.0	10.0
1980	6,596	7.7	35.1	-0.6	13.9	16.6	7.1	22.8	8,249	100.0	10.0	10.0
1981	7,038	6.7	19.7	-3.0	12.5	18.6	14.5	16.4	6,096	84.3	10.0	10.0
1982	6,095	-13.4	9.9	8.8	24.3	14.6	9.2	19.4	5,548	80.3	10.0	10.0
1983	5,882	-3.5	27.3	7.5	34.7	12.0	5.4	24.0	5,556	87.5	18.0	18.0
1984	6,241	6.1	19.9	9.1	27.8	12.3	10.7	24.3	5,075	83.1	24.0	24.0
1985	6,509	4.3	30.7	9.8	16.3	16.8	8.3	28.1	5,107	77.2	26.0	26.0
1986	6,900	6.0	19.5	5.0	13.5	17.1	6.9	29.1	5,524	85.8	20.0	20.0
1987	7,355	6.6	19.9	1.5	12.2	19.4	4.3	30.3	6,637	89.4	20.0	20.0
1988	7,892	7.3	14.7	-0.1	10.9	20.3	0.7	34.6	8,614	108.2	15.0	20.0
1989	8,697	10.2	17.0	-1.2	9.1	23.1	3.1	35.1	9,416	110.8	15.0	15.0
1990	8,958	3.0	26.0	0.7	9.6	24.6	2.8	34.3	9,188	110.0	15.0	15.0
1991	9,504	6.1	21.8	-1.0	7.4	21.7	-0.2	33.3	9,470	112.6	15.0	15.0
1992	10,483	10.3	15.4	-0.5	6.0	23.7	1.7	30.8	10,281	106.9	11.0	11.0
1993	11,112	6.0	12.7	-1.0	4.6	26.5	5.1	27.8	9,202	97.6	11.0	11.0

* Includes quasifiscal operations.
** Includes emergency employment programs.
*** Fixed capital formation.
Sources: Central Bank of Chile (1994) and Bosworth, et al. (1994).

9

Political Reform and Economic Liberalization in Colombia

Francisco E. Thoumi

Introduction

In 1990 Colombia began an economic liberalization program similar to those undertaken by other Latin American and Caribbean (LAC) countries. It includes measures to decrease the role of the state as a producer of goods and services, to relax economic regulations, to eliminate most price controls and subsidies, to reform capital markets, to lower tariffs and nontariff barriers to international trade, and to liberalize the labor legislation.

Although the Colombian reforms are similar to those of other countries in the region, there were two important differences in the process that led to the policy changes. First, during the 1970s Colombia borrowed very cautiously in the international markets and escaped the debt crisis that affected the rest of LAC, avoiding drastic balance of payments and external debt crises, sharp increases in unemployment, and higher inflation rates. During the Latin American debt crisis of the 1980s, Colombia was the only country in the region that experienced no decrease in income and the only one that did not reschedule its external debt payments. Thus, Colombia did not have most of the economic difficulties that led to economic liberalization programs in the rest of LAC.

During most of the postwar period, Colombia enjoyed a relatively satisfactory and stable income growth; however, GDP growth rates declined sharply during the 1980s when they averaged about 3.2 percent, compared with the 1967–80 average of about 5.75 percent. Concern about the flagging GDP has been posited as the main justification for establishing the program to open the economy that began during the Virgilio Barco administration (Departamento Nacional de Planeación, 1990) and was continued by the César Gaviria administration. That is, the current Colombian reforms were motivated by a desire to resume a relatively high growth rate, while in most of the other LAC countries these policies have been established in response to deep economic crises.

Second, the Colombian economic reforms must be seen as part of a wider social reform package. Colombian social and economic development in the postwar has been quite paradoxical: while the level of economic comfort of most Colombians has increased, many fundamental quality of life indicators have deteriorated badly. On one hand, income per capita, life expectancy, and nutrition, health, and education levels have improved substantially and infrastructure growth has been spectacular.[1] The country, which at the turn of the century had been a collection of fairly isolated, almost totally self-sufficient small regional economies, became an integrated national market. Furthermore, available data show that, during the last twenty years, income distribution has improved substantially, mainly as a result of a decline in the salary gap between unskilled and skilled workers (Londoño, 1990, 1992). Macroeconomic policy management has been prudent, with policies changing only gradually, avoiding the drastic changes and fads followed by other LAC countries.[2] Indeed, during the last 40 years, Colombia's economic growth was more stable than that of the United States (García-García, 1991). Colombia has transformed itself from a mostly rural and traditional society into a mainly urban and dynamic one. These economic successes were accompanied by political ones. When compared with the rest of LAC, Colombia has an outstanding record of elections and transfers of power between civilian governments;[3] and the country avoided the populist episodes experienced by most large LAC countries (Urrutia, 1991).

On the other hand, persistent, troubling socioeconomic characteristics have marred Colombia's progress. Violence has been very high by any standards, even during times considered peaceful, and has increased dramatically during the last decade (Losada and Vélez, 1989, and Thoumi, 1987). While the army, police, guerrilla, and paramilitary groups have been actors in the increased violence, the level of violence unrelated to political activity has been much higher than in other countries. This is one of the most difficult-to-explain characteristics of Colombia. Colombians seem to have few internal constraints regarding the use of violence and are quite prone to attempt to solve conflicts violently. The common explanations include the very unequal political power and income distributions; failed land and tax reforms; frustrated rising expectations; widespread corruption; a very inefficient government; an almost nonfunctioning judicial system;[4] and the rapid growth of criminal and noncriminal underground economies, particularly marijuana and coca (and more recently poppy) growing and cocaine manufacturing and exporting. These developments have weakened the state as successive governments have become increasingly unable to enforce the law, respond to the needs of the citizenry and be accountable to it, and perform some of the most fundamental functions, such as providing justice and a conflict resolution system, police services and a minimum level of personal security. The political system has become marked by clientelism[5] and can no longer channel the fast changes of the Colombian society in a creative way to democratize it (Leal, 1989, and Leal and Dávila, 1990).

These factors have contributed to the delegitimation of the regime, creating a situation in which the majority of the population does not accept the authority of the current system or accord it respect (Thoumi, 1992b). This delegitimation expresses itself in a growing gap between the legal system and its laws and regulations and the socially accepted behavior, that is, between *de jure* and *de facto* behavior.

The current policy reforms must be placed within this paradoxical context of Colombian development. The main challenge for any Colombian government is to reform the political and economic system to provide the basis for the development of a democratic capitalist regime and a modern stronger state, with anonymous and efficient markets in which rent seeking activities are minimized.

To that end, the economic liberalization program should be evaluated according to two criteria: first, how does it affect economic growth, and second, how does it affect the legitimacy of the regime and the degree of democracy in Colombia.

Colombian Economic Development Highlights

After World War II, Colombia followed a traditional import substitution development strategy supported by the conventional wisdom of the time. Manufacturing was protected, maintaining exchange controls and a fixed exchange rate system that did not adapt to fluctuations in export revenues and led to periodic foreign exchange crises. After one such crisis in 1967, the country changed its fixed exchange rate policy, instituted a creeping peg,[6] established export subsidies, and succeeded in maintaining remarkably continuous exchange rate and other macroeconomic policies.[7]

The 1967 policy changes encouraged the expansion of nontraditional exports, which also benefitted from the expanding global demand. At the time of the November 1973 international oil price increase, Colombia had a small oil trade balance, and its international reserves had increased to the point that it weathered the oil crisis without major problems.

The early 1970s witnessed an interesting policy change. The Miguel Pastrana administration (1970–74), under the influence of the ideas developed earlier by Lauchlin Currie (1966), made urban construction (mainly housing) the leading growth sector. The main idea behind this policy was that in order to increase the rural standard of living, rural labor productivity must be increased. This meant that nonagricultural jobs must be generated for the excess rural labor. Remarkably, this was done at a time when the conventional wisdom encouraged policies to slow rural-urban migration. The promotion of urban construction required significant capital market changes and led to the creation of the Unidad de Poder Adquisitivo Constante, or "UPAC," (constant purchasing power unit) system[8] that indexed savings and loans. Until then, real interest rates in the official capital market tended to be negative. The financial system captured very few domestic savings and acted mostly as a funnel for Central Bank or external funds channeled to industry and manufacturing. The UPAC increased the amount of domestic savings captured by the financial institutions, encouraged the growth of the financial sector, and forced agriculture and industry, the traditional "productive" sectors, to compete for funds with construction.

During the mid-1970s an international coffee boom brought the country unprecedented amounts of foreign exchange. This was followed by a marijuana boom in the late 1970s and a greater cocaine boom also starting in the late 1970s. These booms changed the nature of Colombian macroeconomic management issues as the country went from a foreign exchange constrained economy to one in which foreign exchange was quite abundant.

The capital market liberalization process continued in the mid–1970s as both foreign exchange availability and underground income increased. The financial sector grew substantially in a very loose regulatory environment. The formation of financial groups with very large investments in other sectors led to large loans to the firms owned by these groups and other financial mismanagement. The result was a financial sector crisis and a weakening of the financial structure of the industrial sector during the early 1980s (Echavarría O., 1983; Jaramillo, 1982; Montenegro, 1983; and Restrepo, Serna, and Rosas, 1983).

The consolidated public sector deficit during the twenty years before 1980 had usually remained under 3 percent of GNP, and in most years it had been below 2 percent. The Julio César Turbay administration (1978–82) undertook a massive infrastructure program (mainly electricity and some higways) and ran very high (by Colombian standards) fiscal deficits, financed with extensive use of foreign borrowing at a time when the central bank was accumulating reserves at a very fast pace.[9] This administration is responsible for a substantial proportion of the current external debt of Colombia.[10] At this time, the government also promoted the development of several very large mining projects in petroleum, coal, and ferronickel that substantially changed the sectoral composition of investment in the country.

When the Belisario Betancur administration (1982–86) came to power, it faced severe economic problems: a very high fiscal deficit, increasing inflation, and a financial sector crisis. The growth of underground exports and the financial sector produced highly speculative investments and some fraud. The government was not prepared to cope with these developments. It lacked regulatory legislation and foresight. Several large financial institutions failed and were taken over by the government that socialized many of the losses. The Betancur administration's main economic accomplishment was its success in controlling the fiscal deficit and the financial sector crisis.[11]

By 1982 cracks in the political system were also evident. Guerrilla activity had gained strength, and the growth of political clientelism was obvious. Colombia has had a formalistic democracy with periodic elections and peaceful changes of power. However, the Colombian political system has been controlled by a two-party elite, therefore, "it has been in many ways a limited or qualified democracy, one in which even the constitutional rules of the game have restricted popular participation and the unhindered interplay of competing forces and interest" (Martz, 1992).[12] The elites of the two traditional parties had a long history of conflict and violence that culminated in the infamous "violencia" period that began in the late 1940s and resulted in 200,000 to 300,000 deaths, equivalent to between 2 and 3 percent of the country's population. This undeclared civil war led to the military dictatorship of Gustavo Rojas Pinilla from 1953 to 1957. However, the dictator threatened the traditional elites' control, and they realized the need to negotiate future coparticipation in government. The traditional elites then promoted the successful overthrow of the military government and established a power-sharing system known as the National Front. The system included the even distribution of most government jobs and the alternation of the presidency between the two traditional parties. The National Front amounted to the institutionalization of a power monopoly of a two-party cartel for sixteen years. This monopoly rid the country of the main immediate cause of political violence, but "it also produced a growing electoral and systemic alienation, as the average Colombian well understood the futility of active involvement in politics" (Martz, 1992). When the National Front ended, a constitutional amendment extended the power-sharing agreement under less rigid conditions.

Because the traditional political conflicts had more to do with clientelism and its control of the state than with differences in economic orientation between the two party elites, the National Front agreement permitted the remarkable macroeconomic policy continuity and stability that accounts for the equally remarkable stable performance of the Colombian economy. Since 1967, government policies have demonstrated a continuous pragmatic accommodation to various external and internal forces, including the growing underground economy. Indeed, the political elite clearly understood that although they had an agreement to distribute the bureaucratic pie, a few key institutions that set the main economic policies (particularly, the Central Bank and the National Planning Department) had to remain relatively independent from the political establishment. These institutions are staffed with highly qualified professionals, who have been responsible for macroeconomic policy formulation and for avoiding the big policy changes and macroeconomic policy inconsistencies frequent in other economies of the region. Interestingly, Colombia is the only large country of the region in which macroeconomic policies have not been important electoral campaign issues.

While macroeconomic policy was successful in the sense that it produced satisfactory growth rates, policies that attempted to address the main structural problems of the country or alter the political status quo or that were made in response to rural violence—such as the land reform promoted in the early 1960s and the attempts to open the political system undertaken during the Betancur and Barco (1986–90) administrations during the 1980s—have been much less effective. The country has also struggled since 1974 through a succession of seven tax reforms, which have increased short-term tax collections and allowed underground money laundering, but have failed to provide a stable long-term tax base.

Beginning in the mid-1970s, the illegal drug industry developed at a fast pace, contributing substantially to the growth of an already significant underground economy. Government response to the illegal drug industry was ambivalent: it was attracted by the foreign exchange generated by drug trafficking, but did not want to allow the illegal drug capitalists to attain political power and social respectability. The establishment's opposition to these illegal drug businessmen's attempts to invest in farmlands in areas with active guerrillas and left-leaning peasant populations that were targeted by the government's land reform program became a source of social conflict and violence.

The increased education levels of the population, the growing urbanization, the development of communications and the media, the growth of an "emergent" class of illegal drug capitalists, and the failure of distributive reforms, coupled with the exclusionary characteristics of the political system, provided fertile grounds for the growth of political alienation and violent opposition to the system, mostly from left-leaning guerrilla movements and illegal drug businessmen who demanded access to political power.

The Colombian political system allowed the traditional elites to control the state, but while the system provided short-term stability, its dynamics guaranteed long-term instability and turmoil. Colombian political scientists have long recognized this reality and have prescribed political "opening" or democratization of the system. Mainstream economists have perceived a deterioration of economic performance as economic growth declined during the 1980s, and in their search for answers, they have endorsed an economic "opening" or liberalization. Recent Colombian presidents, beginning with Belisario Betancur (1982–86), have been increasingly aware of the need to open the regime and have made efforts in that direction. However, the political establishment blocked many policies aimed at democratizing Colombian society during the Betancur and Barco administrations.[13]

In 1986, GDP growth appeared to have been brought back to the 5–6 percent range in response to increased coffee prices. However, after prices fell in 1987, GDP slowed again in 1988 and remained low. During the late 1980s, coal and oil exports grew in response to the earlier investments, and when the international Coffee Agreement collapsed in July 1989 and international coffee prices fell by about 50 percent, the increase in coal and oil exports more than compensated for the coffee revenue downfall. The government then had to confront a low growth situation that could not be attributed to severe fiscal or foreign sector imbalances. Total factor productivity slowed during the 1970s and declined in the 1980s, indicating the development of long-term growth problems that needed to be addressed.[14]

During the Barco administration, the increased level of violence—particularly, the assassination of three presidential candidates and other notables in 1989 and 1990—galvanized public opinion regarding the need for deep systemic changes to resolve what was increasingly seen as an institutional, rather than a policy, crisis. President Barco promoted a referendum that approved convening a constituent assembly charged with rewriting the 1886 constitution, which had survived with several reforms. The new constitution, approved in July 1991, opened the political system and instituted programs designed to make the state more accountable and responsible to the citizenry.

The Gaviria reform program follows that of the Barco administration (in which President Gaviria was first Finance and then Interior Minister) and includes first, a "political opening" of which the new constitution is the keystone. In an attempt to break the power duopoly held by the two traditional parties, the constitution attempts to weaken the clientelism that defines Colombian politics and to open channels for the political participation of small political groups. Second, the program advocates an increase in regional autonomy, in which the decentralization of government decisions and the strengthening of local governments play an important role. The reforms also include, third, a "social opening" implemented through increases in social sector expenditures and, fourth, an "economic opening" package. The most important element of the economic package is an international trade liberalization program initiated in February 1990 by the Barco administration, but it also includes several other market liberalization measures (Hommes, 1992). All these reform policies are meant to increase the degree of democracy in Colombian society and to decrease economic privileges and rents.

Policy Reform and Economic Growth

In their search for a higher growth rate, the Barco and Gaviria administrations fully accepted the "Washington consensus," which attributed low growth rates and total factor productivity stagnation to the lack of competition in domestic markets, the high degree of government regulations, and the low level of international trade that reflected the closed nature of the Colombian economy.[15] The new policies include a fast international trade liberalization program that lowered tariffs substantially and eliminated most non-tariff trade barriers; an elimination of the exchange control system that freed foreign exchange transactions and international capital flows; the weakening of the restrictions on direct foreign investment; drastic changes in the labor code to make labor markets more flexible;[16] and more capital market liberalization measures. These measures have been complemented with a very aggressive trade liberalization program with Venezuela and Ecuador, as well as an agreement with Venezuela and Mexico to form a regional common market (the Group of Three, or G-3).

The drastic policy changes begun during the last year of the Barco administration were followed by the Gaviria administration, inaugurated in August 1990, in a remarkable example of policy continuity. The new administration was committed to controlling the fiscal deficit and lowering the inflation rate, which was seen as one of the main obstacles to the reforms' success. Thus, tight fiscal and monetary policies were implemented. In late 1991, another tax reform, granting amnesty to those who had illegally acquired assets and had income abroad, was implemented to complement the elimination of the exchange control system.

The Gaviria administration clearly gambled on the success of the market liberalization policies to regain GDP growth rates in the 5 to 6 percent level. These policies have been accepted by most Colombians and questioned by few economists. The mainstream economics policy rationale for the reforms is that the country had become increasingly closed to international competition, a process that led to increased resource allocation inefficiencies and a decline in the growth rate. The evidence supporting this rationale included: a) During the Betancur administration, tariffs were raised a few points in response to balance of payments problems. However, these increases did not raise official tariffs to the levels achieved during the high growth 1960s and 1970s. b) Official data indicate that exports as a percentage of GDP declined secularly from the 1920s on.

Liberman and Hanna (1992) argue that the lack of manufacturing export growth and the decline in total factor productivity in the sector is primarily explained by the anti-export bias of the trade regime, the poor infrastructure supporting exports, the policies that have inhibited direct foreign investment (DFI) and technology import. Using the experience of some of the successful NICs, Liberman and Hanna propose a blueprint for an industrial restructuring program that includes selecting manufacturing subsectors to be evaluated. These include some that need "defensive restructuring" —that is, subsectors that do not have, and are unlikely to develop, an international comparative advantage—and some that need "positive restructuring" in which the country has or may develop a comparative advantage to produce "indicative strategies for restructuring and modernization." These studies will be discussed by working groups consisting of representatives of the government, industry, the financial sector, and the *gremios*,[17] to produce a consensus within the government and trade associations on the necessary policy changes to open up the industrial sector in Colombia and provide a stimulus for change. Technical assistance funding should also be available for a Labor Adjustment Assistance Program, environmental pollution control, and a project management unit to support the government administration of the program.

There is, however, other evidence that raises substantial questions about the logic behind the mainstream view. First, during the 1970s and 1980s, marijuana and cocaine exports grew dramatically and these are excluded from official data. The foreign exchange revenues from these exports that entered the Colombian economy annually are likely to have been in the $1.5 to $2.5 billion range, compared with official goods exports of about $3 billion in the early 1980s, which rose to $6 billion in 1989. Thus, Colombia was substantially more open to international competition than official figures suggest (Thoumi, 1992a).[18]

Second, in 1920 the domestic market was very segmented because of the great difficulties in domestic communication and transportation. As the appropriate infrastructure developed and the domestic market became increasingly integrated, the share of exports in GDP should have declined anyway.[19]

Third, since 1986 official exports have increased substantially (Ocampo, 1992), and GDP growth did not increase proportionally, questioning the link between exports and growth.

The decline in total factor productivity during the 1980s is explained by Ocampo (1991, 1992) in different terms. His arguments are based on historical data and a three gap model developed by Villar (1991). Ocampo (1992) points out that the "post-war growth of the Colombian economy can be best understood as the result of the interplay between foreign exchange shortage and the dynamics of structural change, with factor productivity playing an accommodating role. It argues that neither the balance of payments nor factor growth will be binding constraints in the next few years, but that the economy will be subject to a severe domestic financing constraint."

Protectionist trade policies, inadequate infrastructure for foreign trade, and high industrial concentration have been constant features of the Colombian economy and consistent with high growth periods. Thus, while it is important to open up the economy to international trade and to improve the export infrastructure, it is not possible to attribute the growth decline to those factors. Ocampo attributes the decline in growth to the misguided economic policies of the Turbay administration (1978–82) that resulted in large fiscal deficits and heavy external borrowing, to the "contamination by the Latin American crisis," and to the lack of a defined industrial policy.

Following Echavarría (1989), Ocampo argues that manufacturing growth, rather than export growth, was the major determinant of factor productivity growth from 1925–80. Until the mid-1970s, industrial policy was well defined. From the postwar period until the mid-1960s, import substitution policies were in place: these included not only tariff protection, but also credit and technological support to new industries. This period was followed from 1967 to the mid-1970s by a mix of export promotion and protection to the producers for the local markets. However, in the mid-1970s, the country experienced an external coffee price boom, followed by a illegal drug export boom, and since then industrial growth has declined. "The structural crisis can be traced to the lack of a consistent industrial policy since the early 1970s. Given the objective difficulties faced by manufacturing development once the early and intermediate stages of import substitution had taken place, this policy vacuum became a fertile ground for the severe short-term shocks which the industrial sector experienced since the mid-1970s, including the 'Dutch disease'."[20] Ocampo argues that the Dutch disease effects of the export booms, while important in the late 1970s, cannot explain why industrial growth remained low after the booms passed. Ocampo contends that in the early 1970s the structural change stopped as the share of manufacturing in GDP stagnated, and technological absorption and adaptation slowed down although the national market was already integrated and no new economies of scale developed. According to this view, these two factors caused the stagnation in total factor productivity and slowed the rate of GDP growth. It must be noted that both Liberman and Ocampo coincide on the need for industrial policy.

Ocampo provides valid explanations for the long-term growth decline. However, there are several questions raised by his arguments. First, he shies away from discussing the importance of the illegal drug export industry, but his arguments imply the illegal drug boom peaked in the early 1980s. Indeed, United States wholesale cocaine prices peaked around 1983 and have declined by about 75 percent since then in response to very large increases in exports. However, as shown by Urrutia (1990), unexplained capital inflows in the balance of payments are not related to cocaine prices, but to devaluation expectations and real interest rate differentials between Colombian and international markets. The point is that the illegal drug revenue inflows did not peak in the early 1980s.

Second, structural change did not stop in the early 1970s, as Ocampo contends. It is true that the GDP share of manufacturing stopped growing; however, the productive structure continued changing as mining became the leading sector during the 1980s. Still, in agreement with Ocampo, while mining productivity was increasing, the backward linkages of that sector were very minor. Thus, it did not generate as many positive externalities as the manufacturing sector previously had. The point is that not all structural change contributes to GDP growth rate increases, even when it introduces new high productivity technologies.

Traditional economic explanations of the economic growth slowdown do not give weight to institutional elements. However, there are many institutional reasons why Colombia's growth has slowed down: first, the growth of political clientelism led to a need to devote an increasing share of the budget to pork. Second, the growing inability of the state to carry on some of its most fundamental functions led to increases in the amount of resources devoted by the private sector to protect property rights and to rent-seeking activities. Third, the increase in violence led to increases in the military, police, and security expenditures in the government budget at the expense of social sector and infrastructure expenditures and to increases in protection expenditures in the private sector. Fourth, kidnappings lowered investment, particularly in rural areas, and have been likely to have lowered direct foreign investment. Finally, the growth of the illegal drugs industry and the speculative growth of the financial sector raised the expectations of high short-term profits and encouraged speculative investments (Thoumi, 1987).

The point is, Colombia has experienced a profound institutional crisis, and Colombian institutions have increasingly become an obstacle to economic growth. This crisis has produced a growing gap between *de jure* and *de facto* behavior that has contributed to the growth rate decline (Thoumi, 1994). Many of the elements of the crisis are difficult to quantify and therefore may be dismissed by traditional economic analysts. However, the government does not have the luxury of dismissing the institutional crisis, a fact reflected in the policies discussed below.

In conclusion, it is highly doubtful that the official diagnosis of the low growth crisis and the implemented policy prescription will bring the country back to a fast growth path. Indeed, since 1991 several worrisome signs have appeared in the economy. At a time when the international interest rates, especially those in the United States, were declining sharply, while the Colombian rates remained very high because of tight fiscal and monetary policies aimed at lowering a stubbornly high inflation rate, the international trade and capital liberalization programs resulted in a very large influx of foreign exchange. The programs also caused a de facto revaluation of the black market exchange rate of about 10 percent despite the Central Bank's willingness to buy foreign exchange and a very fast accumulation of reserves.

Extremely large investments in energy during the early 1980s account for a substantial share of the Colombian external indebtness and produced a hypertrophied electricity sector. Despite these investments, maintenance mismanagement and corruption resulted in grave electricity shortages that persisted for over a year, beginning in late 1991, and caused great disruption to daily activities in Colombia.

Policy Reform and Democracy

Beginning with the Betancur administration, the Colombian governments have tried to open the political system. President Betancur began a dialogue with guerrilla organizations to attempt to bring them into the mainstream. The process of discussions with and the partial assimilation of guerrilla groups have continued since then with varying success, although negotiations with some groups that have the power to create important disturbances have been very difficult and unsuccessful. This has been the case of the negotiations with the National Liberation Army (ELN) that controls an area through which the main export oil pipeline runs. The ELN bombs the pipeline continously, resulting in large exports losses and extremely grave environmental damage.

The Barco and the Gaviria administrations encouraged the constitutional reform approved in July 1991. The constitutional reform process allowed broad political representation as all marginal sectors of the population were represented in the Constitutional Assembly.

Since the Betancur administration, the government has attempted to increase political participation and has tried to decentralize the government's economic decisions. Today, mayors and governors are elected; before, they were appointed by the government. Among other changes, municipal finances are being strengthened, most senators are elected on a national basis in an attempt to weaken clientelism, and social expenditures are being increased. These programs were designed to make the state more accountable and responsible to the citizenry and to increase participatory democracy.

Political reform, however, has been full of pitfalls. The attempts to strengthen local democratic processes granting greater autonomy to local governments may fail, given the traditions of authoritarianism and clientelism at the local level. One likely result of electing mayors is the increased control of some municipal governments by those who have the ability to buy elections, particularly individuals related to the illegal drugs industry.

The new constitution has shown some significant weaknesses. It establishes important entitlements to education, health services, and other basic needs, and thus, raises expectations about the ability of the government to provide them. However, it does not explain how to finance any of these entitlements. Chances are that the government will be unable to meet these financial costs, with ensuing social unrest. Also, one of the new constitution's anticlientelism measures was the elimination of the "situado fiscal," an allowance received by each congressman that could be disposed of at their own will. However, Congress has found a loophole that allowed it to reinstate those appropriations.

Negotiations with both drug traffickers and guerrillas have proven to be inconclusive. A large number of guerrillas have become assimilated, and several notable traffickers have turned themselves in. However, violence levels remained very high during 1991, and human rights violations remained widespread (Americas Watch, 1992). "Narco-terrorism" has increased dramatically. Many assimilated guerrillas and their sympathizers have been assassinated, and those still fighting have become increasingly daring. For example, in October 1992, they blocked the most important highway from the eastern prairies into Bogotá, cutting important food supplies to the city. And all the while, the ELN continues bombing the oil pipeline, disrupting oil exports. In 1992 there were approximately 30,000 homicides (de Roux, 1993). During early 1993 Colombia again suffered large bomb explosions resulting from the government's pursuit of drug kingpin Pablo Escobar. Since his death in December 1993, the violence associated with narco-terrorism appears to have abated.

If one accepts the government's fundamental inability to implement many policies, then some of the economic policies of the Barco and Gaviria administrations are consistent with needed policy reforms. However, prior institutional changes are required so that they do not increase the concentration of wealth and power and the inequity of the system. For example, capital markets should be made more competitive, but as restrictions are eliminated, the power of the large economic actors should be controlled to avoid greater wealth and rent concentration.[21] Another example of policy coincidence is the lowering of international trade barriers that decrease the bounty creation by the government and increase competition. There is also a coincidence both in the labor legislation changes that made the labor market more flexible and in the moves to make the process of bidding to supply the government more transparent.

Unfortunately, the obstacles to the establishment of a capitalist democracy in Colombia are many. Among them perhaps the most important is the illegal PSAD (psychoactive drugs) industry, which because of its size, behavior, and illegality adds a particularly complex dimension to any democratic capitalist reform. A democratic capitalist system requires a much smaller and weaker underground economy, an accomplishment unlikely to be achieved as long as the illegal PSAD industry continues to flourish.

Furthermore, even if the illegal drug flow is stemmed, the illegal PSAD businessmen are already extremely rich and sooner or later would have to be assimilated into the mainstream of Colombian society. However, this assimilation creates fundamental problems for the government. At a time when the basis for a democratic capitalism is most needed, the illegal PSAD industry generates forces in the opposite direction. The large growth and size of an industry with a very concentrated income increases the income concentration in the country. The drug traffickers' investments in rural areas have increased the income and wealth distribution in those regions, and the windfall gains and the illegality of the industry's profits have contributed to the widespread rent seeking and predatory behavior that pervades Colombia. The assimilation of the illegal PSAD industry capital legitimizes those behaviors.

The background and values of many drug traffickers creates another problem. Many have violent criminal backgrounds and have shown highly paternalistic behavior patterns that conflict with the development of a capitalistic democracy (Thoumi, 1994). Frequent actions of the illegal PSAD industry, such as its significant contributions to the development of paramilitary groups and its violent repression of left-leaning political activists, are important obstacles to the governments' attempts to open up the political system, a precondition to any democratization project (Leal, 1990, and Melo, 1990).

Conclusion

The current economic liberalization program in Colombia has been taken as part of a social reform package to cope with an economic growth slowdown and important social problems of violence and regime illegitimacy. Mainstream economists see the economic reforms as independent of the political and social ones and forecast an increase in the rate of GDP growth as a result of the economic reform implementations. Structural economists see a more complex problem and argue that a more proactive economic policy is necessary to achieve the necessary structural changes in the economy to regain a high growth rate. The institutional interpretation to which this author adheres argues for deep institutional reforms to cope with the high violence and increased underground economy. Most of the policies followed by the current administration coincide with the needed ones for institutional change. However, they do not go far enough. The main problem is not that Colombia is a large and inefficient state, but rather, that it requires a deep transformation to become successfully proactive. That is the main policy challenge, which transcends traditional economic policies. Such reform faces many obstacles—among which the most important is perhaps the illegal drug industry—that make policy success quite improbable.

Notes

1. Urrutia, ed. (1990) presents a set of articles by several authors that summarizes the most significant improvements in the Colombian standard of living.

2. See Revéiz and Pérez (1986) and García-García (1991) for analyses of the continuity and success of Colombian macroeconomic policies and the relative economic stability they have produced.

3. During the first three years of this century the country experienced a bloody civil war between the two traditional parties (liberal and conservative), but since 1903 it has been ruled by elected presidents, except for a short period (13 June 1953–10 May 1957) during which a military dictatorship held power and a shorter one (10 May 1957–7 August 1958) during which an interim military junta held power. However, it should be noted that when the military overthrew the civilian government in 1953, it did so to stop another bloody confrontation between the two traditional parties and had the support of most of the population.

4. Many judges and supreme court magistrates have been killed and police and security systems have been "privatized" as paramilitary groups have gained strength and private security services have become a growth industry.

5. Clientelism is a political system in which the state is not accountable to the citizenry, and politicians mediate between the state and the people. In its extreme forms, this system provides services and affords rights to the people only through politicians. The vote loses its meaning as an expression of public opinion and becomes the citizens' means to press claims with the politicians who control the state. The Colombian clientelistic system resembles the patronage systems that have prevailed at times in some American cities.

6. A method of controlling exchange rates, "creeping peg" (or "crawling peg") is a general term applying to any proposal with the characteristic that par values—the official exchange rate as declared by the International Monetary Fund (IMF)—can be adjusted over time. In the case of Colombia, the goal was to avoid the large periodic devaluations that caused domestic inflation to be higher than the international inflation rate.

7. Díaz-Alejandro (1976) provides the classic analysis of the 1967 policy changes in Colombia.

8. A system in which the nominal value of saving and other financial accounts increased automatically by a certain percentage determined by the inflation rate. This was designed to eliminate the erosion of purchasing power of financial balances caused by inflation and, thus, to encourage financial savings.

9. The consolidated public sector deficit rose to 5.8 percent of GDP in 1981, peaked at 8.7 percent in 1982, and averaged 6 percent during the following three years before it was brought down in 1986 to 1.6 percent (García-García, 1991).

10. Total external debt increased from $4.06 billion in 1978 to $10.27 billion in 1982, a 153 percent increase (García-García, 1991).

11. Clavijo (1992) surveys the development of the financial sector and concludes that substantial improvements have taken place, and the remaining repressed market characteristics are in part related to the weak competition within the sector. Because the recent policy changes are designed to increase the degree of competition, even allowing direct foreign investment in the sector, the outlook toward future financial developments in Colombia is quite positive.

12. The Colombian formalistic democratic system has been characterized by several authors as "elitist rule" (Berry, 1971); "oligarchical democracy" (Wilde, 1978); and "consociational" (Dix, 1980; Hartlyn, 1985, 1988). These references always imply a deeply unequal society, in which the state is controlled by a group and used to achieve the group's goals.

13. Martz (1992) summarizes the attempts of presidents Betancur and Barco and concludes: "In short, Barco's proposals for *apertura* were effectively gutted as Liberals and Social Conservatives leaders joined to block all measures which might challenge their customary rule."

14. Clavijo (1990) provides a long-term series of total factor productivity estimates.

15. This view had the support of the multilateral lending agencies and the American administration and was reinforced by World Bank studies (World Bank, 1990a and 1990b).

16. These changes included: the possibility to have an "integral salary" without fringe benefits for higher paid employees, allowing firms to hire people for temporary periods of up to three years; the elimination of the legislated tenure after ten years of work that had led to the firing of qualified workers as they got close to that threshold; and other measures that made it easier to hire and fire workers.

17. *Gremios* are producers' associations, which are the strongest lobbies in Colombia.

18. Hallberg and Takacs (1992) indirectly support the contention that the Colombian economy was much more open than it appeared. They provide a detailed analysis of an auctioning of import licenses system, which was established in early 1990 as a first step to determine the importance of quantitative trade restrictions. The results of these auctions were quite surprising as the demand was much lower than expected, and the "extra tariffs resulting from the auction process were also relatively low." Hallberg and Takacs attribute these results to several factors, including widespread contraband on many items opened for bids. The auction results are likely to have encouraged the government to speed up the liberalization process during 1991.

19. It is well known that the share of international trade in GDP is inversely related to the size of a country's domestic market. See, for example, Inter-American Development Bank (1982), part one.

20. "Dutch disease" refers to some of the effects that primary resource booms have on the rest of the economy. The effects include a real revaluation of the exchange rate that makes imports cheaper and other exports unprofitable. When this occurs, sectors that do not export or compete with imports (e.g., the real estate sector) grow while the rest of the economy stagnates.

21. The 1970s experience showed that capital market liberalization—when most banks are owned by large economic groups that lend mainly to their own firms—increased concentration and led to large bankruptcies. It is necessary to insure that small savers are paid positive real interest rates on their savings, and small entrepreneurs have access to capital.

References

Americas Watch, 1992, *Political Murder and Reform in Colombia*, Human Rights Watch.

Berry, R. Albert, 1971, "Some Implications of Elitist Rule for Economic Development in Colombia," in Gustav Ranis, ed., *Government and Economic Development*, New Haven: Yale University Press.

Clavijo, Sergio, 1990, "Productividad Laboral, Multifactorial y la Tasa de Cambio Real en Colombia," *Ensayos Sobre Política Económica*, No. 17: 73–97, June.

———, 1992, "Overcoming a Financial Crisis During the Transition of a Repressed System to a Market Based One: Colombia 1970–89," in Alvin Cohen and Frank R. Gunter, eds., *The Colombian Economy: Issues of Trade and Development*, Boulder, Colorado: Westview Press.

Currie, Lauchlin, 1966, *Accelerating Development: the Necessity and the Means*, New York: McGraw Hill, Inc.

Departamento Nacional de Planeación, 1990, "Programa de Modernización de la Economía Colombiana," *Revista de Planeación y Desarrollo*, Vol. XXII, Nos. 1 and 2, January–June.

de Roux, Francisco José, 1993, "Prólogo," *Violencia en la Región Andina*, Bogotá: CINEP.

Díaz-Alejandro, Carlos F., 1976, *Foreign Trade Regimes and Economic Development: Colombia*, New York: National Bureau of Economic Research.

Dix, Robert, 1980, "Consociational Democracy: the Case of Colombia," *Comparative Politics*, Vol. 12, April.

Echavarría, Juan J., 1989, "External Shocks and Industrialization in Colombia, 1920–1980," Oxford University, mimeo.

Echavarría O., Hernán, 1983, *El Escándalo de los Fondos Grancolombiano y Bolivariano en el Gobierno del Dr. Turbay Ayala*, Medellín: H. Echavarría O.

García-García, Jorge, 1991, "Macroeconomic Crisis, Macroeconomic Policies and Long Run Growth: the Colombian Experience 1950–1986," Washington, D.C., March, mimeo.

Gunter, Frank R., 1991, "Colombian Capital Flight," *Journal of Interamerican Studies and World Affairs*, 35, 1, spring.

Hallberg, Kristin and Wendy E. Takacs, 1992, "Trade Reform in Colombia: 1990–94," in Alvin Cohen and Frank R. Gunter, eds., *The Colombian Economy: Issues of Trade and Development*, Boulder, Colorado: Westview Press.

Hartlyn, Jonathan, 1985, "Producer Associations, the Political Regime, and Policy Processes in Colombia," *Latin American Research Review*, Vol. XX, No. 3.

————, 1988, *The Politics of Coalition Rule in Colombia*, Cambridge: Cambridge University Press.

Hommes, Rudolf, 1992, "Challenges to the Private Sector in the 1990s: Colombian Economic Policies and Perspectives," in Alvin Cohen and Frank R. Gunter, eds., *The Colombian Economy: Issues of Trade and Development*, Boulder, Colorado: Westview Press.

Inter-American Development Bank, 1982, *Economic and Social Progress in Latin America: the External Sector, 1982 Report*, Washington, D.C.

Jaramillo, Juan Carlos, 1982, "El Proceso de Liberación del Mercado Financiero en Colombia," *Ensayos Sobre Política Económica*, No. 1: 7–19, March.

Leal, Francisco, 1989, "El Sistema Político del Clientelismo," *Análisis Político*, No. 8: 8–32, September–December.

————, 1990, "Estructura y Coyuntura de la Crisis Política," in Francisco Leal and León Zamosc, eds., *Al Filo del Caos: Crisis Política en la Colombia de los Años 80*, Bogotá: Tercer Mundo Editores.

Leal, Francisco and Andrés Dávila, 1990, *Clientelismo: el Sistema Político y su Expresión Regional*, Bogotá: Tercer Mundo Editores.

Liberman, Ira W. and James C. Hanna, 1992, "Colombia: Industrial Restructuring and Modernization," in Alvin Cohen and Frank R. Gunter, eds., *The Colombian Economy: Issues of Trade and Development*, Boulder, Colorado: Westview Press.

Londoño, Juan L., 1990, "Income Distribution During the Structural Transformation," unpublished Ph.D. dissertation, Harvard University.

———, 1992, "Had Kuznets Visited Colombia....," in Alvin Cohen and Frank R. Gunter, eds., *The Colombian Economy: Issues of Trade and Development*, Boulder, Colorado: Westview Press.

Losada, Rodrigo and Eduardo Vélez, 1989, "Tendencias de Muertes Violentas en Colombia," *Coyuntura Social*, No. 1, December, Bogotá: FEDESARROLLO and Instituto SER de Investigación.

Martz, John D., 1992, "Contemporary Colombian Politics: the Struggle Over Democratization," in Alvin Cohen and Frank R. Gunter, eds., *The Colombian Economy: Issues of Trade and Development*, Boulder, Colorado: Westview Press.

Melo, Jorge O., 1990, "Los Paramilitares y su Impacto Sobre la Política," in Francisco Leal and León Zamosc, eds., *Al Filo del Caos: Crisis Política en la Colombia de los Años 80*, Bogotá: Tercer Mundo Editores.

Montenegro, Armando, 1983, "La Crisis del Sector Financiero Colombiano," *Ensayos Sobre Política Económica*, No. 4: 51–89, December.

Ocampo, José A., 1991, "The Transition from Primary Export to Industrial Development in Colombia," in Magnus Blomstrom and Patricio Meller, eds., *Diverging Paths: Comparing a Century of Scandinavian and Latin American Economic Development*, Inter-American Development Bank.

———, 1992, "Prospects for Medium-Term Growth in Colombia," in Alvin Cohen and Frank R. Gunter, eds., *The Colombian Economy: Issues of Trade and Development*, Boulder, Colorado: Westview Press.

Restrepo, Juan C., Juan G. Serna, and Manuel G. Rosas, 1983, "Inflación, Financiamiento y Capitalización Empresarial," *Ensayos Sobre Política Económica*, No. 4: 153–198, December.

Revéiz, Edgar and Maria J. Pérez, 1986, "Colombia: Moderate Economic Growth, Political Stability, and Social Welfare," in Jonathan Hartlyn and Samuel A. Morley, eds., *Latin American Political Economy: Financial Crisis and Political Change*, Boulder, Colorado: Westview Press.

Thoumi, Francisco E., 1987, "Some Implications of the Growth of the Underground Economy in Colombia," *Journal of Interamerican Studies and World Affairs*, 29, 2: 35–53, summer.

———, 1992a, "The Economic Impact of Narcotics in Colombia," in Peter Smith, ed., *Drug Policy in the Americas*, Boulder, Colorado: Westview Press.

————, 1992b, "Why the Illegal Psychoactive Drugs Industry Grew in Colombia," *Journal of Interamerican Studies and World Affairs*, 34, 3: 37–63, fall.

————, 1994, *The Political Economy of Colombia and the Growth of the Illegal Drugs Industry*, Boulder, Colorado: Lynne Reinner.

Urrutia, Miguel, ed., 1990, *40 Años de Desarrollo: su Impacto Social*, Bogotá: Biblioteca Banco Popular.

Urrutia, Miguel, 1990, "Análisis Costo-Beneficio del Tráfico de Drogas para la Economía Colombiana," *Coyuntura Económica*, 20, 3: 115–126, October.

————, 1991, "On the Absence of Economic Populism in Colombia," in Rudiger Dornbush and Sebastian Edwards, eds., *The Macroeconomics of Populism in Latin America*, Chicago: The University of Chicago Press.

Villar, Leonardo, 1991, "Las Restricciones al Crecimiento Económico: un Modelo Sencillo de Tres Brechas," in E. Lora, ed., *Apertura y Crecimiento: el Reto de los Noventa*, Bogotá: Tercer Mundo-FEDESARROLLO.

Wilde, Alexander, 1978, "Conversations Among Gentlemen: Oligarchical Democracy in Colombia," in Juan J. Linz and Alfred Stepan, eds., *The Breakdown of Democratic Regimes: Latin America*, Baltimore: Johns Hopkins University Press.

World Bank, 1990a, *Colombia: Industrial Competition and Performance*, Washington, D.C.

————, 1990b, *Colombia: Policies for Efficient Growth in the 1990s*, Report No. 8346-CO, Washington, D.C.

Part IV

Trade Liberalization Beyond Frontiers

10

Mexico/NAFTA and Central Europe/European Community: A Comparative Analysis

William Glade

Save for the episode that briefly put Maximillian on a Mexican throne, there would seem little connection between the southernmost partner of NAFTA and Central Europe—at least since the days of Charles V and his far-flung realm. True, some have detected a link between the development doctrines propounded by the Economic Commission for Latin America, which found considerable resonance in contemporary Mexico, and those of the Romanian Mihail Manoilescu, an economist who wrote during the interwar period.[1] For that matter, Manoilescu's predilection for corporatism suggests a further parallel with the Mexican system of political economy. More directly, in terms of policy genealogy, a few of the pioneers of modern development studies had in mind the needs and possibilities of postwar Eastern Europe when they began to elaborate policy models that, in time, were influential in Mexico and elsewhere in Latin America.[2] Ironically, the legacy was, in a sense, repaid when economists and other social scientists in Hungary and Poland later took an interest in the development experience of Mexico and other Latin American countries as a way of talking about policy options—and external economic relationships—that could not be openly addressed in the party-controlled environment of Soviet satellite regimes.

These curiosities aside, however, there are today relatively few economic connections between Mexico and the emerging Central European democracies with which we are primarily concerned in this discussion: Poland, the Czech and Slovak Republics, and Hungary, to which one could add Slovenia, Croatia, and the three Baltic nations as plausible extensions of the Central European economic region, though these last five will not be covered in this review. There have been virtually no investment flows either way, and even the commerce between them never amounted to a great deal, either before or after the exodus of these erstwhile centrally planned economies from the Soviet bloc. Some have speculated that the opening of the former Council for Mutual Economic

Assistance (CMEA) economies and their eventual economic rehabilitation might eventually create new markets for the exports of
other newly industrialized and developing economies, at least the
more dynamic ones,[3] but there would appear little basis at present
for assessing what this might mean for Mexico. By the same token,
the prospects for reciprocal commercial flows, from Central
Europe to Mexico, are obscure but, in all likelihood, relatively inconsequential. This being the case, a word of explanation seems
clearly in order for dealing with Mexico and the Central European
region in the same chapter.

The Basis for a Comparative Analysis

Both Mexico and the Central European states are semi-industrialized regions that share a proximity to the great economic power-
houses: the United States and Canada on the one side of the
Atlantic and the European Community (EC) on the other. Their
respective economic destinies will clearly depend on the kinds of
ties they are able to cultivate with these industrially advanced
nations. At least nascently, then, they are to some extent trans-
oceanic economic rivals. For example, to the degree that the
capital markets of the North Atlantic industrial economies are not
highly segmented, Mexico and the Central European countries
are, and will increasingly be, competitors for the supplies of ex-
portable capital that are generated therein—a concern that is
shared, for that matter, by Portugal and Greece within the EC.

For the moment, it is not clear that this potential rivalry has
begun to operate with any intensity, although Mexico and Central
Europe are both tapping capital markets on each side of the
Atlantic. Along with European capital, U.S. and Canadian capital
have continued to flow into Mexico, in anticipation of further
growth in the Mexican home market and of improved access, with
NAFTA, to the even larger markets of the other two NAFTA
members. It is also notable, in this connection, that beginning in
the late 1980s Mexico, together with a few other Latin American
countries, was able, through bond sales and private placements, to
return to the Eurobond market $2.2 billion in 1990. The following
year Mexican corporations not only sold $2.6 billion in bonds but
also raised another $300 million through Euronote sales.[4] Mean-
while, both U.S. and EC investments have moved into the former
CMEA region, although the volume of the flow has generally
been somewhat under what had been hoped for, if not actually

expected. Also, somewhat surprisingly, the amount of U.S. capital invested has constituted the largest single country share: some $8 billion out of a total of around $28 billion for the former CMEA area as a whole. (Italy, also surprisingly, has invested over $7 billion, though all of these figures include the whole of Eastern Europe and the former Soviet Union.) Even in Hungary, the most investment-ready of the countries, problems have been greater than was anticipated during the first bloom of liberation. The competition that could be expected in capital markets, therefore, is more a matter for the future, once the economic reconstruction program is farther along in Central Europe. At the same time, Mexico, having been graduated some years ago from the cohort of countries eligible for economic and technical assistance, does not compete with the Central European countries on that score.

In time, too, both of these economic end zones could conceivably grow more competitive with each other in selling goods and services into what could be viewed as the world's most affluent and largest market economy areas: the Single European Market or Economic Community, on the one hand, and, on the other, the free trade area that joins the United States and Canada. (Following long-time usage by the United Nations Economic Commission for Latin America, we shall refer to the combined market area that comprises the EC and U.S./Canada as the "Industrial Center.") How either Mexico or Central Europe will fare in this effort is still a matter for conjecture, though to date their experience has been heartening.

Mexican experience in this respect has been well publicized. Only a short while ago, it was expected that the Central European economies might be unable to export much to the market economies of the West because these economies are equipped with CMEA transaction-specific capital: i.e., capital goods (and, by extension, production organization) that could only turn out products that were acceptable in the managed trade of the CMEA.[5] Thus far, however, the supply response from Central Europe to improved market access to the West has been surprisingly strong on the whole, as will be noted below, though there is some evidence, for Poland at least, that the recent performance of firms is related to their previous hard currency exports.[6] It may be, therefore, that the capacity to increase Central European exports will reach a temporary ceiling and that further expansion will have to await extensive, and difficult, reorganization and retrofitting of the area's capital plant. As of now, though, the evidence for a hiatus of this sort is inconclusive.

Whatever transpires about the production capabilities in Central Europe, it will be interesting to compare and contrast them with the supply elasticities of traded goods in Mexico as trade liberalization and other economic reforms expose long highly protected economies to international competition in their home markets and give them enhanced opportunities to sell more abroad.[7] In Mexico and Latin America as a whole, it has been a reasonable presumption that production costs, product design, and product quality in these nationally sheltered workshops had endowed much of the established manufacturing capacity with something of the same transaction-specific character that has been posited for the erstwhile CMEA members—hence, the sporadic efforts to enlarge national markets through protected regional integration schemes.

For the time being, both Mexico and Central Europe are counting on some of the same factors in their hopes for enlarging their participation in the markets of the Industrial Center. Both expect to capitalize on their lower labor costs. The Central Europeans received a substantial boost in this respect when, for political reasons, German reunification set wages in the former German Democratic Republic at around 70 percent of the West German level, even though productivity in the *funf neuer Länder* (five new states) was only about 30 percent of that of West Germany. In banking on a labor advantage, which in both cases may turn out to extend well beyond the unskilled and semiskilled levels, both have also aroused apprehension among some producers within the Industrial Center, particularly in the Iberian peninsula and Greece. In the case of the EC, though, this seems to have abated somewhat with a realization that the comparative advantages the Central Europeans bring to the table may be different from those of the less developed EC members. More likely to be affected by a Central European economic resurrection is that applicant-in-waiting, Turkey. Be that as it may, for the time being it would appear that Mexico and the three Central European countries with which we are primarily concerned share a revealed comparative advantage in nonelectrical machinery as well as in iron and steel. Mexico has a revealed comparative advantage, not shared by Central Europe, in transport equipment, chemical elements, and nonmetallic mineral manufactures. Poland, Czechoslovakia, and Hungary, in turn, appear to enjoy a stronger revealed comparative advantage in footwear and clothing and are closer to having such an advantage in textiles, yarns, and fabrics.[8]

Neither side, of course, has yet had to factor into the structure of its production costs the environmental protection charges that producers in the Industrial Center have for some time had to assume. At some point, however, each will have to carry out heavy social investment programs to deal with air pollution, restore water quality, accelerate reforestation, and clean up contaminated soils—along, at least in Mexico's case, with repairing the results of decades of soil erosion. Both Mexico and Central Europe think of themselves as having special institutional/locational advantages as gateways to markets lying farther from the industrial heartland, from which they hope eventually to extract some economic benefit. More immediately, each, of course, enjoys already a substantial locational advantage, on account of low transport costs, in supplying the neighboring portion of the affluent Industrial Center market with a variety of agricultural products and low-skilled/labor-intensive manufactures, together with tourism services and, where possible, the services of temporary migrant workers, whether documented or unauthorized. At present, the access of Central European agricultural exports to the smaller European Free Trade Area (EFTA) markets is much greater than it is to the EC market, while Mexican agriculture, excepting chiefly its far-from-robust sugar industry, enjoys reasonably clear entry into the U.S. market. Nevertheless, the EC may sooner or later relax its present restrictions on the admission of Central European agricultural products, at least gradually, as part of its program of assistance in preparing these countries for eventual incorporation into the Community.

Even before NAFTA, the barriers on Mexican trade with the United States were fairly low. NAFTA represents an historically unprecedented experiment in bringing together countries so disparate in their level of economic achievement. For their part, the Central European economies have all entered into a process of association with the European Community, though their actual admission is, fairly clearly, some years away. When and if, the Central European economies are incorporated into a single European Market, that process will have to deal with disparities in economic attainment that are equivalent to those that separate Mexico from the other two NAFTA members and, at least to some extent, reenact some of the disparity-resolving policy solutions that are likely to emerge in NAFTA. Pending that event, the Central European economies have already begun to enjoy the advantages of enhanced market access to the Industrial Center, much as has Mexico.

Hungary, for example, has held most favored nation (MFN) status with the United States for some years, MFN status was restored to Poland in 1989, and in 1990 Czechoslovakia was accorded the same privilege. All three—counting the Czech and Slovak Republics as one for this and subsequent purposes—also enjoy Generalized System of Preferences (GSP) benefits in the United States, and the Trade Enhancement Initiative for Central and Eastern Europe promised further improvement in market access, as did a renegotiation of textile quotas under the Multi-fibre Arrangement (MFA). On the other side of the ocean, a few concessions in market access were made early on by some of the EFTA countries, especially Austria, pending completion of a free trade agreement between EFTA and Poland, Czechoslovakia, and Hungary. Associate membership in the EC bestows, at least implicitly, the abolition of tariff and nontariff barriers on Central European manufacturing exports, save for textiles and steel products, the two product categories that are exceptions in the EFTA relationship as well—along, of course, with agricultural products in both groupings. Hence, thanks to these concessions, the Central European countries and Mexico now find themselves roughly equivalent in their relations to the Industrial Center despite their very different starting points.

Besides the foregoing parallelism in economic situation, a number of other factors justify our taking a comparative look at Mexico in relation to NAFTA, on the one hand, and Central Europe in relation to the EC, on the other. The combined population of the nine countries of the expanded Central European region, around 79 million, is not too different from Mexico's 86 million, and all of the countries are in the middle income category as defined by the World Bank, some a bit above Mexico and some below. Of the Central European countries included in the Human Development Report (Czechoslovakia, Hungary, Yugoslavia, and Poland), all rank above Mexico in the composite Human Development Index and, with one exception, in all the components of that index.[9] The single exception is Poland, which falls somewhat below Mexico in the level of per capita GDP. We can reasonably assume that the composite figure for Yugoslavia conceals a ranking on the higher side for Slovenia and Croatia, considered individually. The three Baltic states are probably not too dissimilar from the average of the other Central European figures for most of the components of the Human Development Index, though they may resemble Poland in the per capita level of GDP. The Slovak Republic would occupy a lower rank than that assigned Czechoslovakia as a whole, putting it somewhat closer to Mexico in a number of variables. These differences aside, all of the countries in the comparison are classified in the same category—that of High Human Development—of the Human Development Index, ranging on the Index from 92, the number for Czechoslovakia, to 83.8 for Mexico.

As the forgoing would suggest, there are additional similarities. Leaving aside the old industrialization of Bohemia and a few other regions, most of the countries in the comparison could be called newly industrializing and have certainly experienced their major industrial growth in the decades following World War II. Regrettably, on both sides of the comparison this growth has coincided with policies that paid scant regard to the environment. Thus, a heavy social charge hangs over developers in both regions as they look for ways to clean up the environment in the future. As the trade of each region with its neighboring advanced industrial partners grows, this circumstance will also render both Mexico and Central Europe vulnerable to charges of social dumping and to retaliation. Indeed, the problems of the EC iron and steel industry have already prompted discussion of the means of limiting the admission of rival products from the East and there is ample reason to believe that U.S. industry will follow suit under the terms of NAFTA. What is more, although both sides of our comparison are clearly semi-industrialized, in each, for quite different reasons, the private sector is characterized by a kind of dualism: the European economies, because of the exigencies of reconstruction, have lately begun to generate an informal sector, something Mexico has had for years.

Besides what has already been remarked, there are other differences to be kept in view. At least as of now, the distribution of income and wealth is more equitable in the Central European cases than in Mexico, and none of these countries has the substantial number of people living in poverty that Mexico has—nor the hyperurbanization of the latter. Generally speaking, the differences between urban and rural areas are fewer in Central Europe than in Mexico. On a number of other measurements—energy consumption per capita, the share of energy in GDP, a variety of health indicators, female enrollment in secondary education, and so on—Mexico ranks below the Central European countries.

However, in one notable respect, population growth rate, Mexico comes out well ahead of the others, saddling it with a problem from which the Europeans are exempted.

From what has been said, it should be evident that the basis of the approach taken in this comparative inquiry leans toward the similarity-of-systems strategy, even though it is precisely the design of systemic organization that becomes the variable to which the most attention will be paid. To the extent possible, we are including among the intersystemic similarities the general level of development that has been achieved, the size of the systems under consideration, their current common involvement in extensive economic restructuring, and the nature of the anticipated engagement between the systems under scrutiny and the systems into which eventual incorporation is sought. In this connection, it must be kept in mind that although the amount accomplished thus far varies widely, each of the countries included has undertaken some measure of structural adjustment, partly in preparation for the anticipated integration but also simply to place their once faltering economies on a sounder footing. The intersystemic differences that are of interest, then, focus on the institutional fabric that must be altered to attain the desired policy objectives. An understanding of the implications of these differences for the nature of the structural reform process is, consequently, the central objective of this inquiry.

Trade into the European Markets

Export markets in the European Community are not an insignificant share of Mexico's total exports, even though the United States, which takes around two-thirds of Mexican exports, is far and away the largest purchaser of Mexican goods and services. In 1990, for example, of Mexico's $36.8 billion (U.S. currency [cy]) total exports, 5.4 percent went to Spain, 2.0 percent to France, 1.3 percent to Germany, 0.8 percent to Italy, and 0.7 percent to the U.K.[10] Other EC countries consume smaller amounts. The year-to-year variation in relative terms has not been great. The 1990 total share for the five countries listed above was 10.2 percent; for 1989, 10.0 percent; for 1988, 11.0 percent; and for 1987, 12.3 percent. The twelve country total for the EC has generally run in the neighborhood of 15 percent. In aggregate value, Mexican exports to the five large EC members rose only from $2.5 billion to $2.7 billion between 1987 and 1990.

In contrast to Mexico's trade links with the countries of the EC—from some of which Mexico also receives important investments—the trade of Mexico with Central European countries counts for much less. Aggregate Mexican exports to the United Kingdom in 1990, for instance, amounted to $184 million, the smallest volume of the five large EC trading partners. Czechoslovakia was, in the same year, the largest of the Central European purchasers of Mexican exports with $4.8 million, a volume that had increased somewhat from earlier years. Poland, the second largest of the region's importers from Mexico, bought only $2.9 million, a figure that was a bit smaller than the imports for 1989 ($3.7 million) and 1987 ($4.1 million) and quite a bit smaller than the purchases in 1988 ($12 million). Only in this latter year did trade with any of the Central European economies, that with Poland, reach 0.1 percent of Mexican exports. Except for this aberration, less than half of this percentage represented the share of each country in Mexican exports over the 1987–1990 period. Meanwhile, although exports to Hungary peaked at $5.3 million in 1989, they varied between $1.0 and $1.15 million for the other years. Capital flows in either direction are, as noted earlier, virtually nonexistent.

In manufactures, Western Europe's share of Mexican exports typically runs somewhat under its share of total exports from Mexico. Four of the Standard International Trade Classification (SITC) categories can serve as a surrogate for more detailed breakdowns as they suffice to indicate the general magnitude and directions of change and to give an idea of the comparable movements in the trade of Central Europe with the EC, which bulks as large with these countries as the U.S. market does with Mexico. Fifty-six percent of Poland's exports, for example, go to the EC, while another 18 percent are sold to the EFTA countries. Similarly detailed scrutiny of the exports of Central Europe and Mexico to the markets of the United States and Canada is not necessary in that Mexican products hold the overwhelming advantage on this part of the Industrial Center. Exports from Central Europe to North America may grow rapidly in the years ahead. Although imports are likely to outpace exports, they do so from a small base.

In Chemicals and Related Products, for example, the five country total for Germany, the U.K., Spain, Italy, and France came to 7.3 percent of all Mexican exports ($1.8 billion) in this branch of production in 1990. This represented a significant improvement on the 4.5 percent of such goods the five countries had purchased from Mexico in 1987, at which time the aggregate Mexican exports of such products stood at $1.1 billion. Hence, the absolute gain was not inconsiderable. It is revealing, however, to line up Mexican export volumes with the comparable figures from Central Europe. Mexico's sales to Germany in this product category reached $40 million in 1990, up from $14 million in 1987; in 1990, Germany bought $219 million of such products from Poland, $182 million from Czechoslovakia, and $115 million from Hungary. With some fluctuations, German imports of chemicals and related products from Central Europe have been generally increasing, as they have been from Mexico. Mexico's next most important EC customer in the same product category was the United Kingdom, which bought just over $37 million in 1990, a marked gain on the $11 million it purchased from Mexico in 1987. On the other hand, British purchases of these goods in 1990 from Central Europe amounted to $59 million from Poland, $31 million from Hungary, and $20 million from Czechoslovakia—again with a significantly increasing trend parallelling that for similar imports from Mexico.

Mexican exports in 1990 of chemicals and related products to the other three EC markets ran lower: $19 million to Spain, $17 million to Italy, and $15 million to France, a gain on the $5 million, $12 million, and $9 million sold to these three countries respectively in 1987. In comparison, Spain purchased $38 million of such products in 1990 from the three Central European suppliers (up from $28 million in 1987), Italy bought $207 million (up from $107 million), and France imported $221 million (up from $83 in 1987).

In the aggregate, Mexican exports of Machines and Transport Equipment grew from $4.3 billion in 1987 to $6.7 billion in 1990, 5.4 percent of this, in 1987, having been shipped to the five major Western European countries. In 1990, the five countries' share of the total of this export category stood at 4.6 percent. Germany and France were, by a large margin, the most important European customers in this line, importing $166 million and $101 million respectively in 1990, compared with $150 million and $45 million respectively in 1987. In the later year, the United Kingdom bought only $19 million of these goods from Mexico, Spain took $11 million, and Italy $7 million. Again, Mexican sales were overshadowed by those of the Central European economies. German imports from these sources amounted to $883 million in 1990, France and Italy each purchased about $205 million, the United

Kingdom some $147 million, and Spain $64 million. The five country total imports of Central European machines and transport equipment, which reached $731 million in 1987, grew to $1.5 billion by 1990—a contrast with Mexican sales to the same countries of $233 million and $304 million in those years.

Basic Manufactures were exported from Mexico in the amount of $2.4 billion in 1987, a figure that climbed to $3.1 by 1990—allowing for a modest increase in the five EC countries' share of these exports from 4.7 percent in 1987 to 5.8 percent in 1990, most of which went to the United Kingdom, Italy, and Germany. Altogether, the five EC countries purchased from Mexico $177 million of these products in 1990, versus $115 million in 1987. Between the two years, U.K. imports of basic manufactures from Mexico increased from $42 million to $73 million; Italian imports, from $21 million to $45 million; and German purchases, from $20 million to $31 million. Sales of these goods to Spain and France, not very large initially, actually declined between 1987 and 1990. Central European sales of basic manufactures to the five were considerably larger: $1.6 billion in 1987 and $2.9 billion in 1990. Of these, in the latter year, Germany purchased $905 million from Poland, $545 million from Czechoslovakia, and $487 million from Hungary, a gain on the $367 million, $334 million, and $240 million purchased from the same countries respectively in 1987. Italy was the next largest EC importer of Central European basic manufactures in 1990, buying $158 million from Czechoslovakia ($104 million in 1987), $148 million from Hungary ($70 million in 1980), and $95 million from Poland ($28 million in 1987). For the same year, the United Kingdom held the third position, with $180 million in imports from Poland ($108 million in 1987), $75 million from Czechoslovakia ($55 million in 1987), and $20 million from Hungary ($31 million in 1987). France was not far behind the United Kingdom, with $120 million in imports of basic manufactures from Czechoslovakia, $91 million from Poland, and $47 million from Hungary, the comparable figures for 1987 being $79 million, $49 million, and $33 million respectively. Spain brought up the rear with notably lesser amounts in both years.

Miscellaneous Manufactured Goods accounted for a much smaller portion of Mexican exports, although they were increasing vigorously: from $614 million in 1987 to $1.0 billion in 1990. Of these, the five Western European countries—led by Germany, France, and Spain—received 6 percent in 1987 and 6.9 percent in

1990. The volume figures for these three in the miscellaneous manufactures category came, in 1990, to $20 million for Germany (410 million in 1987), $19 million for France ($8 million in 1987), and $16 million for Spain ($10 million in 1987), with $11 million in the sales of such items to the United Kingdom and only $3 million to Italy. The contrast with Central Europe's position is notable. Germany, for instance, purchased $721 million in miscellaneous manufactures from Poland in 1990 (up from $308 million in 1987), $496 million from Hungary (versus $305 million in 1987), and $243 million from Czechoslovakia (compared with $165 million in 1987).

Other EC imports of miscellaneous manufactures from Central Europe were generally below the German levels, but even so they surpassed the sourcing from Mexico. The United Kingdom bought, in 1990, $97 million of such products from Poland ($74 million in 1987), $67 million from Czechoslovakia ($54 million in 1987), and $46 million from Hungary ($34 million in 1987). For France the comparable amounts for 1990 were: $95 million ($55 million in 1987) from Poland, $86 million from Hungary ($56 million in 1987), and $71 million from Czechoslovakia ($48 million in 1987). Italian imports ran, in 1990, $29 million from Poland ($15 million in 1987), $20 million from Czechoslovakia (1 million over the 1987 level), and $26 million from Poland (versus $10 million for 1987). Spain imported $10 million in miscellaneous manufactures from Czechoslovakia in that year (a gain of 2 million over 1987), $5 million from Poland (five times the 1987 level), and $3 million from Hungary (with negligible imports in 1987). What is more, although for some reason the U.K. imports from Poland, in this category, decreased in 1991, in every other case the 1991 levels exceeded 1990 levels, sometimes by a quite substantial amount—indicating the growing Western European commercial traffic with Central Europe.

Trade Prospects

Looking ahead, one would suppose that Mexican manufacturing exports to the U.S. market might exhibit much of the dynamism that has characterized them in recent years, in which a half or more of the U.S. imports from Mexico have consisted of manufactures. Mexican manufactures should also find a growing demand in the Canadian market. On the other side of the Atlantic, sales of Mexican manufactured goods to the EC will also continue to increase, albeit much more moderately than in the North American market. Besides the direct exports from Mexico to Western Europe, there may well be an additional growth in indirect exports, i.e., in the Mexican-supplied components of U.S. manufacturing exports to the EC. Even without NAFTA, it is reasonably certain that the U.S. investment in the Mexican manufacturing sector would have increased and that the copro-duction of an expanding range of products likewise would have increased in relative importance. Already business alliances are being formed between firms in the two countries, supplementing the establishment and expansion of wholly-owned subsidiaries and joint ventures that have linked the two business communities for some time. Quite apart from the maquiladora plants, other Mexican operations have been sourced by U.S. manufactures for components for some years—picking up on a development that was gaining ground just before the oil boom of the 1970s reached full steam and arrested this growth through a Western Hemisphere version of the Dutch disease. With the ratification of NAFTA, Canadian exporters of manufactured goods to the EC will very probably incorporate a rising percentage of Mexican-made components as well. Hence, as these developments proceed apace and bring about an ever greater articulation of the production structures of the three members of NAFTA, the extensive marketing networks of U.S. companies—and in lesser measure Canadian firms—in Europe will become the springboard for in-creased Mexican penetration of the EC market, piggybacking on U.S. and Canadian marketing efforts, though how important this will be cannot be foreseen with accuracy just yet.

In addition, there is every reason to expect that the increased competence in production and export management that Mexican firms gain from competing successfully in the U.S. and Canadian markets will eventually spill over into their capacity to sell effectively in Europe and elsewhere—and not only in manufacturing. No doubt, for instance, the joint venture of Televisa and Venvision in the U.S. market will in time enhance the capability of these companies to challenge the beachhead that Brazilian exporters of telenovelas have achieved in Western European markets. Meanwhile, the growth of Japanese and South Korean direct investment in Mexico, though premised on the anticipated expansion of the Mexican market as well as access to the markets of Canada and the United States, should also, in the long run, fortify the capacity of Mexican production facilities to reach farther afield, the EC included. Further, it does not seem likely that the flow of Mexican manufactures, through one route or another, to Europe will be subject to abrupt interruption. The direct export of Mexican manufactures to Europe is so small as to be generally nonthreatening, while European policy in respect to the indirect exports is, in effect, buffered by the superior bargaining positions of the United States and Canada.

The general strength Mexico seems likely to enjoy in export markets is indicated by the comparative advantage it shares with Brazil in such "high technology" products as chemicals, medicinal and pharmaceutical products, plastic materials, nonelectrical and electrical machinery, and transport equipment. Together, the two countries account for 90 percent of Latin American exports of such products. For Mexico, these now represent about 60 percent of its exports of manufactures, and a variety of factors have been working to strengthen its position in the future.[11] For these reasons, there would seem to be room for cautious optimism in assessing the prospects for Mexican participation in the markets of the Industrial Center.

In contrast, although the present elasticity of export supply from Mexico is undoubtedly greater, wage differentials between Central Europe and the EC combine with modest transport costs and proliferating business ties—and a relatively bright outlook for foreign direct investment by EC members in Central Europe—to ensure that, with possible exceptions, such as the restriction of steel sales from Central Europe into the troubled EC market for that industry, Central European suppliers will be able to outdistance Mexican firms in a considerable range of manufactures. Foreign direct investment and joint ventures—though not, in all likelihood, business alliances—will provide the institutional highway over which Central European goods, especially in the manufacturing sector, will make their way into the neighboring markets of the Industrial Center. According to a recent World Bank study, in fact, manufacturing exports from the former CMEA members will probably more than double in the medium term and grow around ninefold to tenfold over the longer run.[12]

In time Mexican exporters to Western Europe may well, along with their Central European counterparts, encounter in a number of product lines some measure of competition from new maquiladora-type operations situated in Morocco, Egypt, and other places along the Mediterranean. A codevelopment scheme that grouped the countries of the Arab Maghreb Union (AMU) sought, between 1990 and 1992, to work out a new strategy of economic cooperation with the EC but temporarily ran aground because of conflicts over Libyan terrorism.[13] Despite this, Morocco has begun to explore the possibilities of the maquiladora relationship, and there is some interest elsewhere in doing likewise. Recent negotiations have, in fact, renewed the impetus to establish a special relationship between the EC and the Maghreb.[14] Meanwhile, the policy reforms in Egypt have been setting the stage for a broader export diversification effort centered on manufacturing, and one must keep in mind that wage levels along the southern Mediterranean shores appear promising for expanding the output of lower income goods. On the other hand, it seems quite possible that Turkey, which has positioned itself for a more dynamic export performance, thanks to the policy reforms of recent years, will experience some erosion of its preferential status in the EC market, owing to the concessions that have been made to the Central Europeans.[15]

More distantly, in geographical terms, Mexico and the Central European countries alike will need to compete for sales against imports from the growing number of Asian tigers, including a very large tiger-in-the-making, Indonesia. Over the longer run, all, of course, will have to reckon at some point with the massive social dumping of manufactures that is expected to come from the Chinese economy, where the production regime not only ignores environmental costs but also excludes significant elements of both housing and health costs from the wages bill.

These threats aside, both Mexico and the Central European economies may take some comfort from the fact that they both are in the process of moving from the status of most favored outsiders to insiders in their relations to the Industrial Center. They will eventually be able to benefit from such policy defenses as the two large trading blocs will be able to erect via-à-vis the rest of the world. At the same time, for all the benefits they may reasonably expect to reap from the new scheme of things, a cautionary note is in order so far as concerns expectations of joining the ranks of the prosperous. Recent research by A.J. Hughes Hallett of Strathclyde University, for example, has indicated that even with the substantial subsidy it is receiving from the German government, the former East Germany may not be able to reach levels of prosperity comparable to the rest of the country for some 30 to 40 years.[16] More sobering still is the example of the Mezzogiorno, the object of special ministrations during decades of exuberant expansion in the rest of Italy and Europe generally. Wales, Ireland, Appalachia, and large stretches of the southern United States stand as testimony to the limits of both markets and public programs to level the playing field.

Mexican Experience and Central European Development

Before Central Europe can test how far the rehabilitative powers of a market economy will ultimately extend, many intervening steps must be taken to clean up the institutional debris left by the entropy and subsequent abandonment of the old system. The breakdown of established trading relationships when the CMEA was disbanded and the rapid deterioration of those organizational troglodytes, the state enterprises, with the tremendous drain they have placed on government budgets, have contributed to the general disarray in the macroeconomy. This disarray also springs from a disruption of established fiscal and monetary relationships. Worse yet, if such were possible, the economies undertaking this systemic reform have had to do so with a recognition that almost all domestic economic relationships (and those linking the domestic sector with the rest of the world) were warped by a distorted and opaque structure of prices and that most, if not all, of the inherited industrial structure was shot through with technological obsolescence, counterproductive organization, and work habits that were wholly antithetical to the exigencies of the system sought as a replacement.

The accounting systems that were widely used in the CMEA era were largely useless as sources of the information needed for most business decisions. Also, the capacity of new firms to emerge from the wreckage has been stunted by the lack of a wide range of supporting business services of the sort that lubricate the machinery of product development, production, and distribution in the West. Though there is a tendency to ascribe the rise of the so-called service economy to the income elasticity of consumer demand for various categories of products, a considerable portion of the service sector responds primarily to the ever more sophisticated needs of modern industry. While privatization of retail and wholesale trade, as well as of construction, has not posed insurmountable difficulties for the most part, development of all the ancillary technical services has been difficult and as challenging as the obstacles to privatizing the large manufacturing combines. Simultaneously, the governments have had to work their way toward a new legal framework to govern all transactions and to devise the regulatory schemes needed to deal with the problem of monopoly, to provide a proper operating environment for public utility industries, to secure the foundations of the new capital markets, and to reduce the risk of weakness, or worse, in newly organized financial intermediaries.

While accomplishing much, the shock treatment has unleashed whole new sets of socially and economically, not to mention politically, destabilizing problems. This suggests that Orlowski, along with many others, may have been well advised in advocating more gradualism in the sequencing of reforms. As is universally recognized, the formerly centrally planned economies, in converting into a market regime, have embarked on a truly pioneering course, one with no real precedents.[17] It is sobering to reflect, in this connection, on the unexpectedly difficult task Germany has taken on in trying to absorb the economic decrepitude of the former German Democratic Republic, supposedly the most advanced of the old Soviet satellite bloc. Admittedly, a slower but deliberate approach to reform carries risks of its own, most obviously in the interim misallocations of resources it fosters during the period of transition—and in the enhanced opportunities it may afford for sabotage of the implementation process by entrenched members of the nomenklatura and their political allies. Such may, however, be a greater problem in Russia and some other successor states to the Soviet Union than in the Central European economies with which we are concerned here.

The catalogue of ills associated with this situation is formidable and complicated by the fact that the task of correcting major imbalances comes on the heels of falling economic activity. This decline brought a number of adverse consequences even though a good portion of the lost output actually contributed little or nothing to real social welfare. This is not the place to play Leporello and recite the list, but one aspect of the problem is key to the theme of this concluding discussion. A chief problem in the transition is that of trying to install a market system in the near absence of a collection of constituent institutions and relationships that give market processes their inherent suppleness and spontaneity. Not only are the policy instruments the new governments must use unfamiliar, but they are also being applied to a setting of incompletely developed market forces and an environment characterized by numerous lacunae in market institutions, lacunae that render the response to many policy changes exceedingly problematic.[18] The reliability of policy instrumentation is reduced accordingly, transactional costs are elevated, and behavioral responses—say, of management accustomed to a soft budget constraint—are quite different from what is normally expected in a Western-style mixed economy. The operation of monetary policy, for instance, is influenced by the limited range of effective instruments for credit control, by the limited options for dealing with nonperforming loans, by the limited track record for assessing creditworthiness, and, indeed, by the opaqueness of the enterprise accounting systems still in use. Meanwhile, as indicated above, many more decisions are thrown akilter by the paucity of information of all kinds and a services sector that is, at best, extremely rudimentary and unable to provide much support to the other sectors of production, especially in industry but to a considerable extent in agriculture as well.

There is, in other words, a vast amount of institution building to be accomplished to elicit the kind of enterprise behavior that is needed to raise productivity and income, to generate the human capital and entrepreneurial initiative, and to hone the skills needed by workers and consumers to make markets work. For key sectors to be able to withstand international competition and even earn resources in foreign markets, the transaction-specific capital—both material and organizational, that Hillman and Schnytzer have properly identified as a constraint on economic capability—must enter into a process of wholesale replacement, while in Hungary and Czechoslovakia, at least, privatization must find ways of effecting a significant measure of deconcentration in the structure of industry.[19] As Alfred Chandler's work has shown, there is an important sense in which the market in advanced industrial economies has been shaped by business organization rather than the reverse, and this historical experience would seem indisputably relevant to the agenda of marketization today.[20] Even allowing for the fact that the Central European economies can, in effect, import a great deal of the new price structure they need from the EC, significant modifications therein will be needed to ease the transition, and much else needs attention in order to increase the reliability of policy instruments.

This, finally, is where Mexico may fit into the Central European scheme of things. Over a period of 50 years of virtually unbroken growth, it carried out an extraordinary program of institution building, almost from the ground up. True, remnants of infrastructure from the period of late nineteenth-century (and early twentieth-century) expansion provided a small base on which to reconstruct the national economy, but it is germane to recall that the process that got underway in the mid- to late 1920s was likewise predicated on widespread economic devastation, owing to the disruptions and dislocations of revolution. Building on a very limited expertise in business management, constructing a workable system of financial intermediation, and consolidating new working rules and intergroup relations, the tutelary Mexican state took responsibility for socioeconomic engineering on a massive scale. It did so, moreover, with certainly no greater reservoir of human capital than Central Europe has to draw on today—and, in most respects, much less—and no deposit of institutional experience to tap for mapping the new territory into which it ventured. Neither had it much guidance in the way of development theory, at least for the first couple of decades or so.

What is more, Mexico was able for much the greater portion of this time to carry out its mission with fiscal restraint, monetary caution, convertible currency and realistic exchange markets, and a level of macroeconomic stability that was enviable—only occasionally, before the policy aberrations of the 1970–82 period, running into the balance of payments problems that have been elsewhere so chronic and widespread. The point is worth stressing. Not until the Echeverria and Lopez Portillo administrations, when lack of discipline characterized the public and parastatal sectors and the the oil boom permitted runaway borrowing and fiscal laxity, did things get out of hand. Before that, a conservative approach to monetary policy, because of the priority given to containing inflation, and a notable moderation in fiscal policy ensured that habits of mismanagement did not become deeply engrained in most public enterprises. No small part of the success was also attributable to the professionalism with which the government's lead institution in industrial development, *Nacional Financiera*, managed its role as a pioneer investment banker and industrial entrepreneur—in the days before similar services, and those relevant to industry rehabilitation, were readily available in the international market from private concerns.[21] This policy expedient helped to overcome the so-called agency problem that has afflicted so many public enterprises in other countries and was in some measure reinforced by the nearby example of reasonably good standards of managerial performance in the United States and in U.S.-linked enterprises in Mexico.[22] Even the dampening effects of protectionism on managerial efficiency, in both public and private sectors in traded goods, was most probably tempered by the ever present possibility of contraband trade, thanks to the permeability of the northern border.

Thus, notwithstanding the rickety infrastructure, both organizational and physical, with which Mexico began its "long march" into development, the disruptions of the Great Depression, a brief conflict with the international investor community over the petroleum expropriation, and further dislocations born of wartime conditions, Mexico went a half-century before experiencing a negative aggregate growth rate. Indeed, the very rapidity and success with which the system could be opened and restructured in the past few years, in spite of the crisis of the 1970–82 period and a huge foreign debt overhang, attests to the fundamental success in institution building of the state-led development program that went before. It is this that, in the last analysis, has enabled Mexico not only to carry out its restructuring program with such dispatch but also to contemplate with such equanimity its partnership with Canada and the United States.

Spain and various Asian successes have been recommended as models for Central Europe to emulate. The factors that have justified a comparative study of Central Europe and Mexico, however, and the nature of the agenda for the former suggest that the latter's version of a state-managed, state-designed market system, would be well worth researching for the policy guidance Central Europe could appropriate from it—though this approach flies in the face of the current passion for marketolatry.

Notes

1. See, for example, Joseph Love, "Economic Ideas and Ideologies in Latin America, 1930–1970," in Leslie Bethell, ed., *Cambridge History of Latin America*, Vol. VI, Cambridge: Cambridge University Press.

2. Gunnar Myrdal, the first executive secretary of the UN Economic Commission for Europe, began his long involvement in development with an interest in the problems of Eastern and Southern Europe, but the classic pieces, perhaps, were Paul Rosenstein-Rodan's "Problems of Industrialization of Eastern and Southeastern Europe," which was published in 1943, and Kurt Mandelbaum's *Industrialization of Backward Areas*, which came out in 1947. Besides these, the Political and Economic Planning (PEP) unit at the Oxford Institute of Statistics issued two of the earliest proposals for development programs: see "Economic Development in South-Eastern Europe," *Planning* (1944) and *Economic Development in South-Eastern Europe* (1945).

3. Refik Erzan, Christopher Holmes, and Raed Safadi, "How Changes in the Former CMEA Area May Affect International Trade in Manufactures," Policy Research Working Papers Series on International Trade, WPS 973, Washington, D.C.: World Bank, September 1992, p. 41.

4. Fred Z. Jasperson, "External Resource Flows to Latin America: Recent Developments and Prospects," unpublished paper, Washington, D.C.: Inter-American Development Bank, November 1992, p. 6. The lack of any significant crowding out by Central European borrowing is suggested by the fact that Chile, Venezuela, Argentina, and Brazil have also been able to tap the voluntary lending available in Euromoney markets.

5. Arye Hillman and Adi Schnytzer, "Creating the Reform Resistant Dependent Economy, the CMEA International Trading Relationship," PRE Working Papers Series, WPS 505, Washington, D.C.: World Bank, 1990.

6. Helga Mueller, "Determinants of Export Performance of Polish Enterprises During the Transition Process," mimeo, Washington, D.C.: World Bank, 1991.

7. For several reasons, one must be extremely cautious in using the present structure of market prices and trade patterns to infer what will be the longer term comparative advantages in Central Europe. On this, see Gordon Hughes and Paul Hare, "Competitiveness and Industrial Restructuring in Czechoslovakia, Hungary and Poland," *European Economy*, Special Edition No. 2 (1991), pp. 104–5.

8. Note the caveat in note 7, however, on inferring the longer run comparative advantages of Central Europe from today's trade patterns. These statements about revealed comparative advantage are based on a major recent study of exports of manufactures by Montague J. Lord, "Latin America's Exports of Manufactured Goods," in *Economic and Social Progress in Latin America*, 1992 Report, Washington, D.C.: Inter-American Development Bank, October 1992, pp. 191–279, which also compares the advantages of Latin American countries with those of other regions. At this point, Lord's is the definitive analysis of the topic.

9. United Nations Development Programme, Human Development Report 1991, New York: Oxford University Press, 1991.

10. These and other trade statistics, except where noted otherwise, come from the International Trade Information System that has been developed on the basis of UN data by the Center for International Business Education Research of the Graduate School of Business of the University of Texas at Austin.

11. Lord, p. 213.

12. Erzan et al., p. 19. The estimate is for five Eastern European countries, including Bulgaria and Romania along with the three that figure in this chapter, but the bulk of the gains seem destined to accrue to Poland, Hungary, and Czechoslovakia.

13. Besides the three countries of the Maghreb—Algeria, Morocco, and Tunisia—the AMU included Mauritania and Libya.

14. Michael Sutton, "Euro-Maghreb Partnership: a New Form of Association," *European Trends*, no. 3 (1992), pp. 61–67.

15. Erzan et al., p. 41.

16. A.J. Hughes Hallett and Yue Ma, "Real Adjustment in a Union of Incompletely Converged Economies: an Example from East and West Germany," mimeo, Strathclyde: Department of Economics, University of Strathclyde, August, 1992.

17. Lucjan T. Orlowski, "Present Stages of Economic Reforms and Privatization Programs in Eastern Europe: the Cases of East Germany, Czechoslovakia, Poland, and Hungary," Working Paper 156, Notre Dame, Indiana: Helen Kellogg Institute for International Studies, April 1991. A more comprehensive treatment—one of a burgeoning number these days—of the magnitude and complexity of the challenge of systemic transformation is found in the chapters of Paul Marer and Salvatore Zecchini, eds., *The Transition to a Market Economy*, Vol. 1, Paris: OECD, 1991. Most of the experts in this collection counsel, at least implicitly, a certain gradualism in the transformational process.

18. Rey Koslowski, taking particular note of the dearth of information in the Central European economies, also points to the inadequate policy support provided for the development and nurture of market institutions. See his thoughtful critique of shock therapy in "Market

Institutions, East European Reform, and Economic Theory," *Journal of Economic Issues*, Vol. XXVI, no. 3 (September 1992), pp. 673–705. For a similar and succinct statement of the same critical assessment for the former Soviet Union, see "What is Shock Therapy and Why Has it Failed in Russia and the Other Successor States?", testimony of James R. Millar to the Committee on Armed Forces of the United States Senate, Thursday, 4 February 1993. Hughes and Hare, p. 105, couch the need for intervention in the form of a plea for industrial policy, designed, of course, to strengthen the export sector.

19. David M. Newbery, "Tax Reform, Trade Liberalization, and Industrial Restructuring in Hungary," *European Economy*, no. 43 (March 1990), pp. 80–83. See also, Jozef M. van Brabant, "Divestment of State Capital: Alternative Forms and Timetable," in Kazimierz Z. Poznanski, ed., *Constructing Capitalism, The Reemergence of Civil Society and Liberal Economy in the Post-Communist World*, Boulder: Westview Press, 1992, pp. 117–38, and Friedrich Levcik, "The Thorny Path of Transition from Command to Market Economy," in Sandor Richter, ed., *The Transition from Command to Market Economies in East-Central Europe*, Boulder: Westview Press in Cooperation with the Vienna Institute for Comparative Economic Studies, Yearbook IV, 1992, pp. 57–72.

20. Alfred D. Chandler, Jr., *Scale and Scope: The Dynamics of Industrial Capitalism*, Cambridge: Harvard University Press, 1990. This study shows how improvement in productivity, wealth generation, and the competitiveness of nations is a function of the organizational and financial capabilities of firms and their supporting institutions and how governance structures, managerial systems, and the institutional-legal contexts are critical to industrial outcomes. This monumental work gives powerful validation to the key idea advanced in John F. Tomer, *Organizational Capital: The Path to Higher Productivity and Well-being*, New York: Praeger, 1987, wherein organizational capability as a factor of production is traced in theoretical and empirical studies.

21. *Nacional Financiera*, for example, seems to have functioned with a fair degree of efficiency as the government's lead institution in industrial development: Robert T. Aubey, *Nacional Financiera and Mexican Industry*, Los Angeles: Latin American Center, University of California at Los Angeles, 1966, and the chapter on *Nacional Financiera* by Calvin P. Blair in Raymond Vernon, ed., *Public Policy and Private Enterprise in Mexico*, Cambridge: Harvard University Press, 1964.

22. Although there were notorious exceptions, the government's banks generally adhered to sound management principles and such major undertakings as the Federal Electricity Commission and Petroleos Mexicanos were, before the 1970s, run with a fair level of competence.